MAN:
HIS TRUE NATURE
& MINISTRY

"L'homme est le mot de toutes les enigmas."
De l'esprit des Choses.

Louis-Claude de Saint-Martin
(*"Le Philosophe Inconnu"*)

trans: Edward Burton Penny

British Library Cataloguing in Publication Data

A catalogue record for this book is available from the British Library

ISBN-13: 978-1-908388-25-4

Printed and bound in Great Britain by Lightning Souce UK Ltd., 6 Precedent
Drive, Rooksley, Milton Keynes MK13 8PR.

Cover Illustration: Martinist Pentacle

TRANSLATOR'S PREFACE

Some account of Saint-Martin (*Le Philosophe inconnu*) and his writings has been given in the preface to his 'Correspondence with Baron Liebestorf', recently published*; and it is necessary here only to say that the book of which a translation is now presented to the reader, *'Le Ministère de l'Homme-Esprit'*, was probably the last, as it certainly was the most important, of his works. It was published in Paris, in 1802: he died the following year.

Saint-Martin wrote to his friend the Baron: (Let. cx. of the above 'Correspondence'): "The only initiation which I preach and seek with all the ardour of my soul is that by which we may enter into the heart of God, and make God's heart enter into us, there to form an indissoluble marriage, which will make us the friend, brother, and spouse of our Divine Redeemer ['the violent take it by force:' Matt. xi. 12.]. There is no other mystery, to arrive at this holy initiation, than to go more and more into the depths of our being, and not let go till we can bring forth the living, vivifying root, because then all the fruit we ought to bear, according to our kind, will be produced within us and without us naturally; as we see is the case with earthly trees, because they are adherent to their own roots, and incessantly draw in their sap." These few words suffice to show the scope, intent, or spirit, and point to the modus operandi, of all Saint-Martin's works, and of none more truly so than of the work before us.

In allusion to the above-named recently published 'Correspondence of Saint-Martin', a learned friend (who will doubtless be the interpreter of a numerous class of readers) said to the Editor: "We are on unsafe ground when we leave the old paths of received truth for those of mysticism". - But, without controversy, may it not be asked: Received by whom? And which are those old paths of "received truths"? And are they anywhere visible or recognizable? Have they not been everywhere overgrown with vegetation? And have not as many paths been made through this vegetation, and in as many different directions, as there have been Essayists and Dogmatizers - especially in our own country - of late years? And as all these paths have been virtually authorized as lawful highways, do they not form a legal labyrinth, out of which no exit is found?

Let the reader therefore see if Saint-Martin cannot help him out of the difficulty: and let him not be repelled by the word mystic; the office of such mystics as Saint-Martin is to go to the bottom of mystery, and lead mysticism captive, by laying open the essential, fundamental laws of things, and showing their connection with their Root, which is God.

No doubt when men's minds, looking upon things, as we are all naturally inclined to do, in their outward and visible aspect alone, consider that their

Correspondence between Louis Claude de Saint-Martin and Kirchberger, Baron de Liebestorf. Translated from the original by E. B. Penny. 1 vol. fscap. 8vo. Hamilton & Co. 1863.

reality lies in their materiality, - not in their immaterial essences; in the tangible form or letter, - not in the spirit of things - it is hard for such minds to realize that they themselves are the men who have been looking at shadows, and not at realities. Yet this truth has been affirmed from all antiquity down to the present time, by authorities which they are compelled to respect.

In the present day, when, as we have seen, the old way has been completely overgrown, and we are enclosed in a labyrinth, it would seem particularly opportune that our attention should be called to Nature's landmarks along the way of our regeneration, which cannot mislead us; and that we should be led to dig through the overgrowth of spontaneous vegetation, and plant our feet on the original pavement, laid by God's own hand, all the way from matter, through spirit, to God Himself, from whom we derive.

Of course, these landmarks can be seen by the traveler only as he proceeds on his journey, and the pavement can be cleared and trod upon only by advancing on it; and no fireside traveler can know practically anything of either one or the other, any more than he can know such things in earthly travel:- therefore all men are invited to gird themselves for the journey, and *Go* and *See* for themselves.

It is certain that no good thing is ever acquired without trouble; and, on this journey, much patient endurance is called for. Earthly voyages of discovery are attended with more hardships than most other enterprises. In spiritual voyages it is the same: and they are or may be of two kinds; either of discovery only, or of conquest and settlement, besides. If they are of discovery only, that is, merely intellectual, the labours, fatigues, and calls for self-denial will be of the same order; the mental powers must leave the fleshpots amongst which they have been at ease.

This sort of voyage may be of the greatest use to future settlers, but, except for fame, is of small advantage to the discoverers themselves. Books, as Saint-Martin says, give the means of this intellectual voyage only; and the way, even through Saint-Martin's books, is hard enough, - not only from the nature of the regions they penetrate, but because he was less careful in expressing himself than perhaps he might have been: he thought more of the matter than of the manner; more of the moral conquest, and settlement in those regions, than of the construction of his sentences, or the lines of his map.

The *intending settler*, whose moral and affectional powers are those which leave the flesh-pots, and travel out of Egypt, and who has to find his own resources for his expedition, will be thankful for this map as it is; and, looking at its use and intention, he will overlook its faults of construction.

To lighten the journey for the reader, and break its monotony, in some degree, the Translator has taken it upon himself to place sign posts on the way, in the shape of headings of subjects as they come before the reader: - these were not in the original.

In parts of the work there is an apparent redundancy of illustration, which the Editor would willingly have curtailed ; but, as such parts are nearly always found to cover or lead to something original, little could be done in this way. He has, moreover, felt it his duty to keep as closely as possible to the text, and to render in the simplest language at his command.

The reader will observe that Saint-Martin affects to designate God by the name of His Attribute which is immediately in question or in action: thus we find Him called Supreme Love, - or Wisdom, - or Ruler, - The Principle, - Source, - and such like. In a work which seeks the ground of all things, this is, no doubt, in itself, strictly as it ought to be; - but, if it should sound inharmoniously to some readers, let them remember that Saint-Martin wrote for the French of the Revolution, who had decreed that there was no God, but who had no objection to recognize Him in His Attributes. In this way Saint-Martin undermined the ramparts of infidelity.

With these few remarks the Editor commits the book to the reader, and wishes him God speed.

Topsham, 1864

SUMMARY OF CONTENTS

THIRD PART - The Word

INTRODUCTION

(An Invocation)

When a man of desire, a man who longs for the reign of truth and love, wishes to make himself heard by his fellow-mortals, he is forced to exclaim, "O Sacred Truth, what shall I say to them? I am thy wretched victim, myself ; what can I do but sigh for them?

"Thou hast kindled a burning fire within me, which corrodes my whole being.

"A zeal for the repose of the human family - or rather the imperious necessity I feel of this repose, masters and consumes me. I can neither evade it, nor resist it; it torments me continually.

"The worst of all is, that this unhappy zeal is reduced to feed on its own substance and devour itself, - not finding wherewith to appease the hunger thou hast given me to feel for the peace of souls.

"It ends continually in sobs which choke the sound of my voice.

"It allows me no relief, but to plunge me the next moment into new pains, and leave me a prey to my groaning still.

"And thou callest upon me, in this condition, to lift up my voice to my fellow-creatures!!

"Moreover, how can I make myself heard by men of the stream?

"Principles are all I have to offer them ; and they will answer with opinions, not to say deceptions, and fascination will make them blind to their dishonesty.

"Whatever edifice I build must be founded on their imperishable being, all shining with eternal splendour; and the last word of their science assimilates them to dead earth.

"I would animate them with a glorious desire to renew their alliance with Universal Unity, by inspiring them with some pride for their birthrights; and they are in arms against that Unity, and seem as if they wished to efface its very existence!

"I would wish, by employing only the Word of Life myself, to induce them also not to make use of a single word which is not vitalized by that inexhaustible life-giving power; and they, by closing their ears to this Word of Life, and refusing its aid, have transformed their tongues into so many instruments of confusion and death!"

(The Answer)

What does Truth answer?

"Timidity, also, is uncleanness ; and one most fruitful in mischief ; it may give rise to every error.

"Have confidence in Him who guides you; that confidence will make you clean.

"Do not allow your zeal to be quenched ; let it not be given you in vain: who would insure its being ever rekindled?

"You fear men will not profit by your words! - They are starving for the truth. Who can tell if you may not cause some of your brothers to feel the want that devours them unknown to themselves? Few amongst them are so gangrened as to turn their backs upon truth voluntarily; you cannot estimate the power of a pure zeal nourished by confidence.

"Besides, what fisherman expects to catch with his line all the fish in the stream? When he has caught a few for his food, he is content.

"At all events, look beyond this fleeting life, in which the man of desire must sow his works. To the true husbandry, this life is a season of hailstorms and tempest. Such is not the season in which to look for your harvest.

"The labourer sows for the future; look forward, then, in what you do, to the happy time of harvest; for that is the time when the earth and the landlord will repay the sweat of your brow."

Then the man of desire, the man who longs for the reign of truth and love, resigns himself, and says, " I know that thou art God, concealed in thine own glory ; but thou dost not wish to be unknown ; thou seekest but to display thy power before our eyes, to teach us to fear and love thee.

"Be, then, the Master of my will and my work! Be thou the teacher of those who come to learn from my words !

"Why art thou not the Master of every impulse of men's souls, as thou art, through thy powers, of every movement of Nature, and of every region which has not repelled thy loving hand?"

(Address to the Reader)

The writer of this work has sometimes felt some of the anguish of men of desire; he partakes their desire for the happiness of mankind, and is going to call their attention to what he believes to be the source of all their evils, and to what ought to be the object of all, as images of the First Principle: he addresses himself to Man.

Man! Thou who art become a mere source of bitterness, for thy light shines only through pain; Man, the dearest object of my heart - next to that sovereign Fountain, which can be composed but of love itself, as proved by this sweet and sublime privilege it has given me of loving thee - to thee I now appeal, to second my undertaking; thyself I invite to the most respectable of all partnerships, the object of which is to lay before my fellow-creatures their true titles, that, struck with the greatness of their origin, they may neglect nothing to revive their rights and recover their inheritance.

Reader! You will abuse yourself if you look for matter of recreation here, and come for entertainment only! Expect still less to meet with lying representations to flatter you, and nourish your deceptions and self-love. You have flatterers enough, and accomplices in your delusions, without me.

My part is to exercise a severer and more truthful ministry; the all-important Ministry of Man. Now, the human family are not like kings to whom incense is offered, and who are deceived with praise; and the man who now comes before you, honours his species and respects himself too much, ever to act the dissembler towards his brethren.

Before you proceed further, see if you have the courage, and if you are able, to join me in weeping for the ills of humanity.

The happiness which ought to belong to our species, is now to be seen only as a phenomenon, and a wonder, Our tears are now the only signs of our fraternity; we are relations only in misfortune. This is the fatal bond to which we have, one and all, jointly and severally, become liable, instead of that hereditary peace, to which we should all have had claim, if we had not suffered our original titles to be lost.

Alas! How should we be acquainted with peace? Every human joy, nay, every human impulse arises in blindness, and ends in groans.

O man! Recall your judgment for one moment. I will, for the present, excuse your not yet recognising the sublime destiny you ought to fulfil in the universe; but you ought, at least, not to shut your eyes to the insignificant part you act in it, during the short interval between your cradle and your grave.

That sublime privilege of speech, (*la parole*,) above all. Do you think it was given to you merely to amuse your fellow-creatures, day after day, with details of your monotonous occupations, and narratives of your animal life; to stun them with your noisy eloquence in justification of your ravings and delirium; or to deceive and mislead them with the endless fictions of your fancy?

If a glance is sufficient to convince you of the frivolous and guilty use you make of your faculties, a glance will also suffice to undeceive you as to the results you obtain. Weigh all these results in a balance: you will not find one which does not escape you, or, at least, fall short of your expectations; which does not feed you with disquiet, or end in your tears.

What region, then, is this, where nothing that we are fulfils its law, and where we taste no joy but what cheats us? An imperious fascination, as though it were essential, seems to compose the atmosphere we are in. We are reduced to breathe incessantly, and almost exclusively, this vapour of illusion which surrounds us, and which, after infecting it with our own corruption, we transmit to others; or, if we would secure ourselves from it, we must suspend all our faculties and exist in complete inaction.

In the Alps, the hunter is sometimes caught suddenly and enveloped in a sea of mist, in which he can see neither his hands nor his feet, when he is obliged to stop where he is, as he cannot make a step without danger. What happens to the hunter only occasionally and at intervals, is the permanent situation of man here below. His earthly life is itself the sea of mist which shuts out the light of the sun, and compels him to remain in painful inaction if he will avoid the fracture of his limbs, or being hurled down a precipice.

With men hasty to judge, my writing may not expect to succeed; they will not forgive me for believing a truth wholly, since, by teaching doubt so much themselves, they consent at most to half-beliefs, not to say none at all.

If, however, it should be my happiness to do some good, I shall be content to make no noise. I shall consider myself abundantly recompensed, and not complain of my judges ; and this so much the more, because, if they had thought me worthy of being enrolled under their flag, I should have been obliged to side with the opinions by which they are ruled, and I could not long have served under such banners.

Besides, though I may not expect the suffrages of the majority, my cause will not, therefore, be lost: for it may be brought before a permanent and competent tribunal, whose judgments are not subject to the vacillations of human opinion.

Perhaps, even, the time is not distant, when Europeans will look eagerly at things which they now treat with distrust or contempt. Their scientific edifice is not so established as not to have some revolutions to undergo. They are now beginning to recognise, in organic bodies, what they call *elective attraction*, - an expression which will carry them far, notwithstanding the pains they take not to call the truth by its right name.

The literary wealth of Asia will come to their aid. When they see the treasures which Indian literature begins to open through the 'Asiatic Researches' of the Calcutta Society; when they have studied the *Mahabarat* - a collection of sixteen epic poems, containing one hundred thousand stanzas on the mythology, religion, morals, and history of the Indians, and the *Upnek'hat*, translated by Anquetil, containing extracts from the *Vedas,* etc. - they will be struck with the similarity between the opinions of the East and those of the West on the most important subjects.

In this mine some will seek correspondences of languages in alphabets, inscriptions, and other monuments; others may discover the grounds of all the fabulous theogonies of the Egyptians, Greeks, and Romans; and, lastly, others will find remarkable coincidences with the dogmas published within the last centuries by different spiritualists of Europe, who will never be suspected of having got them from India.

Then, when these dogmas are found to be prevalent over places and distances and epochs so remote from each other, my writings may possibly appear less obscure and repulsive. But, while waiting to know more of this theosophic wealth of India, from which I expect more light myself, I must admonish my fellow-men that it is not in these books, any more than it is in any others, to take them beyond speculative spiritualism; the radical development of our intimate essence alone can lead us into active spirituality.

And on this indispensable foundation is raised the work I now publish, as well as those I have published heretofore.

Descartes rendered an essential service to natural science by introducing the use of algebra in geometry. I know not whether I shall have rendered an equal service to the human mind by applying Man himself, as I have done in all my works, to that living and divine geometry which embraces all things, and of which, the true algebra and universal instrument of analysis, I consider the Spirit-Man to be; this would be a satisfaction I may hardly hope for, even if it were right to wish for it.

This work is divided into three parts: the first treats of Nature; the second of Man; the third of The Word (*parole*) or speech.

THE SPIRITUAL MINISTRY OF MAN

or

The Ministry of the Spirit-Man

FIRST PART - On Nature

Man, not outward nature, the true witness of Divinity

The human understanding, by applying itself so exclusively to outward things, of which it cannot even yet give a satisfactory account, knows less of the nature of Man's own being even than of the visible objects around him; yet, the moment man ceases to look at the true character of his intimate essence, he becomes quite blind to the eternal Divine Source from which he descends: for, if Man, brought back to his primitive elements, is the only true witness and positive sign by which this supreme Universal Source may be known, that source must necessarily be effaced, when the only mirror that can represent it to our minds, disappears.

Then, when praiseworthy writers and well-meaning defenders of truth try to prove that there is a God, and deduce from His existence all its necessary consequences, as they no longer find this human soul sufficiently in harmony to serve as a witness, they go back to Nature, and to speculation taken from the external order. Hence, many excellent spirits in modern times have made use of all the resources of logic, and put every external science under contribution in their endeavours firmly to establish the existence of Divinity; and yet, notwithstanding these numerous testimonies, never was atheism more in fashion.

It must surely be to the glory of our species, and show the great wisdom of Providence, that all the proofs taken in the order of this world are so defective. For, if this world could have truly shown the Divinity, God would have been satisfied with that witness, and have had no need to create Man. In fact, Man was created merely because the whole universe, notwithstanding all the grandeurs it displays to our eyes, never could manifest the riches of Divinity.

A far different effect is produced by those great writers who, in maintaining the existence of God, take Man himself for their proof and the basis of their demonstrations: Man as he should be, at least, if not as he is. Their evidences acquire force and fulness and satisfy all our faculties at once. The evidence drawn from Man is gentle in its effect, and seems to speak the language of our own nature.

That which is drawn from the outside world, is cold and arid, and like a language apart, which requires a laborious study: besides, the more peremptory and decisive this kind of evidence is, the more it humbles our antagonists, and disposes them to hate us.

That which is taken from the nature of Man, on the contrary, even when it obtains a complete victory over the unbeliever, causes him no humiliation, because it places him in a position to feel and partake of all the dignity which belongs to his quality as Man.

And one who is not vanquished by this sublime evidence might, at most, deride it sometimes; but, at other times, he would very likely be sorry not to be able to reach so high a ground, and would certainly never take offence at its being offered to him; and this is enough to show how carefully we ought to sound the depths of Man's being, and affirm the sublimity of his essence, that we may thereby demonstrate the Divine Essence, for there is nothing else in the world that can do it, directly.

...I repeat, that, to attain this end, every argument taken from this world and nature, is unsatisfactory, unstable. We suppose things for the world, to arrive at a fixed Being, in whom every thing is true; we lend to the world abstract and figurative verities, to prove a Being who is altogether real and positive; we take things without intelligence, to prove a Being who is Intelligence itself; things without love, to demonstrate Him who is only Love; things circumscribed within limits, to make known Him who is Free; and things that die, to explain Him who is Life.

Is it not to be feared, that, in committing ourselves to such an undertaking as this, we may imbibe the very defects which are inherent in the means we use, instead of demonstrating to our opponents the treasures of Him we wish to honour?

Two worlds, outward and inward

From the foregoing, we shall see a light arise, which may at first seem strange, but it will not be the less real: it is, that, if man (who, be it remembered, is not of this world) is a sure and direct means of demonstration of the Divine Essence; if proofs taken from the external order of this world are defective and incomplete; and if the hypotheses and abstract truths, which we impute to this world, are taken from the metaphysical order, and have no existence in nature; it clearly follows, that we comprehend nothing in the world we are in, but by the light of the world in which we are not; that it is much easier to attain to the light and certainty which shine in the world in which we are not, than to naturalize ourselves with the shadows and darkness which envelope the world we are in; in short, since it must be said, that we are much nearer to what we call the other-world than we are to this.

It will not even be very difficult to acknowledge, that, to call the other world the world in which we are not, is an abuse, and that this world is the other world to us.

For if, strictly speaking, two things may be respectively the other to each other, there is, nevertheless, a priority between them, either in fact, or conventionally, which requires the second to be considered as the other in respect to the first, and not the first as the other in respect to the second; for, that which is first is one, and can offer no difference, having no point of comparison anterior to itself, whereas that which is second finds that point of comparison before it.

Such is the case with the two worlds in question; and I leave it to the reader to compare the light and certainties we find in the metaphysical order, or what we call the other world, with the obscurities, approximations, and uncertainties we find in the one we inhabit; and I also leave it to him to pronounce whether the world we are not in has not some right to priority over that we are in, as well on account of the perfections and science it affords us, as of the superior antiquity it seems to have over this world of a day in which we are imprisoned.

For none but slaves of ignorance and hasty judgments could think of making mind descend from matter, and, therefore, what we call the other world, from this; whilst this, on the contrary, seems to derive from the other, and come after it.

Thus then, if the world where we are not, the one we call the other world, has, in all respects, the priority over this, it is truly this world, the one where we are, which is the other world, since it has a term of comparison before it, of which it is the difference; and what we call the other world, being one, or the first, carries with it all its relations, and can be a model only, and not another world.

This also shows how much the Spirit-Man must be out of his line of descent, imprisoned in these material elements, and how far these material elements, or this world, is from sufficing to show the Divinity: moreover, strictly speaking, we never do go out of the other world, or the Spirit-World, though so few people believe in its existence. We cannot doubt this truth, since, to give value to the proofs we draw from matter, or this world, we are obliged to lend it the qualities of mind, or the other world. The reason is, every thing depends upon Spirit, every thing corresponds with Spirit, as we shall see in the sequel.

Thus, the only difference between men is, that some are in the other world, knowing it, and the others are there without knowing it; and, on this head, there is the following progression.

God is in the other world, knowing it, and He cannot but believe and know it; for, being the Universal Spirit Himself, it is impossible that, for Him, there can be any separation between that other world and Himself.

Pure spirits feel well enough that they are in the other world, and they feel it perpetually, and without intermission, because they live by the life of that world only; but they feel that they are only the inhabitants of that other life, and that another is its proprietor.

Man, although in the terrestrial world, is still in the other world, which is every thing; but, sometimes he feels its sweet influences, and sometimes he does not; often, even, he receives and follows the impulse of this mixed and dark world only, which is like a coagulation in the midst of that other world, and, in respect to it, a sore, a boil, an ulcer. Hence it is that there are so few men who believe in that other world.

Lastly, lost spirits, whose existence the reflective man can demonstrate to himself beyond all question, by the simple light of his understanding, and without help from tradition, by probing to the quick, those sources of good and evil which combat each other within him, and disturb his intelligence; these lost spirits, I say, are also in that other world, and believe in it.

But, not only do they not feel its sweet influences, nor enjoy the rest and refreshment which even this apparent world affords to man, but they know the other world only by the endless suffering which the acrid source they have opened causes them. If man, through negligence, allows them to enjoy a moment's respite, it is only for a time, and they have always to restore their ill-gotten goods a hundredfold.

What idea, then, should we form of this Nature, or this universe, which makes us so blind to that other world, that spiritual world, - be it good or evil, - which we are never out of? The answer is brief.

Without the evil spiritual world, nature would be an eternity of regularity and perfection; without the good spiritual world, nature would be an eternity of abomination and disorder. It is Supreme Love or Wisdom, who, to assuage the false eternity, has thought right to oppose a ray of the true eternity to it. The mixture of these two eternities composes time, which is neither one nor the other, and yet offers an image successively of both, in good and evil, day and night, life and death, etc.

Supreme Love could employ for this work, powers only which descended from the true eternity, for this reason, on the one hand, everything in time is measured, and, on the other, time itself, both general and particular, must necessarily pass away.

But, as the true eternity has, so to speak, come out of itself to contain the false, and the false eternity, on the contrary, has been thereby forced to draw back; this is the reason why we find it so difficult, in time, to distinguish these two eternities, neither of which is here in its place; and this is the reason why it is so difficult to prove God by nature, in which all is fragmentary and mixed, and in which the two eternities show themselves only under the outward veil of corruptible matter.

Man buries himself in the external world

In the state of apathy into which man sinks, through his daily illusions, and studying only the external order of Nature, he can see neither the source of her apparent regularity, nor that of her disorders; he identifies himself with this external Universe; he cannot help taking it for a world, and even an exclusive and self-existing one.

And, in this state of things, the idea which has the most difficulty of access into man, is that of the degradation of our species, and the fall of Nature herself; he has lost the rights he ought to have had over her, by allowing them to fall into disuse, and ended by confounding this blind dark nature with himself, with his own essence.

Yet if he would, for a moment, take a more correct and profitable view of the external order, a simple remark would suffice to show him, at once, the positive degradation of his species, the dignity of his being, and its superiority over this external order.

How can men deny the degradation of their species, when they see-that they can neither exist, nor live, nor think, nor act, but by combating a resistance? Our blood has to defend itself from the resistance of the elements; our minds, from that of doubt, and the darkness of ignorance; our hearts, from false inclinations; our whole bodies, from inertia; our social state, from disorder, etc.

A resistance is an obstacle; an obstacle, in the order of spirit, is an antipathy, an enmity; and an enmity in action is a hostile combatant power: now this power, continually extending its forces around us, holds us in a violent and painful situation, in which we ought not to be, and, without which, this power would be unknown to us, as if it existed not, since we inwardly feel that we were made for peace and quiet.

No! Man is not in his proper proportions; he has evidently undergone a change for the worse. I do not say this of him because I find it in books; it is not because this idea is generally entertained amongst all people; it is because man, everywhere, seeks a place of rest for his spirit; it is because he wants to master all knowledge, even that of the infinite, and although it escapes him continually, he had rather distort it, and make it bend to suit his dark conceptions, than do without it; it is because, during his transient existence on earth, he appears to be in the midst of his fellow-creatures, like a ravenous lion amongst sheep, or like a sheep amongst ravenous lions; it is because, amongst that vast number of men, there is hardly one who awakes for anything but to be either the victim or the executioner of his brother.

Man's titles higher than Nature

Nevertheless, Man is a great being; if he were not, how could he be degraded?

But, independently of this proof of the former dignity of our being, the following reflection ought to convince us of our superiority over Nature, even now.

Astral earthly Nature works out the laws of creation, and came into existence by virtue of those laws only.

The vegetable and mineral kingdoms have in them the effect of these laws, for they contain all the elementary, astral, and other essential properties; and that with more efficacy, and in greater development, than the stars themselves, which contain only one-half of these properties, or than the earth, which contains the other half.

The animal kingdom has the use of these laws of creation, since animals have to feed, maintain, and reproduce themselves; and they contain all the principles which are necessary for this. But the Spirit-Man has, at once, the effect, the use, and the free direction or manipulation of these laws. I will give only one material example of this, and that a very familiar one, but, by its means, the mind may rise higher.

This example is: First, a corn-field, which has in it the effect of these laws of Nature; Secondly, a granivorous animal, having the use of this corn, and may eat it; Thirdly, a baker, who has the control and manipulation of the corn, and can make bread of it; which, though in a very material manner, shows that the powers of Nature are possessed but partially by the creatures which constitute it; but, that the Spirit-Man alone, and in himself, embraces them all.

As for those material rights which man possesses, and which we have summed up above, in the manipulations of the baker, if we rise in thought to Man's true region, we shall, no doubt, find these rights proved more virtually, and on a grander scale, by sounding the wonderful properties which constitute the Spirit-Man, and exploring the high order of manipulations which these properties may lead to.

If Man has the power to be the workman and handicraftsman of earthly productions, why should he not be the same of a superior order? He ought to be able to compare those divine productions with their Source, as he has the power to compare the total effect of Nature with the Cause that fashioned and guides her, and he alone has this privilege.

But experience alone can give an idea of this sublime right or privilege; and, even then, this idea will ever appear to be new, even to him who is most accustomed to it.

But, alas! Man knows his spiritual rights, and he does not enjoy them! What need is there of any other proof of his deprivation, therefore, of his degradation?

Man may recover his titles

O, Man! Open, then, your eyes for an instant; for, with your rash judgments, you will not only never recover your rights, but you run the risk of annihilating them. You might take a lesson from the physical order: animals are all heart; and it is clear that, though they are not machines, they are without mind (*esprit*), for this is distinct from them, outside. For this reason, they have no alliance to establish, as we have, between themselves and their principle; but, seeing the regularity of their march, it cannot, to man's shame, be denied that, taken altogether, these creatures, which are not endowed with freedom, manifest a more complete and constant alliance with their principle than we can form in ourselves, with our own. We might, even go so far as to say, that all creatures, except man, manifest themselves as so many hearts, of which God is the mind or spirit.

In fact, the world, or lost man, would be all mind (*esprit*), and thinks he can do without his true heart, his sacred divine heart, if he can but protrude his animal heart, and his vainglory.

In God, there is also a sacred heart and mind. Since we are his images, but they are one, as all the powers and faculties of the Sovereign Being are one.

Now, we have the prerogative of forming, after the similitude of the All-Wise, an indissoluble, eternal alliance between our minds (*esprits*) and our sacred hearts, by uniting them in the principle which formed them; and it is only on this indispensable condition that we can hope to become again the images of God; and in striving for this, our conviction is confirmed, as to the painful fact of our degradation, and, at the same time, of our superiority over the external order.

Sentiment of immortality

By striving to become again God's images, we obtain the inestimable advantage, not only of putting an end to our privation and degradation, but of advancing towards what men, greedy for glory, call immortality, and actually enjoying it; for, the vague desire which men of the stream have, of living in the minds of others, is the weakest and most false of all the arguments commonly advanced in favour of the dignity of the human soul.

In fact, although Man is spirit, and, in all his actions, orderly or otherwise, he always has a spiritual motive of some kind; and although, in whatever emanates from him, he can work only by and for spirit; yet the desire of this kind of immortality is only an impulse of self-love, a sentiment of present superiority over others, and a foretaste of their admiration which he promises to himself, and which warms him; and when he does not see his way to realise this picture, his zeal cools, and the works which depended on it are affected accordingly.

And we may affirm that this inclination comes rather of a wish for immortality, than of any real conviction about it; and the proof is, that those who indulge in it, are those who, to realize it, have nothing but temporal works to offer, showing that the ground they go upon is within the limit of time: for the tree is known by its fruit.

If they were really convinced of this immortality, they would prove their conviction by trying to work in and for the true God, forgetting themselves; and their hopes of immortal life would not be disappointed, because they would sow their seed in a field where they would be sure to find it again; whereas, by working only in time, and sowing only in men's minds, to be soon forgotten by some, and never heard of by others, is to go to work most awkwardly and disadvantageously, in building for immortality.

If we would reflect a little, we should find, close at hand, decisive proofs of our immortality. Only consider the habitual, constant dearth in which man leaves his spirit, - and his spirit is not extinguished. He excites himself, he goes wrong, he gives himself up to error, he becomes wicked, he turns mad, - he does evil when he would do good; but, properly speaking, he does not die.

If we treated our bodies with the same carelessness and neglect, if we left them fasting and starved in a similar way, they would do neither good nor evil, they would simply die.

Another indication of our immortality may be noticed in the fact, that, in all respects, man, here below, walks all day long by the side of his grave, and that it can be only from some kind of feeling of immortality that he, all the time, tries to show himself superior to this danger.

This may be said of soldiers, who may receive their death at any time. It may be said of the corporeal man, who may be taken out of this world at any time; the only difference being that the soldier is not necessarily victim to the danger that threatens him, whilst natural men must all fall, without a possibility of escape.

But, in both, we perceive the same tranquillity, no to say carelessness, which makes the warrior and the man of nature live as if no danger existed for them their carelessness being in itself an indication that they are full of the idea of their immortality, though they both walk by the edge of their graves.

In his spiritual concerns, man's danger is still greater, and his carelessness more extraordinary still: not only does the Spirit-Man continually walk by the side of his grave, always nearly being swallowed up in the immortal source of all lies, but, may we not ask, are there many amongst us who do not walk in their graves? And man is so blind that he makes no effort to get out, and inquires not whether he ever shall.

When he is fortunate enough to perceive, if only for a moment, that he is walking in this grave, then he has an irresistible spiritual proof of his immortality, since he has that of his frightful mortality, and even of what we figuratively call his death. Now, how could he feel a horror of this spiritual mortality, if he had not, at the same time, a strong sentiment of his im-mortality?

It is only in this contrast that he finds that he is punished; just as physical pain is felt, by the opposition of disorder to health. But this kind of proof can be got only by experience, and it is one of the first-fruits of regeneration; for, if we do not feel our spiritual death, how can we think of calling for life?

Here, again, we also learn that there must be another and a still more unhappy being, - the prince of falsehood, - since, without him, we could not have had the idea of him; seeing that all things can be revealed only by themselves, as we have shown in "*L'Esprit des Choses*".

Not only does this being continually walk in his grave, not only does he never perceive that he is walking in that grave, - for this he could not do without a ray of light to help him, - but, when we approach that grave, we perceive that he is in continual dissolution and corruption; that is, that he is in the perpetual proof and sentiment of his death; that he never conceives the smallest hope of being delivered from it, and thus his greatest torment is the sentiment of his immortality.

Man's primitive dignity, his degradation, and his high calling, shown in the writer's previous publications

My other writings have sufficiently established the dignity of our being, notwithstanding our abject condition, in this region of darkness.

They have sufficiently shown how to distinguish the illustrious captive, man, from nature, which, though his preserver, is also his prison.

They have sufficiently indicated the difference between the powers, mutually exercised on each other, by the physical and moral orders, the former having over the latter a passive power only, obstructing it, or it leaves it to itself; whereas, the moral has over the physical order an active power, that of creating in it, so to say, notwithstanding our degradation, manifold gifts and talents, which it would never have had of its own nature.

Although I do not flatter myself that I have convinced many of my fellow-creatures, as to our lamentably degraded state, since I first took upon myself to defend human nature, yet I have often attempted it, in my writings, and, I believe I may say, my task is fulfilled in this respect, though this may not be the case with those who have read me.

Those writings have sufficiently shown how the All Wise, from whom Man descends, has multiplied the means by which he may rise again to his primitive state; and, after laying these foundations in man's integral being, so as to be above suspicion, and so that he might, at any moment, verify them by his own observation, they have represented to him the entire heavenly and earthly universe, the sciences of all kinds, the languages, and mythologies of all nations, as so many depositions which he may consult at his pleasure, in which he will find authentic evidence of all these fundamental truths.

They have particularly recommended, as an indispensable precaution, though universally neglected, that all traditional books whatsoever be considered only as accessories, posterior to those important truths which rest upon the nature of things, and the constituent nature of Man.

They have essentially recommended men to begin by firmly assuring themselves of these primary and impregnable truths, not omitting, afterwards, to gather from books and traditions everything that may come in support of them, without allowing themselves to be so blinded as to confound testimony with facts, which must first be known to exist as facts, before depositions of witnesses are received; for, when there are no certain facts, witnesses can have no pretension to our confidence, nor be of any use.

I have not now to demonstrate man's frightful transmigration; I have said that a single sigh of the human soul is more decisive on this point than all the doctrines derived from external things, or than all the stutterings and noisy clamour of the philosophy of appearances.

Hindoo priests may stifle the widow's cries, whom they burn on their funereal pyres; their fanatical songs and the tumultuous noise of their instruments do not the less leave her a prey to the most horrible tortures; and their impostures and atrocious shouts will not make her forget her pains.

No! those only, who make themselves matter, believe they are as they ought to be. After this first error, the second follows as a necessary consequence; for, matter, in fact, knows no degradation; in whatsoever condition it may be, it has still no character but inertia; it is what it ought to be; it makes no comparisons: it perceives no order in itself, nor disorder.

Neither do men, who make themselves matter, discern any better the striking and repulsive contrasts of their state of existence.

Nature is not matter

But Nature is another thing than matter; it is the life of matter; it possesses an instinct and a sensibility different from matter; it perceives its deterioration, and groans under its bondage.

Therefore, if lost men would only be content to make themselves nature, they would have no doubt about their degradation ; but they make themselves matter: and the only torch they have left to guide them, is the blind insensibility and dark ignorance of matter.

A golden age

Moreover, the reason why those glowing descriptions of a golden age, given to us in poetry and mythology, still rank as fable, is that they would seem to represent enjoyments which had been formerly ours, which is not the case; they represent only our right to those enjoyments, which we might even now recover, if we would but avail ourselves of the resources inherent in our essence. And I myself, when I speak so frequently of man's crime, I mean the whole or general Man, from whom the human family has descended.

Original sin

As I have shown, in 'Le Tableau Naturel', we bewail our sorrowful situation here below, but have no remorse about original Sin, because we are not guilty of it; we are under deprivation, but are not punished as the guilty are. Thus, children of an illustrious criminal, some great one of the earth, born after their father's crime, may be deprived of his riches and temporal privileges, but they are not punished personally, as he is, and they may even hope, by good conduct, some day to regain favour, and to be installed in their father's honours.

I have, in my writings, also, sufficiently shown that the human soul is more sensible than nature, which, in fact, is sensitive only. This is why I said that the human soul, when restored to its sublime dignity, was the true witness of the Supreme Agent, and that those who can prove God only by the universe, stand upon a precarious evidence, for the universe is in bondage, and slaves are not allowed as witnesses.

Marriage

I have made it sufficiently clear, that man's thought feeds on and lives only by admiration, and his heart only by adoration and love. And I now add, that, these sacred privileges, being divided in mankind, between the man, who is more inclined to admire, and the woman, who is more disposed to love and adore, both the man and the woman are thus perfected in their holy intercourse, which gives to man's intelligence, the love in which he is deficient, and crowns the woman's love with the bright rays of intelligence which she wants; both being thus brought back to the ineffable law of Unity.

(Here we may say, in passing, that this would explain why marriage, everywhere, except with the depraved, bears a respectable character ; and why this tie, notwithstanding our degradation, is the basis of all political associations, all moral laws, the subject of so many great and small events in the world, and the subject of almost all works of literature, epopee, drama, or romance; finally, why the respect in which this tie is held, with the attacks made against it, becomes, in all civil and religious respects, the source of harmony or discord, a blessing or a curse, and seems to link heaven, earth, and hell, with the marriage of man; for, such extreme results would be astonishing indeed, if this conjugal union had not from the beginning, and from its importance, had the power to determine the happiness or misery of all it embraces, and all that relates to man. And sin has made this marriage subject to very sad consequences, which consist in this, that, everything having gone the wrong way, spiritually, for them both, their spirits are obliged to go out of themselves, if they would mutually attain to that holy unity to which their alliance calls them. And there is nothing which they do not owe to each other, in their intercourse, by way of encouragement and example, that through this medium, the woman may return into the man out of whom she came; that the man may sustain the woman with the strength from which she is separated, and recover for himself that portion of love which he suffered to go out of him. Oh, if mankind knew what marriage really was, how they would at once desire it exceedingly, and fear it! For it is possible for a man to become divine again through marriage, or to go through it to perdition. In fact, if married couples only prayed, they would recover possession of the garden of Eden; and if they will not pray, I know not how they can stand, so constituted we now are of corruption and infection, both physically and morally; above all, if, to their own moral and physical infirmities, they add the corrosive atmosphere of the frivolous world, which attracts everything to the outside, because it cannot live in or by itself.)

I have sufficiently made it appear, that we alone on earth enjoy the privilege of admiring and loving, on which marriage should rest; and that this reflection alone demonstrates both our superiority over everything in nature, and the necessity of a permanent Source of admiration and adoration, by which our need to admire and adore maybe satisfied; it also demonstrates our relations and radical analogy with this Source, whereby we may discern and feel what in it there is to attract our admiration and homage.

Man is the book of God

I have sufficiently expressed my thought of books, in saying that Man was the only book written by God's own hand; that all other books which have come down to us were ordered or permitted by Him; that all other books whatsoever, could be but developments or commentaries of this primitive text, this original book; and that thus our primary task, and one of fundamental necessity to us, was, that we should read in Man, who is the book written by God's own hand.

Sacred writings or traditions

I have been equally explicit as to sacred traditions, in saying that everything must make its own revelation; so that, instead of proving religion merely by traditions, written or unwritten, which is all our ordinary teachers attempt, we have a right to draw directly from the depths which we have within us, since facts, how marvellous soever they may be, must be posterior to Thought; that we ought to have begun with the Spirit-Man and thought, before going to events, especially such as are only traditional; that thereby we might cause to germinate or reveal themselves, both the healing balm, of which we all feel so much need, and religion itself, which should be nothing but the mode or preparation of this sovereign remedy, and never be substituted for it, as it so often is, in passing through the hands of men.

I have sufficiently made it appear that this was the only sure way to obtain natural, and really positive and efficient evidence, to which alone our understanding can yield its confidence.

Thus, I may be excused from returning to these first principles; the more so, that, if we attentively observe the state of men's minds, we shall acknowledge that we ought less to think of those who are hardened, themselves, than of rescuing some of their prey; especially if we reflect how small the number of those hardened beings is, compared with those who are still capable of recovering their sight; for, it is a striking fact that those who speak against the Truth, amount almost to none at all, compared with those who defend it, though it may be awkwardly ; they are fewer still, when compared with those who believe it, even though it be without knowing it, which is the case with most.

Jacob Boehme

Moreover, a German author, whose first two books I have translated, 'The Aurora', and the 'Three Principles', will supply all my deficiencies. This German author, Jacob Boehme, who lived two centuries ago, and was looked upon in his time as the prince of divine philosophers, has left, in his numerous writings, which consist of about thirty different treatises, most astonishing and extraordinary openings, on our primitive nature; on the source of evil; the essence and laws of the universe; the origin of weight; on what he calls the seven wheels or powers of nature; the origin of water (confirmed by chemistry, which teaches that it is a burned body); on the nature of the crime of the angels of darkness; on that of man; on the mode adopted by Eternal Love, for the restitution of mankind in their rights; etc.

I think I do the reader a service, in advising him to make himself acquainted with this author; recommending him, however, to be armed with patience and courage, that he may not be repelled by the unusual form of his works; by the extremely abstract nature of the subjects he treats; and by the difficulty which the author (as he confesses himself) had in expressing his ideas, for the reason that most of the matters in question have no analogous names in our common languages.

The reader will there find that this physical elementary nature is only a residuum, a corruption (alteration) of an anterior nature, which the author calls Eternal Nature; that this present nature constituted formerly, in its whole circumscription, the throne and dominion of one of the angelic princes, called Lucifer: that this prince, wishing to reign only by the power of fire and wrath, put the kingdom (*regne*) of divine Love and Light aside, instead of being guided by it exclusively, and inflamed the whole circumscription of his empire; that Divine

Wisdom opposed to this conflagration a temperate cooling power, which contains it, without extinguishing it, making the mixture of good and evil which is now visible in nature; that Man, formed, at once, of the principle of Fire, the principle of Light, and the Quintessential principle of physical elementary Nature, was placed in this world, to contain the dethroned guilty king; that this Man, though having in him the quintessential principle of elementary nature, was to keep it, as it were, absorbed in the pure element which then constituted his bodily form; but that, showing himself to be attracted more by the temporal principle of Nature than by the two other principles, was overcome by it, so as to fall asleep, as Moses expresses it; that, soon finding himself subdued by the material region of this world, he suffered his pure element to be swallowed up and absorbed in the gross form which envelopes us now; that he thus became the subject and victim of his enemy; that Divine Love, which eternally contemplates itself in the Mirror of its Wisdom, by the author called SOPHIA, perceived in this mirror, in which all forms are comprised, the model and spiritual form of man; that He clothed Himself with this spiritual form, and afterwards with elementary form even, that He might present to man the image of what he had become, and the pattern what he ought to have been; that man's actual object on earth is to recover, physically and morally, the likeness of his first pattern; that the greatest obstacle he here meets with is the astral elementary power which engenders and constitutes the world, and for which Man was not made; that the actual procreation of man is a speaking witness of this truth, by the pains which pregnant women experience in all their members, as their fruit is formed in them, and attracts those gross astral substances; that the two tinctures, igneous and watery, which ought to be united in Man, and identify themselves with Wisdom or SOPHIA, (but are now divided,) seek each other ardently, hoping to find, the one in the other, that SOPHIA which they are in want of; but they only fall in with the astral, which oppresses and thwarts them; that we are free to restore, by our efforts, our spiritual being, to our first divine image, as we are to allow it to take the disorderly, inferior images; and that these divers images will constitute our mode of being, our glory or our shame, in a future state, etc.

Caution to the Reader

Reader, if you resolve courageously to draw from the well of this author's works, judged by the learned in the human order as those of a madman, you will assuredly not need mine. But if, though you may not penetrate all the depths which he will present to your mind, you are not firmly established on at least the main points which I have just passed in review before your eyes; if you still doubt the sublime nature of your being, notwithstanding the decisive proofs you might, on the slightest examination, find in yourself; if you are not equally convinced of your degradation, written in letters of iron in the disquietudes of your heart or in the dark delirium of your thoughts; if you do not feel that your absolutely exclusive work is to concentrate all your time to the re-establishment of your being in the active enjoyment of those ancient domains of Truth which ought to be yours by right of inheritance; go no farther. The object of my writing is not to establish these foundations over again; they have been solidly laid already.

I have the right here to suppose all these grounds admitted, and we are not now called upon to prove them. In a word, this is not an elementary book: I have done my duty in that respect. This work presupposes all the notions I have just laid down, and will suit only such as hold them, or, at least, such as have not absolutely declared against them.

I shall apply myself chiefly to the contemplation of the sublime rights originally granted to us by the Most High, and to deploring, with my fellow-creatures, the lamentable condition in which they now languish, compared with that for which they were destined by their nature. I shall, at the same time, show the consolations which are still in their reach, and, above all, the hope they may yet entertain of again becoming the Lord's workmen, as originally intended; and this part of my work will not be that which is least attractive to me, so great is my desire that, amidst the evils which are eating them up, instead of losing courage and giving themselves to despair, they should begin by seeking strength, not only to bear but to conquer them, and to come so close to Life, that Death shall be ashamed of having thought of making them his prey; so much do I wish, I say, that they should fulfil in Spirit and in truth the object for which they received their being.

How to estimate books

Let all who read this book - you even who may indulge the taste for writing yourselves - learn to reduce your own books and those of your fellow-creatures to their real value. All these productions should be pictures; and pictures, to be worth anything, presuppose real originals, whose features they represent to us, and positive facts, of which they convey a faithful report.

Yes! The annals of Truth ought to be nothing but compilations of its own dazzling lights and wonders; and he who has the happiness to be called to be its true minister ought never to write till he has acted virtually under its orders, and only to tell us of the marvels he may have wrought in its name.

Such, in all times, has been the way of ministers in spirit and in truth of the things of God. They never wrote till they had wrought. Such also should still be man's course, since he is specially destined for the stewardship of the things of God.

What are those enormous heaps of books, the issue of human fancy and imagination, which not only have not waited for works to describe or marvels to relate, but present themselves to us with the puerile and culpable pretension of altogether taking their places?

What are all those writers, whose object is only to make us contribute to their own vain and noisy celebrity, instead of sacrificing themselves for our good? False friends, who are ready enough to talk to us of virtue and truth, but take great care to leave us in peace, in inaction, and falsity; fearful lest if they attempted to pluck us out with sharp words we should desert their school and stand in the way of their glory, and so reduce them to silence and oblivion.

Oh, throw aside those profitless books, and take the way of work at once, if you are happy enough to know what this really means. Give yourself to work at the cost of your sweat and blood, and take not a pen till you have some discovery to relate in the regions of true knowledge, some instructive experience in the works of the spirit, or some glorious conquest gained over the kingdom of darkness and lies.

Inspired writings

This is what, in the books of true stewards of God in all ages, communicates to the man of desire a spirit of life wherewith to quench his thirst at all times. These books are like highways between great cities, affording at once beautiful prospects, hospitable shelter, and protection against danger and evil doers. They are like smiling and fruitful banks of rivers, from the waters of which they derive their fertility, and which they confine in their turn, enabling the navigator to sail peacefully and pleasantly upon them.

Responsibility of writers

All men of God are responsible to the world for their thoughts; for, if they are truly men of God, every thought they receive is intended for the perfecting of things and the extension of the Master's rule.

Therefore, as he who is not a steward of the things that are of God, should distrust his own words, and spare their utterance to others; so, on the other hand, ought he who is one of those stewards, carefully to collect his, and sow them in men's minds, even though they be but as germs sent by the Master for planting in the garden of Eden.

He will have to give a strict account of all those germs which, through his indifference or neglect, may fail to come to flower, for the adornment of man's abode.

Man is the book of books

But, if books of stewards of divine things may render such services to the human family, what might that family not expect from Man himself, reinstated in his natural rights? Those books are but the highways between great cities. Man is himself one of the cities. Man is the primitive book, the divine book; other books are only books of the spirit; they merely contain the waters of the river; Man partakes, in some sort, of the very nature of the waters.

O my brethren, read, then, incessantly, in this Man, this book of books; without leaving unread those written by stewards of divine things, which may render you much daily service! With these great means at your command, open the regions of Divinity, which may be called regions of the Word (*parole*); and then come and relate to us all the life-giving wonders which you meet with, in those regions where all is wonder.

But, do not forget, that, in the state of aberration in which Man is, you have a duty to perform for your fellow-men, more urgent than writing books; that is, so to live and do, as, by your efforts and desires, they may get ears to hear them. This is what is most needed by mankind. If their intelligence do not keep up with your writings, you will do them no service, your work will be dead, and, unfortunately for yourself, your egotism and self-applause will be the only fruit you derive from your undertaking.

Men's minds are blasés

What do I say? Open men's understanding! What would the most perfect books avail for this? Men's understanding is debased, it is darkened, it has become childish. The child, like the savage, can understand only by substantial and gross signs, or even the sight of the object itself. Its thought is yet only in its eyes.

Do not attempt to treat man's understanding otherwise than as that of the child or the savage. Develop within and before him, the active powers of Nature, those of the human soul, those of the Divinity, if you would have him to know God, Man, and Nature. On these subjects, his reason is dead; you will lose your pains if you only speak to him about them.

In fact, the time for books is almost past. Man is blasé by their abundance; like those high-livers to whom the most succulent viands are insipid.

The time is almost past, not only for books of human imagination and fancy; but, it may even be said, for books of men of God; books of human imagination have taken away their value, and almost entirely annulled their power; and nothing but works of overpowering effect, can now awaken the world from its lethargy.

We know that extremes meet; and man and the savage, reduced in their childishness and ignorance to the impossibility of being awakened by anything but signs of imposing effect, retrace to us inversely the true primitive nature of Man, who ought always to have been nourished with effective wonders, and was reduced to making and reading books, only when he lost sight of the living patterns which ought never to have ceased acting before his eyes.

In short, time is advancing towards its dotage; the spirit-age must now come, since miracles wrought by the power of the Most High are now the only means by which He can be made known, and respected by mortals.

This is why I am so pressing that you should go earnestly into the way of work; that is, if you feel called to it; and, if you do not, at least pray the Master to send workmen.

If you are of the number of these workmen, when you have opened the regions of Nature, forget not those of the Spirit, nor even those of Divinity: when you come to relate their wonders, when you take up your pen to describe them, do not forget the price at which you came to know them; that you acquired the right to speak of them only after pouring out your sweat and blood in these laborious and useful researches; do not forget, even, that, when you describe them, you must still pour out your sweat and blood, to gather new pearls from this inexhaustible mine, in which you are condemned to work all the days of your life.

Your task is double now: and your consolations have sorrow for their mother and companion. To you the sounds of joy are no longer separate from those of groaning: it is useless to distinguish between them ; they are forcibly bound together, and not all the joys of your spirit allow any intermission to your sobs.

Man the Universal Rectifier

Of all the titles which may serve to designate Man, restored to his primitive elements, none so satisfies the mind and the vast and laudable desires of the human soul, as that of Universal Rectifier (*améliateur*). For this human soul experiences an urgent want, even to importunity, to see order reign in every class of beings in every region, that every point of existence may contribute to the sovereign harmony which alone can manifest the majesty and glory of Eternal Unity.

It is even the secret presentiment of this universal eternal harmony, which has led men of celebrity, in all ages, to look upon the present state of nature as eternal, in spite of the evils and disorder in which we see it is sunk.

Yes, everything is eternal, in its fundamental ground, but not in the pains and frightful confusion which are visible throughout nature: yes, there is, doubtless, an eternal nature, where everything is regular, and more alive and active than in this our prison; and the strongest proof that this present nature, in which we are imprisoned, is not eternal, is, that it suffers, and that it is the abode of death of all kinds, whereas there is no eternal but life.

Granted, that you teach me great and useful doctrines, who, by your precepts, call men to brotherly charity, to zeal for the House of God, and to the care of quitting this earthly mire, without being infected by its pollutions.

But have you followed these precepts to the fulness of their meaning? As for me, I feel that something is still wanting to fill the boundless desires which devour me. The prayers and truths which are given and taught us, here below, are too little for us; they are prayers and truths of time, only; we feel that we are made for something better.

I can conceive that brotherly charity may find no more sublime exercise than to forgive our enemies, and do good to those who hate us. But, what of men who do not hate us ; and those who are, and ever will be, unknown to us? Is our charity in regard to them to remain inactive, or limited to those vague prayers alluded to when we are told that we must pray for all men? In a word, may not all mankind, past, present, and to come, be the object of our true love?

Granted, that there may appear to be no holier zeal for the House of God, than to publish the divine laws, and to make them honourable, by our example, as well as our preaching. But our God, who is so exceedingly precious to every faculty of our being; this God, who, on so many grounds, may indeed be called our friend, has He no pain, no anguish of heart, by reason that all the wonders He planted in man and the universe are lost to us in clouds of darkness? And should we allow ourselves an instant's repose till we have brought Him relief?

Finally, the duty of preserving ourselves clean from this earthly mire may seem to imply nothing more important than that we should return to our mother country, without contracting the manners and habits of this wicked world. But, after escaping its pollutions, would it not be something still more excellent to neutralize its poison, or even to transmute it into a balm of life? Are we not advised to do good to our enemies? And can we deny that, in many respects, Nature is one of them?

As for those who are called enemies of God, it is for God, and not for us, to dispense to them the justice they deserve; let us disregard His seeming declaration of open and implacable war against His so-called enemies. God has no enemies; He is too meek and loving ever to have had any. And those who call themselves God's enemies, are only their own enemies, and are under their own justice.

A higher ground for the regenerate man

I now come to speak, with the man of faith and desire, of the different privileges which constitute the eminent dignity of man when regenerate. Let your understanding second my efforts; the rights I maintain may be claimed by all men. We ought, originally, all to have had the same task, that of developing our characters of rectifiers, as having all emanated from the Author of all goodness and loving-kindness. I know too well, O man of desire, that your understanding may be dark; but I also know that, with a decided will, and a conduct in conformity, you may obtain from your Sovereign Principle the light you require, and which is grounded on your original titles.

The Father's children

We here clearly distinguish several tasks to be performed in the spiritual course. Most men who come to it, come to seek virtue or knowledge, only for their own improvement, and their own perfecting. And happy, indeed, are those who come with such intentions as these! And how much to be wished is it, that this happiness were the portion of every individual of the human family!

But if these good, pious, and even enlightened men, cause joy to the Father of the family, by seeking to be admitted amongst his children, they would cause him still more, by seeking to be admitted amongst his workmen, or servants: for these may render him real service; the others render it only to themselves.

The Father's workmen

Although far from being able to reckon myself of the number of those sublime workmen, or mighty servitors; yet of them chiefly I shall speak in this writing, having already done so fully, to the best of my ability, of what belongs to the children of the Father of the family.

I again call upon the man of desire to look at the fields of the Lord, and seek to labour therein according to his strength, and the kind of work for which he is adapted; in living works, if this be given him; or in developing man's nature, if he has been led to perceive its depths; or even in plucking up the thorns and briars which enemies of truth and false teachers have planted, and still plant daily in Man, the image of Eternal Wisdom.

For, to teach one's fellow-creatures their true duties and veritable rights, is also, in a way, to be the workman of the Lord ; to provide and put in order the tools and implements of labour, is to be useful to agriculture; only it is necessary to examine very carefully what we are competent to do in any class of work. He who provides implements of husbandry is responsible for what he provides; the sower is responsible for what he sows.

But, as it is impossible to be a true workman in the Lord's fields, without being renewed and reinstated in one's own rights, I shall often dwell upon the paths of restoration through which we must necessarily pass, to be admitted as workmen*.

Heaven taken by violence

Which, then, of all the privileges of the human soul, is that which we should seek to avail ourselves of first, as the most eminent, and one without which all our other privileges would amount to nothing? It is the being able to call God, so to speak, out of the magical contemplation of His own inexhaustible wonders, wonders which have been before Him from all eternity, are born of Him, and are Himself, and from which He can no more separate, than He can from Himself.

It is, in a manner, to drag Him away from the imperious absorbing attraction which eternally draws Him towards Himself, and makes what Is turn continually

---

* I owe likewise some advice to my brethren, when I invite them to qualify themselves for the Lord's service, namely: -

(Advice about Spirit communications.)

Some men, when they hear of living spiritual works, conceive the idea of communicating with spirits, or what is commonly called seeing ghosts.

With those who believe in the possibility of such a thing, this idea often excites nothing but fright; with those who are not sure of its impossibility, it gives rise only to curiosity; with those who deny or reject all about it, it produces only scorn and contempt, as well for the opinions themselves, as for those who hold them.

I think myself obliged, therefore, to say to all such, that a man may go on for ever in living spiritual works, and attain a high rank amongst the Lord's workmen, without seeing spirits. I ought further to tell him who, in the spiritual career, would seek to communicate with spirits, that, supposing him to succeed, not only he would not thereby fulfil the chief object of his work, but he might be very far from deserving to be classed with the Lord's workmen.

For, if he think so much of communicating with spirits, he ought to suppose the possibility of meeting with bad ones as well as good.

Thus, to be safe, it would not suffice that he should communicate with spirits; he should also be able to discern from whence they came, and for what purpose, and whether their errand were laudable or unlawful, useful or mischievous; and, supposing them to be of the purest and most perfect class, be should, before all, examine whether he would himself be in condition to perform the works they might give him to undertake in their Master s service.

The privilege or satisfaction of seeing spirits can never be otherwise than quite accessory to man's real object in the way of living, spiritual, divine work, and his admission amongst the Lord's workmen ; and he who aspires to this sublime ministry would not be worthy of it, if he were drawn to it by the puerile curiosity of conversing with spirits ; especially if, to obtain these secondary evidences, he depended upon the uncertain aid of his fellow-creatures, with usurped, or partial, or even corrupt powers.

away from what is not, and towards what Is, as a necessary consequence of a natural analogy.

It is to awake and force Him, if we may use the term, out of that intoxication which is occasioned by the perpetual mutual experience of the sweetness of His own essences, and that delicious sentiment which the active generative source of His own existence gives. It is, in short, to draw down His divine countenance upon this lost dark Nature, that its vivifying power may restore her to her former splendour.

But what thought can reach Him, if its analogy with Him is not first restored? What thought can accomplish this awakening in Him, if it is not first made alive again, like Him? What thought can make rivers of sweet and healing waters flow out of Him, if it be not first made pure and meek, like Him? What thought can ever unite with what Is, if it become not again like that which Is, by separating from all that is not? What being can ever be admitted into the Father's house, and His intimacy, if he have not shown himself to be a true child of this Father?

O Man! If here you see the most sublime of your privileges, that of making God come out of His own contemplation, you see also on what condition such a privilege may be exercised. If you should ever succeed in awaking this Supreme God, and forcing Him out of His own contemplation, do you suppose it would be a matter of small concern to you what condition He found you in?

Let your whole being, then, become a new creature! Let every one of your faculties be revived, even to its deepest roots! Let the living simple oil be subdivided into an infinity of purifying elements, and let there be nothing in you which is not stimulated and warmed by one of these regenerating and ever living elements!

A Helper and Comforter

If there were no strong One sent to comfort you, and help you to become, like Him, the dutiful child of your heavenly Father, how could you attain to the lowest step of your regeneration? Nor are you ignorant that this Agent exists, since He is the very living focus in which your being reposed when you were made, and who has no more abandoned you since, than a mother can abandon her son in any affliction whatever. Unite with Him, without delay or reserve, and your pollution will vanish and your famine be turned into plenty.

Man must perform his Father's work

Nevertheless, the weight of the work will not cease to be felt, it may even become heavier; for, when the weight of God's hand is on man, and not for his punishment, it must be for work.

In fact, God, having destined man to be the rectifier of Nature, did not give him this appointment without ordering him to fulfil it; He did not order him to fulfil it, without giving him the means; He did not give him the means, without an ordination, nor an ordination without a consecration; He did not give him consecration, without a promise of glorification; nor did He promise this glorification, but because he was to serve as organ to the praises of God, by taking the place of the enemy whose throne was cast down, and opening the mysteries of Eternal Wisdom.

Two kinds of mysteries

But there are two kinds of mysteries. One comprises the natural mysteries of the formation of physical things, their laws, and modes of existence, and the object of this existence. The other comprises the mysteries of our fundamental being, and its relations with its Principle.

The final intent of a mystery cannot be to remain altogether inaccessible, either to the understanding or to the sweet sense of admiration for which our souls are made, and which we have already recognised as a first necessity for our immaterial being to feed upon.

The intent of the mystery of Nature is to raise us, through the discovery of the laws of physical things, to the knowledge of the higher laws and powers by which they are governed. The knowledge of this mystery of Nature and all that constitutes it, cannot then be prohibited now, even since our fall; otherwise its final intent would be missed.

The final intent of the mystery of divine and spiritual things, which is connected with that of our own being, is to move us and excite in us sentiments of admiration, tenderness, love, and gratitude. This mystery of divine and spiritual things ought, then, to be allowed to penetrate to the very ground of our being, otherwise this double mystery, which connects us with divine things, and divine things with us, would fail of its effect.

But there is a great difference between these two sorts of mysteries. The mystery of Nature may be more or less known, but Nature itself hardly touches our essential fundamental being at all; and, if we experience pleasure in its contemplation and in penetrating its mysteries, it is because we then rise above Nature, and ascend, by its means, to regions which are really analogous to ourselves; it is herein like a lantern, showing us the way to these high regions, but unable, in itself, to communicate their sweetness.

The spiritual and divine things, on the contrary, touch our faculties of love and admiration far more than our understanding; it seems even as though it were to prepare us for a still higher measure of admiration, that they will not so readily yield themselves to our perceptions ; for if we could, at will, subject them to our cognizance, we should not admire them so much, and our pleasure would be less: for, if it is true that our happiness is to admire, it is also true that to admire is to feel, rather than to know; which is the reason why God and Spirit are at once so sweet and so little known.

For the opposite reason, we might say that Nature is so cold because it is more adapted to be known than to be felt; thus the plans of Wisdom are so arranged, that things, on which our true pleasure depends, do not so yield to our intelligence as to quench admiration; and things which are intended less for the nourishment of our admiration, i.e. our true pleasures, as having less analogy to us, afford us a sort of compensation in the pleasures of the understanding.

By the way men have managed these domains, they have allowed these two sources, which would have produced delicious fruit, each after its kind, to dry up; that is, human philosophy, treating of natural sciences, and keeping only on the surface, has prevented us from knowing them, and has not given us even the pleasures of the understanding, which they would have so readily afforded; and teachers of divine things, by darkening them and making them unapproachable, have prevented us from feeling them, and so deprived us of the admiration they would not have failed to awaken in us, if they had been allowed to reach us.

The perfection of mystery is, to unite in a true and harmonious combination, what will at once satisfy our intelligence and nourish our admiration; this we should have enjoyed for ever, if we had kept our first estate. For the door by which God goes out of Himself, is the same by which He enters the human soul.

The door by which the human soul goes out of itself, is the same by which it enters the understanding.

The door by which the human understanding goes out of itself, is the same by which it enters the spirit of the universe.

The door by which the spirit of the universe goes out of itself, is that by which it enters into the elements and matter.

This is the reason why the learned, who do not take all these routes, never enter Nature.

Matter had no door by which to go out of itself, nor enter any region inferior to itself ; this is the reason why the enemy could have no access to any orderly region, whether material or spiritual.

Instead of watching carefully at his post, Man not only opened all these doors to his enemies, but he closed them against himself, so that he now finds himself outside, and the robbers within. Can a more lamentable situation be conceived?

Man the mirror of God's wonders

We see why the superb titles which constituted Man so privileged a being, would have made his ministry in the universe of so much importance; he might have made known the Divine Threefold Unity, our likeness to which has been so often remarked, showing thereby that we should not thus have been His image, if we had not the right of representing Him. And everything, even to the angels, was greatly interested in man's keeping the post which was committed to him.

In fact, as animal life, scattered all through nature, knows neither the spirit of the universe in itself, nor the germs of the vegetables, which are its results, and the sensible expression of its properties, and animals know these things only in the flavour of what they feed upon ; so do the angels only know the Father in the Son. They know him neither in Himself nor in Nature, which, especially since the first great change, is much nearer to the Father than to the Son, through the concentration it experienced; and they can know Him only in the divine splendour of the Son, who, in His turn, has His image only in the heart of Man, and not in Nature.

For this reason, Man, who, in the beginning of the Universe, was related, principally, to the Son, the Source of Universal development, knew the Father, both in the Son and in Nature. And, for this reason, Angels seek so much the society of Man, believing that he is still in condition to show them the Father in Nature.

Key to the wonders of Nature

Our task, therefore, since the epoch when Adam was drawn out of the precipice into which he fell, should be to discover, by all possible means, the wonders of the Father, manifested in visible Nature; and this it is the more possible for us to do, because the Son, who contains them and opens them all, restored them to us, by incorporating our first parents in the material form we now bear, and brought the key with Him, when He made Himself like us.

Angels learn by Man

Oh what deep things might we not teach, even to angels, if we recovered our rights! St. Paul says, "We shall judge angels" (1 Cor. vi. 3)*. Now, power to judge supposes power to instruct. Yes, angels may be stewards, physicians, redressers of wrong, warriors, judges, governors, protectors, &c., but, without us, they cannot gain any profound knowledge of the divine wonders of Nature.

What prevents this is, not only that they know the Father only in the splendour of the Son, and that, unlike the first man, their bodily covering is devoid of essences taken from the root of Nature, but also because we close for them the central eye within us, the divine organ, by which they might have had the means of contemplating the riches of the Father in the depths of Nature; and that is why

* Scripture speaks of "evil" angels and "fallen" angels, as well as of holy angels. May not Man well be the touchstone by which the former are tried? and may not even the latter look into Man, to know somewhat of the breadth, and length, and depth, and height of the love of Christ, which passeth knowledge? - ED.

men of God ought to instruct angels, and open to their eyes the depths which are hidden in the corporification of Nature, and in all its wonders. This also is the reason why, in sciences and letters, those men are ranked highest who discover the grand laws of Nature; and, in religion, those who have been clothed with the greatest power from the Spirit.

Since our degradation, this precious privilege of penetrating the depths of Nature, and becoming, so to say, possessors of them, has been, in part, restored to us; it ought even to be an inheritance, inherent in Man's nature, inasmuch as it constitutes his true riches and original property: of this we have several instances in the patriarchal testaments.

Spiritual testaments

But men of matter have transposed these sublime rights, and applied them merely to their testaments of earthly goods; although it might be reasonably objected that a man may not dispose of goods which he would cease to possess at his death, and before his will could be executed.

It was, then, to real possessions that the law of testaments should apply, whereby the testator invests his heirs with a living right which he does not thereby lose himself, but which he takes with him to a region in which this right will still increase, instead of diminishing. And, here, our thoughts may expand, and be enriched by meditating upon the patriarchal testaments.

Man the tree, God the sap

Man is the tree, God is its sap. It is not surprising, then, that when this living sap flows in man, it converts each of his branches into a new tree; nor is it surprising, if some wild branches are grafted on these, that they should soon partake of its excellent properties.

Yes, since the fall, Man has been replanted upon the living root which ought to work in him all the spiritual vegetations of his Principle. For this reason, if he rose to the living fountain of admiration, he might, by his existence alone, communicate a living testimony thereof.

This, moreover, is the only means by which the divine purposes can be accomplished; for Man was born only to be Prime-Minister to the Divinity; even now, the material body we bear is very superior to the earth. Our animal spirit is very superior to the spirit of the universe, through its junction with our soul-spirit, (esprit animique), which is our real soul; and our soul-spirit is very superior to angels.

But man would deceive himself if he thought he could advance in the work of the Spirit-Man, without this holy sap being revived in him, for it has become, as it were, thick and congealed by the universal corruption.

Luminous foundation for Man's building

Thus, O man of desire, whatever you have allowed to coagulate and darken within you, must be dissolved and revealed to the eyes of your spirit. As long as you can see a stain there, or the smallest thing remains to obstruct your view, take no rest till you have dispersed it. The more you penetrate to the depths of your being, the better you will know the grounds on which the work rests.

No other ground but this, re-hewn and shaped, can serve for a foundation to your building. If it is not level and true to the plumb, the building can never be raised. No! It is in the inward light of your being alone that the Divinity, and all Its marvellous powers, can be made perceptible to you in their living glory.

If you dare not dwell in this region yourself; if your view cannot penetrate so far; or if you fear to look there, on account of its difficulty of access; how can you expect the Divinity to be more at ease there than you, and accommodate Itself to your darkness, and the obstructions which repel you? - the Divinity, which is so radically and altogether luminous and pure, and able to develop the wonders of Its existence, only in atmospheres which are cleared of every obstruction, and free as Itself?

The science of Truth is not like other sciences: it ought originally to have been all mere enjoyment for man ; now it is all a mere combat; and this is why the learned and savans of the world have not the least idea of it, because they confound it with their own dark notions, which are acquired passively.

The Universe in pain

The universe is on a bed of suffering, and it is for us, men, to comfort it. The universe is on a bed of suffering, because, since the fall, a foreign substance has entered its veins, and incessantly impedes and torments its life-principle. It is for us to speak to it words of comfort and encouragement, and the promise of deliverance and covenant of alliance, which Eternal Wisdom is coming to make with it.

This is nothing more than what is just and our bounden duty, since the head of our family was the first cause of its pains. We may say that we made the universe a widower; and it will be waiting for its spouse to be restored, as long as things endure.

O Sun of Righteousness! We are the first cause of thy discomfort and disquiet. Thine eye ceases not to survey, in succession, every region of nature. Thou risest daily for every man; Thou risest joyously, in the hope that they will restore to Thee thy cherished Spouse, the Eternal SOPHIA, of whom Thou hast been deprived; Thou fulfillest thy daily course, asking for her from the whole earth, with burning words, which tell of Thy consuming desires. But, in the evening, Thou settest in affliction and tears, because Thou hast sought thy Spouse in vain; Thou hast demanded her from man, and he has not restored her; and he still suffers thee to dwell in barren places and abodes of prostitution.

The World is dead

O Man! The evil is greater still! Say not now that the Universe is on a bed of suffering; say it is on its death-bed ; and it is for you to perform its funereal rites. It is for you to reconcile it with the pure source from which it descends; a source which, though not God, is one of the eternal organs of His power, and from which the Universe ought never to have been separate; it is, I say, for you to reconcile it, by purging it from all the substances of falsehood with which it has been incessantly impregnated ever since the fall, and by washing it from the consequences of passing every day of its life in vanity.

The Universe would not thus have passed its days in vanity, if you had yourself remained in that throne of glory in which you were originally seated, and if you had anointed it daily with an oil of gladness which should have preserved it from sickness and pain; you would then have done for it what it now does for you, by providing you daily with the light and elementary productions to which you have subjected yourself, and which are now necessary for your existence. Come, then, and ask its forgiveness, for you were the cause of its death.

The evil is greater still! You must no more say the Universe is on its death-bed: it is in its grave! Putrefaction has got hold of it, infection issues from all its member ; and you, O man, are to blame! But for you, it would not have thus sunk into its grave; but for you, it would not have thus exhaled infection.

Man must bring the Universe to a new birth

Do you know the reason why? It is because you have made yourself its sepulchre. It is because, instead of being the cradle of its perpetual youth and beauty, you have buried it in yourself as in a tomb, and clothed it with your own corruption. Inject quickly the elixir of life into all its channels, for it is for you to bring it to life again; and, notwithstanding the cadaverous smell it already emits from all its parts, you are charged to give it a new birth.

Natural light itself, that beautiful type of a former world, which is still left us, contains a devouring power which consumes everything; and the artificial lights we use in its stead subsist only at the expense of the substances they feed upon. And we ought to have had none of those lights; they are a monstrosity in Nature, in which insects burn themselves, mistaking them for the natural light, because Nature's creatures know nothing that is out of order.

Yes, our very trades and manufactures (*industries*) are a proof of the injury we have done to the world, since this injury, and these pursuits, proceed from the same source, and thus Nature is every way our victim. Oh, how this Nature, if she could speak, would complain of the little good she derives from the vain sciences of men, and from all their scaffoldings, and labours to describe, measure, and analyse her, when they have in themselves the means to comfort and cure her!

Man himself is dead: how he died

But is not Man himself on his bed of suffering? Is he not on his death-bed? Is he not in his grave, a prey to corruption? And who will comfort him? Who will perform his obsequies? Who will bring him to life again?

The enemy was ambitious from the beginning; he saw into the wonders of glory, and wished to turn their source towards himself, and rule over it. Man's fall did not begin in this way: this was not his crime, for he was to attain these glories only as he accomplished his mission; and, when he first received his existence he did not know of them. He went astray, first, through weakness, as his children do now, in their infancy, when objects of ambition have no effect upon them; and his weakness was, that he allowed himself to be struck, attracted, and penetrated by the spirit of the world, whereas he was of a higher order, and a region above this world.

When he once descended to this lower region, the enemy found it easy to inspire him with ambitious thoughts, which he would not otherwise have had-with none to speak to him of objects of ambition, of which he knew nothing.

Thus, in his first lapse, he was victim of his own weakness; in his second, he was at once victim and dupe of his enemy, who was interested in leading him astray; and he became entirely subject to this physical world, over which he ought to have been the ruler.

Then his crimes increased in a ratio which it frightens him now to think of! Yes, O Man! You have become a thousand times more guilty since your fall. In your fall, you were a dupe and a victim; but since your fall, you have become the universal instrument of evil, the absolute slave of your enemy, and how often, alas, his accomplice?

Man's work must still be done

And in this condition you have, nevertheless, still to visit the Universe on its death-bed, and restore it to life, not forgetting that the first plan of your own original destination remains also to be fulfilled!

O Man! Stop in the middle of this abyss in which you are, if you will not plunge still deeper in. Your work was quite simple when it came out of your First Principle's hands; it has become threefold, through your imprudence and the abominations you have committed: you have now, first, to regenerate yourself; secondly, to regenerate the Universe; then, thirdly, to rise to be a steward of the eternal riches, and to admire the living wonders of Divinity.

In the physical order, we see the remedy comes after sickness, and sickness after health. Now, if sickness leads to the remedy, it must be the same in the spiritual and moral order of man; and, if, here, health likewise preceded his sickness, his malady should lead him to seek the analogous remedy, as physicians seek those for our physical disorders.

The first step, then, towards the cure which man has to work upon himself, is to throw off all those vitiated secondary humours which have accumulated upon him since the fall; humours which have attacked and taken possession of mankind, in the different lapses of the posterity of the first man; those which we inherit from our parents, through the evil influence of vicious generations; and those which we bring upon ourselves by our daily negligence and offences.

Till we have got rid of these humours we cannot move a step towards our recovery, which consists, particularly, in traversing the region of darkness into which we fell, and causing the natural elixir to revive within us, with which to restore the senses of the Universe, which is in a swoon.

Qualification for the work, and test thereof

Here, O Man! A new condition meets you, if you would go further. It is no longer a question of the spiritual nature of your being; of your essential relation to your principle; of your degradation by a first voluntary act; of the ardent love of your generative Source, which led Him, at your fall, and every day since, to come and choose you in the midst of your disgusting filthiness (which the man of the stream may feel, but cannot understand, because he does not look back); it is, in short, no longer a question of the overwhelming evidences of every kind, which depose in favour of these fundamental truths, which prove themselves: these points are settled between us, without which I warned you not to proceed; and if it were not so, you would probably not have come thus far.

But you have to see whether you have purged your being from all those secondary defilements which we daily bring upon ourselves since the fall; or, at least, whether you feel an ardent desire to cast them from you at any price whatsoever, and revive that life within you which was extinguished by the first crime, without which you can be neither God's servant nor the world's comforter.

Try even to feel that, perhaps, the only science worth studying, is to be without sin; for, possibly, if man were in that state, he might naturally manifest all lights and sciences.

Probe yourself, therefore, deeply as to these new conditions; and, if, not only you have not cleansed yourself from the results of all your secondary lapses, but even if you have not pulled up by the roots the remotest disinclination you had for the work, I repeat to you, solemnly, go no farther. Man's work requires new men. Those who are not so, will try in vain to form part of the building; when such stones came to be presented for their places, they would be found wanting in the required dimensions, or in finish, and be sent back to the workshop till they were fit to be used.

There is a sign by which to know whether you have made this self-denudation or not.

It is, to see if you feel yourself to be above every other fear, every other care whatsoever, but that of failing to be universally anastomosed with the divine impulse and action.

It is when, far from looking upon our personal sufferings in this world as misfortunes, we confess that none can happen to us but what are our due, and that all we do not suffer are so many favours granted to us, in consideration of our weakness; so that, instead of complaining that our joys and consolations are taken from us in this world, we ought to begin by being thankful that they were not taken from us before, and that some are still left us.

Supposing, then, the two classes of conditions that we have mentioned complied with, the following is the commencement of man's regeneration into his primitive rights, virtues, and titles.

Order of Man's regeneration

We see that in our material bodies we often feel pain in members which we have lost; now, as in what constitutes our true bodies we have no longer a single member left, the first evidence we can have of our existence as spiritual beings is to feel, either successively or all at once, acute pains in all those members which we no longer possess.

Life must regenerate all the organs we have suffered to perish, and it can do this only by substituting them, through its generative power, for all the foreign and frail organs that now constitute us.

We must feel the spirit making furrows in us, from head to foot, as with a mighty ploughshare, tearing up the trunks of old trees with their roots interlaced in our earth, and all foreign substances which impede our growth and fertility.

Everything that has entered us by charm and seduction, must go out of us by rending and pain. Now, what has come into us is nothing else than the spirit of this very Universe, with all its essences and properties ; they have borne fruit in us abundantly; they have become transformed in us into corrosive salts and corrupt humours, coagulated to such a degree that nothing but violent remedies and excessive perspirations can expel them.

O Man! These essences and properties of the Universe have taken possession of your whole being; therefore must the life-pains of regeneration be felt in your whole being, till these false foundations and sources of your errors, your darkness, and your anguish, be replaced by the spirit and essences of another, the primitive real Universe, which Jacob Boehme calls the Pure Element, from which you may expect sweeter and more wholesome fruits.

For, on simply considering your physical situation in this world, you cannot doubt that the grounds of these pains are in yourself, and constitute your existence in the daily wants they cause you to feel, and the incessant care they give you.

Thus we see all your days consumed in making yourself superior to cold, and heat, and darkness, and even to the stars of heaven, which you appear to bring under your daring sciences by your optical and astronomical instruments.

This clearly proves that your place should not have been in the region of these inclemencies, nor subject to influences which discomfort you; it should not have been below even those superb creations which, notwithstanding their magnificence in the order of beings, must still rank after you.

As these foreign elements have been implanted in your most inward nature, so, in your inmost nature, must the real pains be felt; there, must be developed the real feeling of humility and contrition, which makes us shudder on finding ourselves connected with essences so incompatible with ourselves.

There, in your inmost nature, you must walk in this world, as in a road amongst sepulchres, where you cannot take a step without hearing the dead calling to you for life.

There, by your groans and sufferings, you obtain wherewithal to offer sacrifice, on which the fire from the Lord cannot fail to descend, to at once consume the victim and give new life to the sacrificer, supplying him with powerful assistance, or continually renewed virtualities, for the performance of his universal work.

For, by this meek living substance of our sacrifice uniting with us, our regeneration begins; the purifying sufferings we speak of can only be its initiative; their object being to cut off what is hurtful to us, but not to give what we want.

When we feel ourselves all rent with these excruciating amputations, and blood runs from all our wounds, then the healing balm comes to stanch it, applies itself to our sores, and injects itself into every channel.

Now, as what this balm brings is life itself, we soon feel ourselves born again in all our faculties and virtues, and in all the active principles of our being.

For all these active principles of our being are so oppressed by the weight of the universe, and dried up by the fire which burns them inwardly, that they wait, in eager impatience, for the sole refreshment that can restore their motion and activity.

This refreshing accommodates itself to our littleness. It begins very feebly with man, who is feeble and little; it so bears its care and love towards us, as to make itself child-like with us, for we are less than children, and generally speaking, at every act of our growth, it has to take step by step by our side.

It acts towards us as a mother does towards her child which has bruised itself, or is in pain; she applies all her thoughts to its cure; she throws herself, so to say, altogether into its bruises or suffering members.

She goes into it, as it were, taking the form, and substituting herself for what was bruised or injured in her child ; she goes in, in some sort, with the industry of her creative love, and nothing is too troublesome, nothing too little, for this industrious tenderness; whatever may do good seems to her to be necessary.

These means of all kinds, graduated to all requirements, are in activity in the healing languages guided by the true Word [*sacred books*]. The wonders found in them contain more or less of the activity which was most appropriate to the times in which they appeared.

For this refreshing, after which we all languish, although it may come into us directly, does not disdain to enter by all sorts of ways; and healing languages, with all their denominations and modes of expression, are one of the means it inclines to most, and makes use of in preference.

It is not surprising that it should be necessary for this living active power to come into us to fit us to do its work. Those who know the real state of things are sensible that we must be alive and strong to do this work, or for it to be done in us, for evil is no mere fable, it is a power.

The reign of evil is not to be destroyed by fine speaking, either in nature or in men's spirits. Men and learned doctors may discourse as they will, evil is not thereby put to flight; it even makes progress under this shelter.

Life itself must do all substantially

In this state of death, in which the universe languishes, with all fallen regions, could any kind or order of things subsist at all if there were not a Substance of Life disseminated everywhere? It is assuredly this life-substance which prevents their dissolution, and sustains them in all the shocks and violence they undergo continually.

This is what sustains Nature against the hostile powers which harass her: this upholds the universal world, in spite of the darkness which surrounds it, as the sun upholds the earth, notwithstanding the clouds which hide it from our view.

This is what upholds nations, notwithstanding the disorders and ravages they excite amongst themselves, and one against another.

This is what sustains man in all the ignorance, extravagance, and abominations which he incessantly pours out.

This life-substance can be nothing else than the Eternal Word, incessantly creating itself, as Boehme has abundantly shown, which ceases not to sustain by its power all the regions it created.

This substance is everywhere buried in a deep abyss, and sighs continually for deliverance, and that quite unknown to Nature; and it is because this Substance of Life ceases not to groan that things still subsist, notwithstanding the continuance and extent of the abominations which surround and pollute them; and these evils are so great, that, if we were to tell them to the spirits, we should send them away weeping.

But as the soul, or radical focus of man, is the first and principal seat of this life-substance, it seeks to develop and show itself, especially in him. And if man concurred with it in persevering action, if he felt that he was, by nature, originally nothing less than a divine oratory, where Truth might come at all hours to offer pure incense to the Eternal Fountain of All, it cannot be doubted that he would soon see this substance of life strike root in him, and spread over and around him numerous branches loaded with fruits and flowers.

Then the spirits, elated with the sweet sensations they received from us, would charitably forget the evil we had done them before; for every act of this substance is a florescence, which ought to begin at the root of our being, at what may be called our soul-germ (*germe animique*); thence it passes to the life of our mind or understanding, and then into our bodily life; and, as each of these is related to its corresponding region, every florescence which takes place in us communicates with its own atmosphere.

But, as the object of this substance, in working these three degrees, is only to give us new life, it can accomplish this only by a threefold transmutation, by giving us a new soul, a new spirit, and a new body.

Process of new birth

This transmutation can be effected only by a painful process: it can proceed only by a combat between what is sound and what is diseased, and by the physical action of the true will, opposed to that of our false will.

Our own wills accomplish nothing without their being, as it were, injected by the Divine Will, which is the only will to good, with power to produce it: this seems a very simple remark, but it is not the less fecund and spiritual.

It is by these different acts that life succeeds in substituting a pure essence for the corrupt essences of our spirits, souls, and bodies.

Thereby, our desire forms but one with the divine desire, or hunger for the manifestation of truth, and its rule in the world.

Thereby, our understanding forms but one with the Divine Eye, which sees behind as well as before.

Thereby, our bodies, allowing all the substances of lies, corruption, and pollution with which they are constituted to die out, feel their places taken by diaphanous substances, which render them like transparencies of Divine Light and wonders throughout, as natural bodies are transparencies of natural wonders: this is what they who believe that this life-substance is no barren substance, may hope for.

And if they believe that it is no barren substance, this is what they will have to go through if they would recover their first estate and fulfil their destination.

How should this life-substance be barren? It proceeds from and participates in that generative movement which is without time, in which motive-causes (*mobiles*) cannot be separated, otherwise there would be an interval; but in which, nevertheless, these motives cannot but be distinct, otherwise there would be no life or diversity of wonders.

O you, who are able to conceive these sublimities, take courage; for it is given you to attain to them, and to so identify them with your whole being, that their region and yours may be but one, and have but one language.

Then it is divine hunger lays hold on man, and by making us distinguish between our two substances, revives all our ardour and regulates all our movements.

We, then, breathe only for one object, which is, not to allow the substance of life, which this divine hunger brings to us day by day increasingly, to fade or die away, and to prevent its falling under the yoke and chains of tyrants within us.

Our daily bread

In this spirit even should we take our daily food: if man were wise, he would never take his material repasts without first awaking this divine hunger within him.

He would thereby escape that fatal consequence which is so frequent, so common to us in our darkness, that of choking the divine hunger, by our food, whereas our food was intended, and ought to be, only for the renewal of our bodily powers, that we might be enabled to seek this divine hunger more ardently, and bear it better when it comes in power and feeds us so effectively that bodily hunger becomes less pressing in its turn.

And there are two degrees in this regimen. One is for the use of our spiritualized intents and labours, which ought to be our daily diet, without restriction to times or hours, or kinds of aliment, for our labours themselves will determine these.

The other is for active work, when it thinks fit to take us into its "service; it then serves at once for our guide and for our support.

What I have said of the first degree of this regimen may be said of every other act of our temporal life: we ought never to apply ourselves to anything, without having first awakened within us the divine hunger; because as this divine hunger has to procure for us the true substance of life, we ought to have no aim, no attraction, no thought, but never to allow this fountain of the divine wonders to pass from us, but, on the contrary, employ ourselves incessantly in reviving it, that it may have the sweet delight of satiating itself with the Substance of Life.

Pains of new birth

I shall not surprise you, by here telling you, O man, that this life-substance is to be found only in pains of bitter anguish, and a sense of profound and complete desolation, for our own faults and privations, and those of our fellow-creatures; for the real wretchedness of those who suffer, and, still more, of those who do not suffer; for the sepulchral state of Nature, and the chronic and acute pains of the universal World, seeking to restore, through us, equilibrium and plenitude everywhere; whilst we, by the mode of being we have, through crime, created for ourselves, keep the Heart of God Himself, in us, on its death-bed, and in a grave of corruption.

Now, why is desolation, thus, the generative source of the Substance of Life? It is because, for us, now, it is the only generative source of speech (*la parole*), the Word; as we see in our sicknesses, our sufferings extort cries, and our cries bring assistance and relief.

For this reason, the man who is called to the Work has no need to remove from his place; the disease and the remedy are everywhere, and he has nothing to do but cry. It is not an earthly, but a spiritual change of place, that can serve us.

And, without stirring from our material place, we ought to reflect incessantly, painfully, on the cold, dark, spiritual place we are in, that we may go and make our dwelling in one that is warmer, lighter, and happier.

Cause of Nature's groans

When we observe that the Universe is deprived of speech, it is not hard to see that this is a principal cause of its distress.

The languor which oppresses it, the pestilential venom which gnaws it, and which, as we have admitted, came into its substances only through man's fault and negligence; it would, I say, feel none of this, were it not deprived of speech, for it would, otherwise, have had strength to dissipate them, or even prevent their attacks.

It is, then, this privation, which is the real cause that Nature is in that perpetual distress, by wise men called vanity.

Those men knew that speech, the Word, should fill all things, and they groaned because there was something in which it was not heard.

They knew that the Universe, without the Word, and empty, signified nothing to them, since God alone was full, and signified all things; so that, whatsoever does not partake of the plenitude of His divine Being, can show only the reverse of His universal properties.

They knew that man could not pray without preparation, that is, unless his atmosphere were filled with the Word; or, in the widest sense, unless speech were restored to the universe.

And they complained in their sorrow, and in man's name they said: "This universe, this beautiful picture, which we should admire with transport, were we blind to all it wants ; this universe is speechless, it can take no part in prayer; it is even an obstacle to it, for we can only pray with our brethren. Alas, then! We shall pray at our ease only when the universe has passed away! and we are obliged to wait till the end of all things, to give free course to the ardour which burns us!

Who could endure such grief as this?" And their days were passed in agony!

O Man! Since you are in the world, there is not one of its storms which you may not feel and share in, since your body participates in the divers influences and temperatures of which the elements are at once the medium and the source.

Yes, since you were able to cause the pains of the universe, you are susceptible of feeling them; and, only in proportion as you are allowed to partake of its pains, can you contribute to the development of its faculties: only by movements coincident with its sufferings, can you succeed in restoring its joys, and hope for freedom to be imparted to your prayer.

You will, indeed, one day, have to enter into the storms of the Spirit, and of God, and the Word, both individually and universally; for the rights of your being call you to act co-ordinately, in both these regions ; and then, your new birth will advance, and the Work be enlarged for you.

Creation still groans for deliverance

Man finds something solemn and imposing in solitudes surrounded by vast forests, or watered by some great river; and these solemn and imposing scenes appear to have still more power over him in the shades and stillness of night.

But he may make an observation of another kind, that is, that the silence of these objects creates a painful impression on the soul, which shows clearly the real cause of the vanity we have above alluded to.

In fact, Nature is like a dumb creature, expressing, as well as it can, by its movements, the wants which devour it most, but which, from want of speech, it cannot express as it desires; and this gives a tone of sadness and seriousness to its happiness, and prevents us from completely enjoying our own.

And, in the midst of these grand scenes, we really feel that Nature is weary of being unable to speak; and our admiration gives way to a languor approaching to melancholy, when we give ourselves up to this painful reflection.

This should suffice to make us understand that everything ought to speak; and the conviction that everything ought to speak, brings this conviction also, that everything ought to be diaphanous and fluid, and that opacity and stagnation are the radical causes of the silence and weariness of Nature.

Nature a prison for Man

What sort of dwelling, then, is this, for you, O Man, amidst all these objects which can manifest neither joy nor speech? And do you not see what the term of that imperious want of speech and joy you feel yourself must be, and what awaits you when you are delivered out of this prison of Nature, as well as what sort of office you have to fulfil in the world, if you still think of being its comforter?

Study Nature's universal transudation; this oil of bitterness will teach you evidently enough, that all Nature is but a concentrated sorrow.

But, though Nature be condemned to weariness and silence, observe that it speaks louder by day than by night; this is a truth which you can easily verify, and your intelligence will show the reason; it will show you that the Sun is the verb of Nature, that when its presence is withdrawn, Nature no longer enjoys the use of her faculties; but, when it returns to restore her to life by its fiery word, Nature redoubles her efforts to bring forth all that is in her.

All the creatures which compose this Nature, then strive which can best prove its zeal and activity, in glorifying and praising this ineffable source of light. They thereby clearly point out the work we ought to do in this universe, and what awaits us when we go out of this house of traffic, which is nothing but the grave of eternity, where our task is to exchange our foreign coins for the currency of our own country; death for life.

Nature also rejoices in hope

Take comfort, you men of desire; if Nature's silence is the cause of its weariness, what can be more eloquent than this silence? It is the silence of sorrow, not of insensibility.

The more clearly you examine, the more surely you will observe, that, if Nature has her season of sorrow, she also has her moments of joy, and to you only is it given to discern and appreciate them. She feels life circulating secretly in her veins; and is ever ready to hear, through your organs, the sound of the Word which supports her, and places her as a barrier to the enemy.

She seeks, in you, the living fire which burns in that Word, and which, through you, would convey a healing balm to her sores. Yes! Although the man of earth perceives nothing but the silence and weariness of Nature, you, O men of desire, are well assured that everything in her is vocal, and prophesying her deliverance in sublime canticles.

And, in holy zeal, and by orders from on high, you announce that every thing in man must break into song, to co-operate in this deliverance, and that all people may one day say like you: that every thing in Nature sings.

You are as harbingers of that reign of Truth for which every thing sighs. You advance in that majestic and divinely healing progression, which restores to each epoch its opposite progression of evil.

Whereby, evil, devouring the life-substance of those great periods, which commenced at the beginning, to end only with time, ceases not to fatten on iniquity, till, its measures being full, it is handed over to judgment.

For, in time, evil is only in privation; yet, has it succeeded in extending its prison's bounds, by corrupting its gaoler, by whom alone it could gain some knowledge of what was passing outside.

But, in the midst of this painful progress of the enemy, you triumph in anticipation, because you also see the healing progression advancing towards its term of glory and victory. You hear it in anticipation, pronouncing sentence of execution on the criminal, who knows nothing of it yet, and will continue in this ignorance till the moment of his final punishment arrives.

Finally, you see it in anticipation, singing, through Nature, and in the souls of true men, the songs of joy, which will crown their desires and labors of prayer. For, if it is true that all is choral in Nature, it is still more certain that all prays, since every thing is in travail and distress.

It is necessary to know the ground of action.

How can any one be employed to bring relief to any thing, without knowing its structure and composition? And how can its composition and structure be known, unless the different substances of which it is constituted be also known, as well as the qualities and properties attached to these substances? Lastly, how can these qualities and properties be known, if the radical sources from which they derive be not known?

Instead of profoundly investigating these foundations, men have allowed their thoughts to be lost in idle questions, which, while they lead them away from the paths they ought to have followed, can teach them nothing. Such, for instance, is that puerile question about the divisibility of matter, which keeps the schools as in their infancy.

It is not matter which is infinitely divisible; it is its ground of action, or, in other words, the spirituous powers of what may be called the material or astral spirit. These powers are innumerable. The moment they are required to transform themselves into sensible characters and figures, the substance is not wanting, for they are impregnated with it, and produce it, in concert with the elementary power, with which they unite.

Hence it is, that every thing that exists here below, creates for itself the substance of its own body.

Now the microscopic minuteness of some bodies, animalcule for instance, should not surprise us, though they be so perfectly organized, after their kind. All bodies are but a realization of the plan of the astral Spirit, added to the individual spirituous operation of each body; and, here, we should bear in mind this important truth, namely, that, as Spirit has no knowledge of space, but only degrees of intensity in its radical virtues, there is not a single spirituous power of Spirit, which, whether materially sensible or not, is not so according to the hidden element, or that higher corporification mentioned before, under the name of Eternal Nature.

Birth of matter

The passage from this, to the material region, takes place only by the most extreme concentration and attenuation of that spirituous power of Spirit, over which the elementary power has rights, to help it to form its body or covering. This elementary power has complete authority in its own region, and exercises it with an universal empire over every spirituous basis that is presented to it: they unite only in their minimum, which, here, is inversely, one being the minimum of attenuation, the other the minimum of growth or development. The spirituous basis, in its turn, effects a living reaction on the elementary power; so that, in proportion as this basis develops itself, the elementary power is also developed to overtake it, as is seen in the growth of trees and animals.

When, by this means, this basis has acquired strength enough to free itself from the dominion of the elementary power, it separates from it; as is seen in all blossoms, smells, and colours; in short, in the ripening of any production. They all abandon their matrices when these can no longer retain them, and then the matrices return to their minimum again, not to say annihilation, because they have no longer any spirituous bases to excite their re-action.

Matter is indivisible

Thus, in the first place, matter is not infinitely divisible, considered in respect to its substance, the division of which, as we have shown elsewhere, we cannot even attempt, as we see organic bodies cannot be divided, without their perishing; - secondly, it is not infinitely divisible in its particular actions, for each of these actions ceases, as soon as the spirituous basis which serves for its subject is withdrawn; the retreat and disappearance of this basis puts an end to this action.

As for this infinite divisibility, considered abstractedly, it is still less possible, for it is nothing but our own conception which serves as basis for a pretended matter, which we continually forge; and as long as our mind affords such a substratum or germ, matter appropriates it in our thought, and gives it form and covering.

Thus, as long as we stop at this divisibility, or think of its temporal results, we find it possible and real, since a sensible form always follows the basis we offer it; but, as soon as we turn our minds away from this centre of action, which we approach only intellectually, this form disappears, and there is no longer any divisibility in matter.

Matter, a portrait or picture

If the learned of all times, from the Platos and Aristotles, to the Newtons and

Spinosas, had but remarked that matter was only a representation or image of what was not itself, they would not have tortured themselves, nor erred so much, in telling us what it was.

Matter is like a portrait of an absent person; we must absolutely know the original, in order to know whether it is like; otherwise, to us, it will be but a fancy work, on which one may make what conjectures he likes, without being sure that any one of them is correct.

Magism of Nature

Nevertheless, in this series of formation of things, there is an important point which will not yield to our cognizance; that is, the Magism of the generation of things, and this refuses itself only because we seek by analysis, what can be apprehended only by a secret impression; and even here, we may say, that Jacob Boehme has raised the veil, by opening to our minds the seven forms of Nature, even to the eternal root of all.

The true character of Magism is, to be the medium and means of passage, from a state of absolute dispersion or indifference, which Boehme calls abyssal, to a state of sensibility, in any order, spiritual or natural, simple or elementary.

Generation, or this passage from the insensible to the sensible state, is perpetual. It holds the middle place between the dispersed insensible state of things, and their state of characterized sensibility, and yet is neither of them, since it is not dispersion, like the abyssal state, nor developed manifestation, like the thing which this generation transmits and communicates to us.

In this sense, Nature has its Magism ; for it contains all that is above it in dispersion, or all the astral and elementary essences which have to contribute to the production of things; and it contains, besides, all the hidden properties of the higher world, towards which it ever tends to direct our thoughts.

In this sense, each particular production of Nature has also its Magism ; for each in particular, say a flower, a salt, an animal, a metallic substance, is a medium between the invisible, insensible properties which are in its root, its principle of life, or its fundamental essences, and the sensible qualities which emanate from this production, and are made manifest by its means.

In this medium, all that has to come forth in every production, is elaborated and prepared. Now this place of preparation, this laboratory, into which we cannot penetrate without destroying it, is, for this very reason, a true Magism for us, although we may know all the springs which concur in its production, and even the law that directs the effect.

Ground of the regeneration of Nature

The principle of this hidden process is founded in the Divine generation itself, in which the eternal medium for ever serves as passage to the infinite immensity of universal essences. In this passage, these universal essences are respectively impregnated, that, after this impregnation, they may be manifested in their living ardour, with all their individual qualities, and those they have communicated to each other during their abode in this medium, or their passage through it.

Now, without this medium, this place of passage, there would be nothing manifest, nothing apprehensible to us; thus, all the mediums of Nature as it is, and all the mediums of spiritual Nature, are only images of this primitive and eternal medium; they only repeat its law; and, in this way, every thing there is in time is the demonstrator, the commentator, and the continuer of eternity.

Eternity the ground, created things the manifestation

For, Eternity, or what is, should be considered as the ground of all things. Creatures are only like frames, vases, or active coverings, in which this true and living Essence encloses itself, in order to manifest itself by their means.

Some, such as those that compose the universe, manifest the spirituous powers of this highest Essence. Others, such as Man, manifest its spiritual essences, that is, what is most intimate in this one Essence, this Being of beings.

Thus, though we may be ignorant of the generation of things, yet all knowledge towards which we tend, and of which we avail ourselves when we obtain it, has true Essence for its ground and object: thus, the beauties of Nature, and the useful and gentle properties, which, since God arrested its fall, are still to be found in it, notwithstanding its degradation, also belong to this true Essence, and may still serve for its organ, frame-work, and conductor.

When we bring changes on the existence of these objects, as our false sciences do continually, it is because we do not take time and trouble to seek in them true essence which they must possess, and which tends but to make itself known ; still less can we then revive it in objects in which it is torpid; - and so we prolong the evils we have done to Nature, instead of assuaging them as we ought.

Man, Nature's physician, must know her constitution

Let us repeat then, supposing it true that the universe were on its death-bed, how should we bring it relief, if we were ignorant, not only of what constitutes the universe in itself, but even of the relations which its different parts, and wheels within wheels, forming the whole machine, and regulating its movements, must have with each other?

But, though Man, in his small sphere, is employed in restoring harmony, and a healthy constitution, amongst the elements and universal powers which are at war; though he strives to put a stop to the painful discord which distracts Nature around him; yet the idea of his contributing to the relief of the universe, is one which will probably create astonishment, and, at first sight, appear exaggerated, and far beyond our power; so thick is the veil, which the schools, and, above all, the oppressive weight of the universe itself, under which we bend, have spread over our true rights and privileges.

At the same time, the mere idea of our knowing the structure and composition of the universe, how it was made, and what those bodies are, which circulate so grandly in space, is not open to the same objection.

For, it may be said, that these questions have been the object of curiosity and research of men, eager for knowledge, in all ages, though, to judge merely from the doctrines which fame has handed down to us, on these subjects, a very mediocre light seems to have resulted from their researches.

In fact, the philosophers of antiquity give us very little help on this subject. It is a small thing for them to say, with Thales, that the universe owes its origin to water; or, with Anaximenes, that it owes it to air; or, with Empedocles, that it is composed of four elements continually at war amongst themselves, without ever being able to destroy each other: - supposing, of course, we may judge these doctrines in the absence of whatever demonstrations may have justified them to their authors and partisans.

The least I can do is to suspend my judgment; - and this I must, even on the "qualities" of Anaximander, and the "plastic forms" of the Stoics. They may be obscure, but I fear it would be going too far to tax them as follies, and philosophers' dreams. Sentence cannot, in such cases, be passed by default, and, if these seeming follies have been combated by unbelievers, as, no doubt, they were, it was probably by substituting manifest absurdities for what was merely obscure.

Nor have the moderns much extended our knowledge on these great questions: for, what does Telliamed's system teach us, which makes everything come from the sea; or the monads of Leibnitz; or the integral molecules and aggregates of modern Physics, which are nothing more than the atoms of Epicurus, Leucippus, and Democritus over again?

Unsatisfactory results of human research

Man's mind, unable to penetrate these depths as successfully as he wished, or unable to make others understand the true signification of the progress and discoveries it made, has always returned to the study of the laws which direct the outward course of our globe, or that of other globes accessible to our view: it is from this we have acquired whatever astronomical knowledge we have gained, whether in ancient or in modern times.

Although these grand acquisitions, which have been so astonishingly extended in our day, through the perfecting of our instruments, and the wonderful assistance of modern algebraical analysis, have afforded us an enjoyment all the sweeter because it is based upon strict demonstration; yet, as they teach us only the external laws of the universe, they do not satisfy us altogether, unless indeed we smother or paralyze within us the secret desire, which all have, for more substantial nourishment.

Thus, notwithstanding Kepler's brilliant discoveries of laws of heavenly bodies; Descartes, who was so celebrated for having applied algebra to geometry, sought still to discover the cause and the mode of their movements.

While Kepler demonstrated, Descartes endeavoured to explain: so great is the attraction of man's mind towards the knowledge, not only of the course of the stars, and the laws, and duration of their periodical movements, but even of the mechanical cause of these movements; yet this led that fine genius into those unfortunate systems which people have rejected, without hitherto substituting anything else for them. The knowledge of the laws of astronomy, and even of attraction itself, embraces the movements of the stars, but does not explain their mechanism.

Celebrated men, since Descartes, have endeavoured to penetrate still more deeply into the existence of the heavenly bodies; he tried only to explain their mechanism; they have attempted to explain their origin and primitive formation.

I do not here allude to Newton; for his beautiful discovery of weight and attraction, which applies so happily to every part of the theoretic universe, is still only a secondary law which presupposes a primary law, from which this weight derives, and of which it can be only the organ, and the result.

Hypotheses of Buffon and Laplace

But I speak of Buffon, who, according to savans of the highest rank, is the first, who, since the discovery of the true system of the heavenly movements, has endeavoured to rise to the origin of planets and their satellites. He supposes that some comet, falling upon the sun, knocked a stream of matter off it, which, uniting at a distance, formed globes of different sizes.

These globes, according to Buffon, are the planets and satellites, which, on cooling, became opaque and solid.

The learned Laplace does not admit this hypothesis, because it satisfies only the first of the five phenomena which he enumerates. But he tries, in his turn, to ascend to their true cause; modestly, however, and with wise hesitation, - offering us something which is not the result of observation and calculation.

His idea of this "true cause" is reduced to this, that, for the planets to have received their circular movement, all in one direction, round the Sun, an immense fluid must have surrounded that Orb, like an atmosphere ; and he pretends that this solar atmosphere at first extended beyond the orbits of all the planets, and gradually contracted to its present limits.

He pretends that the great eccentricity of the orbits of comets leads to the same result, and evidently indicates the disappearance of a great number of less excentric orbits; which supposes an atmosphere round the sun, extending beyond the perihelion of all known comets, and which, destroying the movements of those which traversed it during its great extension, re-united them to the sun.

Then, says he, it is clear that only those comets which were beyond that atmosphere during that period, can exist at present; that as we can observe only those which approach the sun in their perihelion, their orbits must be very excentric; but that, at the same time, their inclinations must be as unequal as if these bodies had been shot forth at hazard, since the solar atmosphere did not influence their movements; that thus, the long duration of cometary revolutions, the great eccentricity of their orbits, and the variety of their inclinations, are naturally explained by means of this atmosphere.

But, he then asks, how did this atmosphere determine the movements of revolution and rotation, in the planets? He answers: that if these bodies had penetrated into this fluid, its resistance would have made them fall upon the sun; that we may therefore conjecture that they were formed at successive limits of this atmosphere, by the condensation of its zones, which it had to abandon, in the plane of its equator, in cooling and condensing . . . that the satellites may be supposed to have been formed in like manner, by the planetary atmospheres; finally, that the five phenomena which he had spoken of follow naturally from these hypotheses, to which the rings of Saturn contribute additional probability.

Let us examine these two hypotheses.

That of Buffon, besides the defects remarked by the learned Laplace, offers a still greater difficulty, namely, how we are to know from whence that comet came, which is supposed to have struck the sun, and broken the matter of the planets from it, inasmuch as planets and comets would appear to have had originally a great amity in their movements.

In fact, if these two orders of celestial bodies differ in their excentricity, in their directions, and in their inclinations, they resemble each other in their subjection to the same laws of weight and attraction, of proportion as to speed and distances, and equality of areas ran through in equal times; which gives the means to calculate, by the same method, the course of the planets, and that of the comets, and to apply to them both the magnificent discoveries of Kepler and Newton.

As to the hypothesis of Laplace, if he finds that his five phenomena result naturally from it, he must also acknowledge that, notwithstanding this, it still leaves much wanting.

In truth, it is hard to conceive how the solar atmosphere, which permitted the planets to be formed, only by contracting itself to its present limits, - and, doubtless, our comets in like manner, - as it withdrew, since it originally extended beyond the perihelion of all known comets, and since, according to him, the great excentricity of their orbits leads to the same results; it cannot be conceived, I say, how the solar atmosphere, which, according to his hypothesis, extended beyond the perihelion of all known comets, has, nevertheless, been traversed, throughout its great extent, by a great number of less excentric orbs, the movements of which it destroyed, and which it reunited with the sun, since the existence and formation of these less excentric orbs or comets, in the bosom of this atmosphere, would contradict his whole system.

It cannot be conceived, why, if comets could penetrate into this solar atmosphere, planets, considering their little excentricity, should not have penetrated thither, there to be destroyed likewise; there circulating, even exclusively, till, in their turn, they were precipitated upon the solar mass; since both, according to his hypothesis, owe their origin to the same cause; from which would result, that, for a long time past, we ought to have had no more planets, inasmuch as it is said (p. 301) that this immensely extended fluid must have embraced all bodies, i.e. planets and satellites.

Finally, it cannot be conceived, if the planets owe their formation only to the retreat or shrinking of the solar atmosphere, how the satellites should owe theirs to the retreat or shrinking of that of their planetary principals, since these satellites which are supposed to be of exactly the same nature as their principals, must owe their origin to a simultaneous cause, and the solar atmosphere, in retiring or shrinking, is supposed to leave no atmosphere at all behind it.

Nature's laws are complex

Without carrying further the examination of these defective hypotheses, I will say, in general, that what militates against the correctness and truth of all hypotheses born of the human mind, is the secret bias men have to seek for all natural phenomena, an uniform mechanism, and a single element, merely because these appear to be what is most regular and perfect.

In all explanations, what is most perfect is what is most true, how multiplied and complex so-ever the causes may be, which the explanation may undertake to account for.

Forgetfulness of this truth, it may be said, is what has most retarded the development of our knowledge, and there is hardly a science which has not been, and does not continue to be sensibly injured by it.

As the progress of astronomy suffered from the opinion, entertained by the savans before Kepler, that the orbs described only circular orbits, because this is what they thought most simple and perfect; so may the belief of unity in the radical causes and data serving for basis in the formation and movements of orbs, retard the knowledge of the sources from which they really are derived.

Another observation which supports this, and is no less true, is that the laws of external results are more easy to catch than that of the organs by which these results are transmitted; and that the law of these organs is more easy to find, than that of the causes which constitute and govern these organs themselves; because, the deeper we penetrate below the surface of things, the more we find their faculties pronounced, and the greater their contrast and diversity.

Thus, to determine the course and periods which the hands of a clock describe over its dial, we have merely to observe with our eyes, and follow their monotonous movements, because, here, there is only one fact, and one formula is sufficient to describe and explain it.

If we look into the interior of the clock, we find several and diverse agencies, the laws of which are necessarily more numerous, and their explanation is less simple, for, here, there is a sort of conflict and opposition of agencies.

If we go further, and examine what sets the wheels of the clock in motion, calculate the movements, and the force and resistance which govern all these agencies, and if we decompose the various substances used in this piece of mechanism, to judge which answers best; we see how these branches of knowledge multiply, and how far we should be from the truth if we attempted to bring all these different branches under one law, and subject them all to one explanation.

This is why, when the genius of man has observed, with attention, the external movements of the stars, he has arrived at those admirable discoveries of modern times, and those grand axioms, by which he describes, with the simplest laws, the true march of the heavenly bodies.

But, here, he has been occupied only with the dial of the clock, and, instead of giving, what savans call the true system of the universe, he has really given only its itinerary ; and even in this, he has forgotten, what is very essential in travels, namely, to tell us whence the traveller comes, and whither he goes.

And, when, after describing the movements of the heavenly bodies, man has attempted to describe their organic and primitive motive powers (mobilité), that is, penetrate into the interior of the clock, we see by the above two hypotheses, (Buffon and Laplace,) what difficulties he has met with, and how far short he has come.

The difficulties became greater still, when, not satisfied with inquiring into the primitive and organic moving power of the heavenly bodies, he has sought to account for the original formation of these bodies themselves ; as we have seen by the two hypotheses in question.

I do not fear to repeat, that the reason of this is, that, as we penetrate beneath the surface of the operations of Nature, we find that different moving powers show themselves distinctly, and yield to no one law, nor one action, nor, consequently, come under any general explanation, which may be applicable to the monotony and uniformity of the external phenomena, which are merely servile results.

Another hypothesis

If the authors of the two foregoing hypotheses were not restrained from publishing them, though so far from explaining the origin of the stars, I may, in my turn, venture to propose a third, even though it should meet with no better success.

At all events, this hypothesis will not be liable to the objections of analysts, as, like the other two, it will not be given as the result of observation and calculation.

Besides, its object will not be to describe the course and movements of stars; this, in our day, would be superfluous; the exact sciences have carried our knowledge, on this head, to a degree of perfection, which, unless to extend it, we can, at least, no longer question or resist.

Nor will it be presented as seeking to explain the kind of convulsion or impulse which may have put the heavenly bodies in motion, in the way we now see them circulate. To undertake this, I should have, first, to be agreed with the savans as to whence this world comes, and whither it goes, a thing that they do not trouble themselves about, believing it impossible to know it. The hypothesis in question will, then, simply follow the principle laid down above, viz. that the laws of creation increase in number, and the properties of things increase in energy, in proportion as we penetrate their depths.

But its principal object will be to give an idea of the origin of the heavenly bodies, and formation of these we call planets; and, in doing this, we shall apply the principle alluded to.

Before stating the hypothesis, I must remind the reader that its author, Jacob Boehme, took for granted the existence of an Universal Principle, at once the Supreme Ruler and Source of everything that is; that he recognised the nature of thinking Man, as distinct from the animal order; and the degradation of the human species, which has extended to the universe itself, and converted it into a mere prison and tomb for us, instead of being our abode of glory, etc.

Boehme's hypothesis

Boehme was persuaded, like the savant Laplace (p. 261), that everything is connected in the immense chain of truths: therefore, in developing his system, he made use of every ground and data which embrace all things; because if, in idea, we were to separate a portion of the universal system, to make of it a system apart, we could never succeed in divining the springs which connect this partial system with the general.

He believed that primitive, or, as he calls it, Eternal Nature, from which this present disordered transient Nature descended by violence, reposed on seven principal foundations, or seven bases, which he calls sometimes powers, sometimes forms, and even spiritual wheels, sources, and fountains, for he wrote in a day when none of these terms were proscribed, as the "plastic forms" and "qualities" of ancient philosophers are in our days; expressions, withal, which have probably not been better understood than those of our author are likely to be.

He believed that these seven bases or forms existed also in this present disordered Nature which we inhabit, but only under restraint, and counteracted by powerful trammels, from which they used every effort to disengage themselves, to vivify the dead elementary substances, and produce all we see that is sensible in the universe.

He endeavours to give names to these seven fundamental qualities or forms in our languages, which he says are degraded, as well as man himself, and the universe.

I would willingly abstain from giving this nomenclature, on account of the difficulty of its acceptance on the part of the reader; but as, without it, it would be still more difficult to understand the original formation of the planets, according to the author's system, I must even speak his language.

The first of these powers he calls astringency, or coercive power, as comprising and inclosing all the others. Thus, all that is hard in nature, bones, kernels of fruits, stones, appear to him to belong principally to this first form or astringency. He extends this denomination also to desire, which, in all creatures, is the basis and spring of all they do, and, by its nature, attracts and embraces all that should belong to their work, everything according to its kind.

The second form he calls gall, or bitterness, and he pretends that this, striving with its penetrating activity to divide the astringency, opens the way of life, without which everything in Nature would remain dead.

The third form he calls anguish, because life is compressed by the violence of the two preceding powers; but, in their conflict, the astringency is attenuated, becomes mild, and turns to water, to give passage to fire, which was shut up in astringency.

The fourth form he calls fire, because, from the conflict and fermentation of the three first, it rises through the water like a flash, which he calls fiery light (éclair igné), heat, etc., which agrees with what passes before our eyes when fire darts in flashes through the water of our thunder-clouds.

The fifth form he calls light, because light comes after fire, as we see in our hearths, fireworks, and other physical phenomena.

The sixth form he calls sound, because sound, in fact, comes after light, as we perceive when a gun is fired, or, as we are supposed to speak, only after having thought.

Finally, to the seventh form he gives the, name of being, substance, or the thing itself; because, as he pretends, it only then discloses the fulness of its existence; and, in fact, the works we give birth to by our words are supposed to be the complement of all the powers which preceded them.

These seven forms, which, in the course of his works, he applies to the Supreme Power itself, to the thinking nature of man, to what he calls eternal primitive Nature, to the present Nature in which we live, to animals, plants, and all created things - to each, in the proportions and combinations suitable to their existence and employment in the order of things: these forms, I say, we must not be surprised if he apply them to the planets and all heavenly bodies, which all inclose within themselves these seven fundamental bases, just as does the smallest production in the universe.

When he applied them to the nature of the planets, he applied them to their number as well; therein partaking the opinion which ruled universally over the world, and has given way only since recent discoveries, that is, nearly two centuries after his death.

But the application of his doctrine to the supposed number of seven planets was only secondary in his system; and, if the existence of the seven powers or seven forms was real, his system would still remain unshaken, though the number of known planets be increased since he wrote, or should still increase hereafter.

In fact, when it was believed that there were seven planets, nothing was more natural than that this author should think that each of them, though inclosing in itself all the powers or seven forms in question, might, nevertheless, more particularly express one of these seven forms, and derive therefrom the different characters which seem to distinguish the planets themselves, were it nothing more than their diversity of colours.

Even though the catalogue of planets actually exceed the number of seven, the predominance of one or other of the seven forms of Nature would not, therefore, cease to have effect in each; only several of them might be so constituted as to present to our eyes the impress and predominance of one and the same form or property.

The number of functions does not vary; that of functionaries only would increase, and that, doubtless, in such proportions as would still help us to distinguish the ranks of those employed in the same function: it would not be probable that all would be absolutely alike, for Nature offers us nothing such. Now we will proceed with the hypothesis in question.

Boehme's hypothesis continued

The original generation or formation of the planets and all stars was, according to our author, in no other way than that according to which the wondrous harmonical proportions of Divine Wisdom have been engendered from all eternity.

For, when the great change took place in one of the regions of primitive Nature, the light went out in that region, which embraced the space of the present Nature; and this region, which is the present Nature, became as a dead body, and had no more motion.

Then, Eternal Wisdom, which the author sometimes calls SOPHIA, Light, Meekness, Joy, and Delight, caused a new order to take birth in the centre, in the heart of this universe or world (*monde**), to prevent and arrest its entire destruction.

This place, or centre, according to our author, is the place in which our sun is kindled. Out of this place or centre all kinds of qualities, forms, or powers, which fill and constitute the universe, are engendered and produced, all in conformity with the laws of divine generation; for he admits, in all beings, and eternally in the Supreme Wisdom, a centre in which a sevenfold production or subdivision takes place. He calls this centre the Separator.

He considers the sun as the focus and vivifying organ of all the powers of Nature, as the heart is the focus and vivifying organ of all the powers of animals. He considers it as the only natural light of this world, and pretends that, besides this sun, there is no other true light in the house of death; and that, although the stars were also depositaries of some of the properties of the higher and primitive Nature, and although they shine in our eyes, yet they are hard bound under the hungry fire of Nature, which is the fourth form; that all their desire is towards the sun, and that they get all their light from it. (He did not then know the opinion since received, that the stars are so many suns; which, however, as it is not capable of proof by strict calculation, leaves the way free for other opinions).

To explain this restoration of the universe, which yet is temporary and incomplete, he pretends that, at the time of the great change, a barrier was placed by the Supreme Power between the light of eternal Nature and the conflagration of our world; that thereby this world then became a mere dark valley; that there was no longer any light that could shine in what was shut up in this inclosure; that all powers and forms were there imprisoned, as in death; that by the great anguish they experienced they heated themselves, especially in the middle of this great inclosure, which is the place of our sun.

He pretends that when the fermentation of their anguish in this place attained its height, by force of heat, then that light of Eternal Wisdom, which he calls Love, or SOPHIA, pierced through the inclosure of separation, and came to balance the heat; because, in an instant, a brilliant light arose in what he calls the power, or the unctuosity of water, and lit the heart of the water, which made it temperate and healing.

He pretends that, by this means, the heat was taken captive, and that its focus, which is the place of the sun, was changed into a suitable mildness, and was no longer a horrible anguish; that, in fact, the heat being kindled with light, deposited its terrible fire-source, and was no more able to inflame itself; that the bursting forth of light, through the barrier of separation, did not extend further in this

(**Monde* and *univers* appear to be used synonymously by our author, and to apply generally to our solar system, exclusively of the sidereal étoiles.-ED.

70

place and that, on this account, the slim did not become larger, although, after this first operation, the light may have had other functions to perform, as we shall see further on.

THE EARTH. - When, at the great change, light was extinguished in the space of this world, then the astringent quality was the most hungry and austere in its action, and it mightily restricted the working of the other powers or forms. Hence proceeded the earth and stones.

But they were not yet brought into a mass, they were scattered abroad in this immense profundity; and, by the powerful and secret presence of light, this mass was presently conglomerated and collected together from all space.

The Earth is a condensation of the seven powers or forms; but the author looks upon it only as the excrement of everything that was made substantial in space, at the universal condensation, which does not prevent there having been other kinds of condensation in other parts of space.

The central point, or heart of this conglomerated mass, belonged originally to the solar centre. But that is no longer so. The Earth has become a centre of itself. It turns, once in twenty-four hours, round itself, and, once a year, round the sun, from which it gets revivification, and seeks virtuality. It is the fire of the sun that makes it revolve.

When it has recovered its plenitude, at the end of its course, it will belong again to the solar centre.

MARS. - But if the light mastered the fire in the place of the sun, the shock and opposition of the light occasioned, in the same place, a terrible igneous eruption, by which there was shot forth from the sun, as it were, a stormy frightful flash, having in it the rage of fire. When the power of Light passed from the Eternal Source of the superior water, through the in-closure of separation, in the place of the sun, and kindled the inferior water, then the flash shot out of the water with a frightful violence; hence the inferior became corrosive.

But this flash of fire could go no further than where the light, which went after and pursued it, was able to reach it. At that distance, it was taken prisoner by the light.

There, it stopped, and took possession of that place; and, it is this flash of fire that forms what we call the planet Mars. Its particular quality is nothing but the explosion of a poisonous bitter fire, which shot out from the sun.

What prevented the light from catching it sooner, was the intense rage of the flash, and its rapidity; it was not made captive by the light, till the light had completely impregnated and subdued it.

There it now is, like a tyrant; it struggles and gets furious, at being unable to penetrate further into space; it is a pricking goad, throughout the whole circumscription of this world: for, in fact, its office is to agitate all things, by its revolution in the wheel of Nature; from whence every thing receives its reaction.

It is the gall of Nature, a stimulant, which helps to light the Sun, as the gall in the human body stimulates and lights the heart. Hence, results the heat, both in the Sun, and in the heart; hence, also, life has its origin in every thing.

JUPITER. - When the hungry flash of fire was imprisoned by the light, this light, by its own power, penetrated still further into space, and reached the rigid cold seat of Nature. Then, the virtuality of that light could extend no further, and it took that place for its abode.

Now, the power that came from the light, was much greater than that from the flash of fire; and, on this account, it rose much higher than the fire-flash, and penetrated to the bottom in the rigidity of Nature. Then, it became powerless; its heart became, as it were, congealed, by the hungry, hard, cold rigidity of Nature.

There it stopped; it became corporeal. So far, the power of vital light from the Sun, now reaches, and no further; but the shining or brightness, which has also its virtuality, reaches to the stars (*étoiles*), and penetrates the universal body.

The planet Jupiter came from this power of congealed or corporified light, and the substance of the place in which that planet exists; but it continually inflames that place by its power.

Still, Jupiter is in that place, as a domestic servant, a valet, whose office is always to wait in the house which does not belong to him; whereas the Sun has its own house. No planet, besides the Sun, has a house of its own.

Jupiter is, as it were, the instinct and sensibility of Nature. It is a gracious, amiable essence; the source of sweetness in all that has life; it is the moderator of furious and destructive Mars.

SATURN. - Although Saturn was created at the same time as the universal wheel of this present Nature, yet it does not take its origin or extraction from the Sun; but its source is the severe, astringent, hungry anguish of the whole body of this universe.

For, as the luminous power of the Sun could not relax, or moderate the hungry rigidity of space, especially in the height above Jupiter, therefore, this same entire circumference remained in a terrible anguish, and no warmth could wake up in it, on account of the cold and astringency which ruled there.

Nevertheless, as the power of motion had extended even to the root of all the forms of Nature, by the eruption and introduction of the power of light, this prevented Nature from being at rest; it underwent the pains of labour, and the rigid hungry region, above the height of Jupiter, engendered from the spirit of hunger, the astringent, cold, austere son, the planet Saturn.

For the spirit of heat, from which come light, love, and meekness, could not be kindled there, and nothing was engendered, but rigidity, hunger (apreté), and rage. Saturn is the opposite of meekness.

(I will observe in passing, that Saturn's rings, detached from the body of the planet, and presenting something like fissures and fractures in their thickness, would seem to support this explanation of its origin in hunger and rigidity. Cold isolates generative powers, instead of harmonizing them; it works only under constraint, as at intervals and by jerks; and, on the bodies it is able to produce, it engenders breaks and cracks; a consequence of the state of division and violence its productive powers are in).

Saturn is not tied to its place, as the Sun is; it is no foreign circumscription, corporified in the immensity of space; it is a son engendered out of rigid anguish, hunger, and cold, and the chamber of death.

It is, nevertheless, a member of the family, in the space in which it revolves; but has nothing of its own, except its corporeal property, like a child just born. Its office is, drying up, and contracting the powers of Nature, thereby bringing every thing into corporeity; it is an astringent power, which especially engenders bones in creatures.

As the Sun is the heart of life, and one origin of what are called spirits, in the body of this universe; so, it is Saturn, which commences all corporeity. In these two orbs, resides the power of the whole universal body. Without their power, there could be no creature, no configuration, in the natural universal body.

(Uranus was not known in our author's time, and is plunged still deeper in the space of rigidity and cold; and may, according to the doctrine we have just read, have had the same origin as Saturn. As to the two new planets, Ceres and Pallas, between Mars and Jupiter, they may derive, more or less, from the original causes of their two neighbours, namely, light and fire.)

VENUS. - The gentle planet Venus, the moving-power (*mobile*) of love in Nature, originates in effluvia from the Sun.

When the two sources of motion and life rose to the place of the Sun, by the kindling of the unctuosity of the water, then meekness, by the power of the light, penetrated into the chamber of death, by a gentle friendly impregnation, descending beneath itself, like a spring of water, and in an opposite direction to the rage of the flash.

From thence came gentleness and love in the sources of life. For, when the light of the Sun had impregnated the whole body of the Sun, the power of life, which arose from the first impregnation, mounted above itself, as when we light wood, or strike fire out of a stone.

We first see light, and from the light, the fire explodes; after the explosion of the fire, comes the power of the burning body; the light, with this power of the burning body, rises immediately above the explosion, and reigns much higher and more powerfully, than the explosion of the fire; and thus must the existence of the Sun, and the two planets, Mars and Jupiter, be conceived.

But, as the place of the Sun, that is, the Sun, as well as all other places, had in them all other qualities, after the similitude of the Eternal Harmony, thus it

was, that, as soon as the place of the Sun was kindled, all the qualities began to act and spread in all directions; they developed themselves according to the eternal law which has no beginning.

Then the Light-Power, which, in the place of the Sun, had made the astringent bitter powers or qualities supple and expansive like water, descended below itself, being of a character opposed to that which rises in the rage of the fire. From this came the planet Venus, which, in the house of death, introduces meekness, lights the unctuosity of water, gently penetrates hardness, and enkindles love.

In Venus, the radical order, or bitter heat, which is fundamental in this planet, as in all things else, desires Mars; and the sensibility desires Jupiter ; the power of Venus makes raging Mars tractable and more gentle ; and it makes Jupiter moderate and modest; otherwise the power of Jupiter would pierce through the hungry chamber of Saturn, as it does through the skull (*boîte osseuse*) of men and animals, and sensibility would become audacity, contrary to the law of eternal generation.

Venus is the Sun's daughter; she has a great ardor for the light; she is pregnant with it; this is why she shines so brilliantly, compared with the other planets.

MERCURY. - In the superior order of the harmonic laws of the seven eternal forms, Mercury is what the author calls sound. And this sound, or Mercury, is, according to him, in all creatures of the earth, without which nothing would be sonorous or make any noise. It is the separator; it wakes up the germs in every thing; it is the chief worker in the planetary wheel.

As to the origin of Mercury in the planetary order, the author attributes it to the triumph gained over astringency by the Light-Power, because this astringency, which held sound, or Mercury, shut up in all the forms and powers of Nature, set it free by its own attenuation.

This Mercury, which is the separator in every thing that has life, the principal worker in the planetary wheel, and, as it were, the speech (*parole*) of Nature, could not, in the conflagration, take a seat far from the Sun, which is the focus, centre, and heart of this Nature, because, being born in the fire, its fundamental properties opposed it, and retained it near the Sun, from whence it exercises its powers upon every thing existing in the world.

It transmits its powers into Saturn, and Saturn begins their corporification.

The author pretends that Mercury is impregnated and fed continually by the solar substance ; that in it is found the knowledge of what was in the order above, before the Light-Power had penetrated the inclosure into the solar centre, and into the space of the universe (which may be the secret cause of so many curious researches about the mineral mercury).

He pretends, moreover, that Mercury, or sound, stimulates and opens, especially in women, what, in all creatures, he calls the tincture, and that this is the reason why they are so inclined to talk.

THE MOON. - This is the only satellite the author treats of. He says that, when the light made the power in the place of the Sun material, the Moon appeared, as had happened with the Earth; he says that the Moon is an extract from all the planets; that the Earth frightens it, on account of its fearful excrementary state, since the great change; that the Moon, in its revolution, takes or receives what it can from the powers of all the planets and stars; that she is as the Sun's spouse; that what is subtile and spirituous in the Sun, becomes corporeal in the Moon, because the Moon assists corporification, etc.

The author does not mention comets. In "*L'Esprit des Choses*", I have compared them to aides-de-camp, communicating with all the parts of an army, or a field of battle. This will make the tracks of comets, in all directions, - so different from the planets, - appear less extraordinary.

But, the system we have been considering, if true, would help us to the origin and the destination of these comets. For the author gives us sufficiently to understand that the Light-Power acted a great part in the formation of our planetary system, as the Fire-Power did in that of the stars, which he looks upon as being in the hungry ebullition of fire.

Now, as harmony can exist only in the union of the powers of light and fire, the comets might have been originally composed of both, but in different degrees, as presumable from the great variety of their appearance and colour.

From thence it might be imagined that the functions of these comets would be to serve as organs of correspondence, between the solar region and that of the stars ; and this conjecture might be thought to be supported, by observing that, in their perihelion, they approach the sun; and that, from the prodigious exentricity of their ellipses, they may convey the solar influences to the sidereal regions, and bring back the reaction of the stars, to the Sun.

It would not be even necessary for the comets to approach very near to the starry region, when they ascend towards it; as, when they come into our solar region, we see that they keep, even in their perihelion, at a considerable distance from the Sun.

Remarks on Boehme's system

Such is the hypothesis that I thought I might present by the side of those of the two celebrated authors mentioned before. I have given it greatly abridged. To give a complete idea of it, it would be necessary to analyze all the works of its author; and even then, I could not flatter myself that it would be safe from objection.

But I should be able to say to the savans alluded to, that, if it had its defects, their systems had perhaps still more, in that they offer us not one of the vital bases which seem to serve as principle and pivot in Nature; I might add, that they have glory enough from their other sciences, which are not conjectural, not to be humiliated, if another has hit nearer the mark than themselves, in what is not susceptible of analysis.

There are many branches in the tree of human intelligence; - and, though severally distinct, they all serve, not to injure each other, but to enlarge our knowledge.

Place a lyre, for instance, before different men; one of them may delineate exactly all its external dimensions.

If another go a step further, and, taking it to pieces, gives me an exact idea of all its component parts, and the preparations and manipulations they had to undergo before they were fit for the use they were intended for, this will not prevent the description given by the first observer, from being very correct, and to be admired.

Then, if a third draws out the sounds of this lyre, and charms my ear with its melody, neither will his talent detract from the merit of the other two.

Therefore, I may be allowed to present the foregoing hypothesis, to men learned in the exact sciences, because, notwithstanding the immense field it embraces, it will never detract from the importance of their own discoveries of exterior astronomical facts, or prevent their marvellous powers of analysis from leading them daily, and with a sure step, to a knowledge of the fixed laws which govern, not the heavenly bodies only, but also all the physical phenomena of the universe.

And, the greater the progress they make in this, the more I shall be gratified, persuaded as I am that they will advance so much the further towards the frontiers of other sciences, and no longer hesitate to connect them indissolubly with each other, when they see the titles of fraternity they all possess.

I will further remark, that we should not be surprised, if notwithstanding its new and unexpected features, the hypothesis in question should still leave voids; the man who opens an extraordinary career, may well be excused if he do not traverse it all.

The history of science teaches us that, although the theory of the Earth's motion dissipated most of the circles with which Ptolemy had perplexed astronomy, Copernicus still left several, to explain the inequalities of the heavenly bodies.

It teaches that Kepler, led astray by an ardent imagination, neglected to apply to comets, the grand laws he had discovered, of the relation between the squares of the periods of revolution of the planets and their satellites, and the cubes of their great orbital axes, because be believed, with the vulgar, that comets were only meteors, engendered in the ether, and neglected to study their movements.

It teaches us, that Newton himself, notwithstanding all the treasures he collected on the different phenomena of our system, the cometary movements, and the inequalities of the lunar movements, arising from the combined action of the sun and the earth on that satellite, merely broached these discoveries; and, amongst the perturbations which he observed in the lunar movements, the evection of that orb escaped his research.

I would add that, supposing the hypothesis true, some voids, or even some errors, should not prevent our gathering some fruit from it; since, even in the exact science of the heavenly movements, astronomers advanced very far, and calculated correctly, without knowing all the bodies of our planetary system.

Thus, before the discovery of the new planets, the ignorance we were in of their existence, did not prevent astronomers from foretelling, with tolerable exactness, the return of the comets; because those unknown planets, being either too distant or too small, could not produce any sensible perturbation on comets passing by them.

Inhabitancy of the Planets

I will not quit the subject of astronomy, without examining the conjecture commonly accepted, that, as the other planets have several points of similarity to our earth, they are probably inhabited likewise.

I have said, in "*L'Esprit des Choses*", that the Earth would not exist the less, even if it were not inhabited, since this property of inhabitancy is only secondary, as it were, and foreign to its existence. Thus, although we see it inhabited, this is not a decisive reason that the other planets should be so also, notwithstanding the analogy which authorizes the conjecture.

We see that vegetation is not a constituent and necessary property of the earth, since it is barren in many climates; and sands and rocks, which are earthy substances, are symbols of sterility.

We see also, that the sun is the direct means which develops this vegetation in the earth, which increases in luxuriance, according to its proximity to that orb, and is barren where too remote from it; but we also see that, when it approaches too near, and the sun takes the preponderance, then the earth becomes calcined, and turns to sand and dust; that is, it becomes barren.

From all this we may presume, that, being susceptible of vegetation, it has been placed, in the series of planets, in the rank which was necessary, and at exactly the right distance from the sun, to accomplish its secondary object of vegetation; and from this we might infer that the other planets are either too near or too remote from the sun, to vegetate.

Much light might doubtless be gathered, in regard to the question of vegetation in the planets, from their difference in density; and, perhaps, this might throw some light on the nature of those bodies themselves, to all of which we can hardly refuse a fundamental identity of substance, since we find a perfect analogy between the earth and the other planets, in the laws of their movements, weight, and attraction; and this is the guide in those beautiful observations in astronomy and mathematics, which are continually made, as to the march of those great bodies, and all their exterior properties.

But, while we wait for this light, we must, at least, in general, suppose an individual and distinct destination to each planet, whether inhabited or not, if we would arrive at anything satisfactory about them; for, the probable sterility of the other planets, on account of their too great proximity to, or distance from the sun, would seem to be also a reason for presuming that they are not inhabited.

The destination of the Universe and Man must first be known

Now, on this subject, no system can be presented, without first supposing a destination to the universe, and knowing what it is; and human sciences pretend that it is impossible to know this.

For the same reason, no destination can be accepted for the universe, without first agreeing as to the nature of Man; that it may be known whether this destination and Man are not co-related.

Now, human science also pretends that it is impossible to know Man's nature; or, to speak with more precision, it confounds him with animals; and this again plunges Man into that state of darkness and uncertainty in which these sciences place all Nature, namely, under the sentence that its destination cannot be known.

In short, to know the destination of Man, we should also know what to think of that General Principle of things, that Supreme Power, to which the name of God has been given ; and human sciences blot this Power out of the order of beings. Discouraged by the schools of religion, in which more is affirmed than proved, they have confounded the principle with the abuse, and proscribed both.

Moreover, the masters of these human sciences, applying, as they do, so successfully, their physical, mathematical, and analytical knowledge, to the exterior properties of the universe, and using these external means only, and, naturally well pleased with the results they obtain; being not only unacquainted with any other means, - and having no need to know of any other, for the external objects they pursue, - but contemptuously shutting their ears to any observation out of the circle in which they have inclosed themselves, - how can we expect to naturalize them with questions and truths of another order?

This I will not attempt, and the few remarks I have made on the other planets, must therefore suffice. But, condemned, so to speak, ever since I could think, to walk in paths which are little trodden, and full of thorns, I must still submit to my lot, and treat, according to my ability, the important question of the destination of our globe. I will offer some means of conciliation to the learned of the world, which, without detracting from the credit they deserve, or rejecting any of the knowledge they have acquired, may induce them to agree, that the circle in which they inclose themselves, might possibly be less exclusive and contracted, than their sciences make it.

I will try to make it apparent, that the regions, in which man has both the right and need to walk, cannot be so inaccessible as they pretend; and, were it only to fill the measure of our intelligence, we require a complement, which they do not give us, notwithstanding the wonders they daily discover.

Destination of the Earth

Men have often made an objection worthy of notice, as to the small space which our Earth occupies amongst the heavenly bodies, and the superiority attributed to it, in regard to its destination, which the boundless aspect of the universe would account for by our pride, if we took counsel only of our eyes.

The reason why observers refuse to give our earth a distinguished destination amongst the heavenly bodies, is all reduced to this, that it is but a small planet, almost imperceptible in the vast extent of the solar system, which itself, since the discovery of the nebulosities, and the common opinion, that the stars are all suns, is but an invisible point in the immensity of space.

If the visible size of things were the only sign or rule by which to judge of their real value, this objection would be unanswerable. But we have many examples to prove that this law is far from being universal, or without exception.

The eye is not the organ which occupies most space in the human body, and yet it does not rank the least amongst the organs, since it is the guardian, the security, the educator of the whole body. The diamond is infinitely small, compared with the terrestrial mass; yet it holds in our eyes a far greater value than other masses far more voluminous.

These simple reflections may, I acknowledge, only arrest the difficulty, and do not solve it. We will therefore proceed to make some observations, which, to some minds, may have more weight. But, as, according to the celebrated savans I have quoted, all truths touch each other, I shall here have to make use of all the data I have advanced, and supposed to be admitted by the reader.

I shall, then, take for granted, the degradation of Man, whose fallen state and humiliation I have never ceased to call to mind.

I shall see the Love and Justice of the Most High engraving by turns, their decrees, upon the sorrowful abode we inhabit.

Lastly, I shall repose on the religious privileges, the powerful evidence of which the Spirit-Man may develop in himself, without borrowing anything from tradition, and which, being unknown to the Material Man, proves at least, that the cause he defends is not yet sufficiently ventilated on his part, for him to expect a judgment in his favor.

The Earth a prison for Man

Starting from the principle that Man is a degraded being, clothed in garments of shame, we may, without inconsistency, consider our Earth as a prison or dungeon for us; and, to say nothing of the continually overflowing miseries of all mortals, where is the Man, who, descending into his inmost secret being, will not bear witness to the correctness of this painful conclusion?

Now, if the Earth is a prison for Man, it is hardly to be wondered at that it is so little remarkable amongst the stars; for, even in our human justice, we give but little space and poor accommodation in our prisons for convicts.

The Earth, which is represented by our German author as but the excrement of Nature, and which, according to the principle of Man's degradation, is only a prison, has no occasion to be the centre of the astral movements, as the ancients and Tycho Brahé believed: a dung-heap or a prison is not commonly the centre or chief place of a country.

We see further, it is true, that governments feed their prisoners, but not with fine bread and delicate meats; in the same way we see that our Earth vegetates, is fruitful, and productive, because, in spite of our quality of prisoners, Supreme Justice is still quite willing to give us our food.

But we see at the same time that, as its prisoners, Supreme Justice allows our Earth to produce, naturally, nothing but imperfect fruits, and feed us with a bread of affliction, a wild bread, and, only by the sweat of our brows can we succeed in ameliorating a little our mode of life; as, in human justice, the prisoner is reduced to the commonest diet, and allowed nothing beyond his rations but what he pays for.

If, in our human justice, prisoners are reduced to so miserable an existence, we also see the succours of benevolence and charity, from time to time, penetrate to their confinement; and, how repulsive soever their dungeons may be, we see sacred and religious consolations are brought to them daily. In short, the eye of compassion, even to the highest in authority, some-times visits these dens of crime, however vile the condition of the convicts maybe. What, then, must it not be, when the prisoner is nearly related to the Sovereign?

All this is a sure sign that if, on the one hand, we are subjected to the severity of a rigorous bondage, it is, on the other, tempered by love and gentleness; as, in fact, is exemplified physically by the place the Earth occupies, which, as every one knows, is between Mars and Venus.

Succours given to Man in his prison

If, then, the Spirit-Man would open his eyes, he would soon recognise in himself the innumerable succours that the beneficence of the Supreme Divine Authority sends him, even in his place of confinement. He would see that, if, in consequence of its smallness, it was wrong to take the Earth for the centre of the heavenly movements, this mistake was excusable, in that he ought, himself, to be the centre of the Divine movements in Nature; and these errors all originate in this secret sentiment of his own greatness, which led him to misapply to his prison the privileges which he ought to attribute to his person, and of which he has nothing left but painful souvenirs in his memory, instead of the glorious traces which they ought to afford.

I believe, then, that if the Spirit-Man followed attentively and with constancy the guiding thread which is offered him in his labyrinth, he would positively succeed in solving all the remaining problems of the prison in which he is confined.

The openings he would thereby arrive at would cause him to feel that, if he is no longer in the first rank of beings in the universe, in respect to glory, he has been replaced in that rank in respect to love; and as his prison necessarily experienced something of this alleviation, it must still show convincing signs of the destination to which it is called.

Now, this destination is nothing else than to be the Temple of purification, in which Man may not only reinstate himself by means of the assistance which is abundantly given him, but in which he may also receive and manifest all the treasures of the Supreme Wisdom which formed him, and disdains not to pour out His own Love and Light upon him, so greatly does He desire to preserve His image in Man.

The knowledge of Man and that of Nature must advance together

But, to attain a correct knowledge of what the Earth is, under all these aspects, it is more essential still to study Man, in relation to all that concerns him; and if he do not, with persevering zeal, cultivate the sacred germs which are daily planted in him for this end, he will again fall under the common ignorance and blind conclusions respecting both the earth and himself.

The Universe and Man form two progressions which are bound to each other, and proceed abreast, and the last term of the knowledge of Man would lead him to the last term of the knowledge of Nature. Now, as human sciences entirely discard this active or positive knowledge of Man, who alone can and ought to teach us all, it is not astonishing that those sciences remain so far short of a true knowledge of Nature.

In fact, although the wonders of the natural sciences, especially those of astronomy, afford us pleasures, which lift us, so to speak, above this narrow and dark world, and enable us to enjoy and feel the superiority of our thinking faculty over our sensible being; yet, it must be confessed, these wonders still fail to satisfy all the wants of our Spirit-Man; and, if we may know Nature, experimentally, by our senses, - if we may measure it by our sciences, - a third power would seem to be wanting to put it in action.

For, if we have desires, intelligence, and a great stock of inward activity, as is evident from all our acts, there ought to be nothing unemployed in us: Nature being our appanage, we ought not, as suzerains, to limit ourselves to mapping our domains, we ought also to have the right to dispose of them at pleasure.

Thus, our most celebrated savans in natural science, our most famous astronomers, ought, from this single observation, to be convinced that they do not enjoy their full rights as spiritual men.

Final causes

What will it then be, if we turn our eyes to what are called final causes?

Everything has, 1st, a principle of action, which we may call its basis of existence, which answers, in the social order,' to the quality of member of the community.

2ndly, A mode of action, according to which it works out what is entrusted to it by its basis, and answers, in the social order, to the administrative power.

3rdly, The instrument, or agent, which performs this action, and answers, in the social order, to the executive power; in the physical, to all the blind powers of Nature.

4thly, An aim, a plan, an object to which this action tends, and for which it is ordained; which may be easily exemplified in any order.

There is not one of these four parts which we ought not to know, particularly in regard to the existence of Man; since it is natural that, as an active thinking power, we should know from whence we receive this power; how we ought to use it; by what agency we ought to work; and to what aim or end we ought to act. But we have also a right to contemplate, and analyse, and know these four parts, in every order of existence.

These are, in general, what may be called final causes, and we see that they are not limited, as is commonly supposed, to the reason of a thing's existence, whether general or particular, since we may go on to the knowledge of its principle, as well as that of its mode of action.

Human sciences turn in circles

Human sciences turn in circles round these foci of knowledge, but never enter within, and then they pretend they cannot enter. They certainly, in a way, try to find out the mode of action; and this is the object of all mathematical and physical researches, whether purely scientific or practical. And, as a consequence of this right which we possess, they even try to ascend to the principle of that action; but, seeking it only in its results, and not in its source, - in forms, and not in the bases concealed in those forms, - they lose sight, at once, of the existence of things, of the mode of their action, of the agent which operates this action, and the aim or end of this existence.

Then, instead of searching from whence things come, whither they go, and how they tend towards their term, they concentrate themselves altogether in the consideration of how they are made. Hence they remain ignorant alike of the source of things, of their true mode of action, of the wherefore of their action, and their true how, which is inward and hidden, and they exhaust themselves in showing us a false how.

The more difficult they find it to advance in these paths, the more obstinate they are. And this is what fixes them, like posts, in these erroneous ways, and makes them such enemies to, and so contemptuous of the wherefore of being; which wherefore, however, is the very first knowledge we should seek, even before we think of the true how.

What, then, can we expect from our researches after the false how, to which they exclusively restrict us?

All our productions of art have a wherefore, and we take care to make it known, that they may be accepted. The person to whom we show them does not enquire how they are made till after he knows their wherefore.

The artisan who produces them first thinks of their wherefore, and only after this comes to the question of how he is to make them; and, in doing his work, he assuredly does not lose time about the false how of mere outside, but seeks the true and active how, which can best succeed or realise the end, or wherefore, which he proposes to himself.

Those who believe in a Supreme Source of existence, ought to suppose that He must be at least as intelligent as we are, and that, in the production of His works, He must do as well as we do in ours.

Now if, in our works, we always show, not only a wherefore, but also an interior how, which is the pivot of the work, and a mode of action connecting the two; I say, if we disclose these secrets to those to whom we exhibit our works, Providence can never have intended to hide from us these same secrets in the works which He exhibits to us, and our ignorance in this can be only attributed to our own want of address.

The Word only can open the central reason of things

You who would like to know the reason of things, remember that this is not to be found on their surface; it is not even in their exterior centre, which is the only one which human sciences can open. It can be found only in their inward centre, because there only their life resides; but, as their life is the fruit of the Word, so only by the Word can their inward centre be opened. Without this medium the prize lately offered on the subject of a very famous fluid may indeed be obtained, but will never be gained, because that fluid, though a proper subject for study, and it may lead to great discoveries, is still, to use the words of Boehme, shut up in the four forms of Nature, and the Word alone can open its prison.

The repose of Nature, the Soul, and the Word, should come from Man

Here I conclude what I had to say of the astronomical bodies, and proceed to the main object of this work, which is to treat of the repose of Nature, that of the Human Soul, and that of the Word; to all of which the Spiritual Ministry of Man should contribute.

Man takes different characters at each step of this sublime undertaking. At the first, he may be regarded as Nature's master, and he ought to be so, in fact, for her to derive any comfort from him.

At the second, he is simply the brother of his fellow-creatures, and, rather as a friend than as a master, he devotes himself to their relief.

Lastly, at the third, he is nothing more than a servant, a mercenary to the Word, to which he ought to bring relief; and it is only when he enters the lowest rank that he becomes specially the Lord's workman.

But, to contribute to Nature's relief, Man must begin by ceasing to torment and injure her. Before his breath can recover power to purify and revive Nature, he must first make himself sound enough not to infect the universe, as he does daily.

Man's habitual influence on Nature

What is it, that Man, in fact, habitually does on the earth? When pure air comes to us, and finds an entrance into our dwellings, can it be merely to bring us a new medium of life? May it not also be to receive its own freedom from us, and deliverance from the corrosive action to which it has been subject, ever since the first crime? And we, by our putrid exhalations and poisonous miasms, and, still more by the infection of our thoughts, add to its corruption and destructiveness.

The earth we walk upon opens to us all its pores as so many mouths, asking for a balm to heal its wounds, and, instead of giving it repose and new life, what we give to quench its thirst withal, is men's blood, which we shed in our furious and fanatical wars, and which, poured into its bosom, steaming with the wrath and rage of men, can only exasperate its pains.

Like the Goddess, under whose feet, flowers sprang up on Mount Ida, we also may fill our gardens with beautiful plants, and magnificent trees; but, instead of restoring to them the life of the trees and plants of Eden, we come, in idle crowds, to walk amongst them.

We fill the surrounding atmosphere with effete, if not mortiferous words; we intercept the powerful influences of Nature; and, for fear, even that the fine trees which constitute the chief ornament of these gardens, and almost reproduce in Nature, the Elysium of the poets, should preserve their vigour too long, we burn them to their very roots, with what is most corrosive, without once reflecting whether chaste and modest eyes may not be near, to blush at our immoral, and revolting indecencies.

Alas! O depraved man! In the mob, wandering with yourself, under the hospitable shade, in those public gardens, hardly any chaste and modest eyes now remain, to blush at your immorality. The death which is in your morals, has seized also the morals of those thriftless ones, whose number you come to increase.

With our astronomical instruments, we penetrate the vast depths of heaven; we there continually discover new wonders which fill us with admiration; and, when it would seem that the mighty springs which animate all those heavenly bodies, and the space they are in, are opened to us, only that we may, as far as in us lie, restore to them those still more mighty springs from which they are separated, - what do we?

Instead of showing zeal, to restore their alliance as of old, we increase their melancholy, by saying that they have no other estate to sigh after; that they now enjoy all the repose they have to expect, and that it is in vain for them to invoke any power but their own; in a word, when they come to ask us to bring them nearer to that Being, who is so high above their abode, without whom no creature enjoys peace, our profound sapience fills the majestic vaults in which they float, with our blasphemies, and we proclaim, under the heavenly portals: There is no God!

Is it to men, in such moral and intellectual aberration as this, that we may speak of the true Ministry of Man in Nature? Would they be capable of fulfilling it? They would not understand a single word of anything relating to that important ministry, and every instruction offered to them, would only irritate them, and excite their scorn and contempt.

But, to such as have stemmed the torrent, I will talk of this grand subject with confidence, and I will take my stand with them on the notions and beliefs we have in common.

The Sabbatic rest of the Earth

The great sin of the Jews, according to Moses, was, their not having given rest or sabbath to the earth. After the calamities and total dispersion, with which he had just threatened them, Moses adds: (Lev. xxvi. 34) "Then shall the land enjoy her Sabbaths as long as it lieth desolate, and ye be in your enemies' land, then shall the land rest ; As long as it lieth desolate, shall it rest, because it did not rest in your sabbaths, when ye dwelt upon it".

Compare with this, the idea we ought to have of the people of Israel who are the Lord's inheritance (Is. xix. 25.). Compare the people under this splendid title, with the idea we should form of Man, who ought to be preeminently the Lord's inheritance when this universe which now contains us, arrives at its term.

Lastly, compare the high Ministry which we are endeavouring to retrace to the eyes of Man, with the work the children of Israel had to accomplish in the land of Judæa, which was, to give sabbath or rest to the earth, and we shall find that Man, and the Jewish people, had the same destination and employment, the same title and qualification.

If there is any difference, it is in Man's favor. Israel was but a sketch or epitome of Man. Man is Israel *en grand*. Israel was charged to give rest to the promised land; Man is charged to give rest to the whole earth, not to say, to the whole universe.

But, it is essential that we should understand this word sabbatic rest, that we may better know what we ought to understand by the Spiritual Ministry of Man.

We can hardly avoid the belief, that, independently of the earthly fruits which the earth bears for us so abundantly, it has other fruits to produce, besides these. The first indication we have, of this, is the difference we observe between the wild fruits which the earth bears naturally, and those we cause it to bring forth by cultivation; which, to seeing eyes, proclaims that the earth wants only man's help to bring forth still more interesting marvels.

A second indication is, that there are few pagan nations who have not rendered religious worship to the Earth.

Lastly, Mythology comes to support the conjecture, by the fable of the golden apples in the garden of the Hesperides; by teaching that men were instructed in the art of agriculture, by a Goddess; and, according to Hesiod, that the Earth was born immediately after chaos; that she married Heaven, and was the mother of Gods, and Giants, of Goods and Evils, of Virtues and Vices.

If, from these natural and mythological observations, we pass to traditions of another order, we see, (Gen. iv. 11 and 12) that, after the murder of Abel, it was said to Cain: "And now thou art cursed from the earth, which hath opened her mouth to receive thy brother's blood from thy hand; when thou tillest the ground, it will not henceforth yield unto thee her strength".

Now, we do not see that the earth must be cultivated only by the hands of the righteous, under pain of sterility. Nor that men's blood prevents its fecundity. The fields of Palestine were saturated with the blood of the inhabitants, whom the children of Israel were ordered to exterminate; and the fertility of those plains was one of the promises, and part of the recompense that the Jews were entitled to claim, if they obeyed the laws which were given them.

Neither do we observe that, in our wars, the ground in which we bury the dead in heaps, is struck with barrenness. On the contrary, it is remarkable for fertility. Thus, while human blood unjustly shed, calls for vengeance from heaven, we do not find that the terrestrial laws of vegetation on our globe are inverted or suspended, in consequence of homicide.

When, therefore, we see it said to Cain, that when he tilled the ground it would not yield its fruit, we have every reason to believe that, by the tillage here spoken of, another than the ordinary cultivation was meant; now what idea can we form of this other tillage, than that it was part of the true Spiritual Ministry of Man; that high privilege which was given him, to make the earth enjoy her sabbaths? A privilege, however, which is incompatible with sin, and which must cease, or be suspended, in those who walk not in the paths of righteousness.

But we cannot well penetrate the meaning of this word sabbatism, without recurring to the notions of which we have previously given some account, and taking, at least for granted, the seven forms or powers, which our German author establishes as the ground or basis of Nature.

We must, besides, agree with him, that, as a consequence of the great change, these seven forms or powers are buried in the earth as well as in the other stars, concentrated, as it were, or in suspension; and that this suspense is what keeps the earth in privation or sufferance, since only by the development of these forms or powers, can it produce all the properties of which it is depository, and which it is desirous of bringing forth ; an observation which may be applied to all Nature.

Finally, we must picture to ourselves, Man, announcing an universal tendency to improve everything on the earth, and as commissioned by the All-Wise, (Gen. ii. 15), to cultivate the paradise of bliss, and watch over it.

Now, what could this culture be, but to maintain in activity, in right measure and proportion, the working of these seven powers or forms, of which the garden of paradise had as much need as other places in creation?

Man must have been the depositary of the moving power of these seven forms, to be able to make them act according to plans marked out for him, and keep that chosen place in repose, or enjoying its sabbath, since there is no rest or sabbath for any thing, but in so far as it can freely develop all its faculties.

In our days, although the mode of men's existence is prodigiously altered in consequence of the great change, the object of creation has no-wise altered on that account, and the Spirit-Man is still called to the same work, which is, to make the Earth keep its sabbaths.

All the difference consists in this, that now, he can perform this task only in a way which is both difficult and painful; and, above all, he can do it only through that same active medium which was formerly appointed to give motion to the seven fundamental powers of Nature.

So long as Man does not discharge this sublime function, the earth suffers, because it does not enjoy its sabbaths.

It suffers still more, if man reacts criminally upon it, by trying to develop from it, powers which are blameworthy or corrupt, and contrary to the plan he received. In the one case, the earth endures man, notwithstanding his negligence; in the other, it casts him out, as happened with the children of Israel.

The rainbow and the lesson it teaches

We see a sensible image of those seven powers, now shut up in the Earth, and in all Nature, in the physical phenomenon exhibited to our eyes, when the clouds dissolve in rain, in sunshine.

The aqueous substance, (which, according to some profound and true observations, is, in every order, the conductor or propagator of light), by filling all space, presents a natural mirror to the sun's rays.

Those rays, penetrating into this aqueous element, marry their powers to those of which this said element is depository; and, by this fruitful union, the sun and water, that is, the superior and inferior regions, manifest to our sight, the septenary sign of their alliance, which is, at the same time, the septenary sign of their properties, since results are always analogous to the sources from which they derive.

This sensible physical effect in Nature, affords us a most instructive lesson, as to the state of concentration and invisibility in which these seven powers are, in Nature; on the necessity there is, that their trammels must be broken, before they can recover their freedom; on the constant action of the sun, which works only to aid their deliverance, and thus show to the universe, that it is the friend of peace, and that it exists only for the happiness of all creatures.

When this rain, thus fecundated by the sun, descends upon the earth, it comes to work there, by its own marriage with the earth, the salutary results of vegetation, which we second by our own labours, and from which we derive such happy fruit; and thus, life, or the material sabbath of Nature, is propagated, by a gentle progression, from the solar source, to us.

But, this physical figurative phenomenon, with all its results, is produced without the aid of Man's Spiritual Ministry, and yet it is for Man to give sabbatic rest to the earth; therefore, we admitted above, that it looked to him for another cultivation, which, now, he can accomplish by hard labour only.

In what the earth's sabbath of rest consists

I fear not to affirm that this glorious sabbath, which the Spirit-Man is commissioned to bring to the earth, is to help it to celebrate the praises of the Eternal Principle, and that, in a more expressive way than it can, by all the fruits it brings forth.

This is the real term, to which all things in Nature tend. Their names, their properties, their seven powers, their language, in short, all is buried under the ruins of the primeval universe; it is for us to second their efforts, that they may again become harmonious voices, capable of singing, each after its kind, the Canticles of Sovereign Wisdom.

But, how should they sing these Canticles, if this All-Wise, which is so much above them, did not employ an intermedium, a representative and image of itself, by which to cause its sweetness to reach them?

We have not here to show that Man is this intermedium; all that has been said, has had no other object but to establish this fact; and, notwithstanding the dark clouds which overhang the human family, and the overpowering weight we have to bear, since we were plunged into this region of death, I flatter myself, that some amongst my fellow-creatures will be found, who, in this sublime destination, will see nothing which their true nature will disown; and there may, perhaps, be some, who will not contemplate its charm without a thrill. We will here, therefore, merely try to find, at what price man may succeed in acquitting himself of this important Ministry.

Hidden powers in Man

It can be only by making use of those same powers, which are hidden in his corporeal being, as they are in all other creatures in Nature; for Man, being an extract from the divine, the spiritual, and the natural regions, the seven forms or powers, which are the basis of all things, must act in him, though in different ways, and degrees, according to his natural, spiritual, and divine or divinized being.

But, for them to act in any of these his constituent orders, these powers must be themselves restored, in him, in all their original freedom.

Now, when Man looks at himself under this aspect, when he considers to what state of disorder, disharmony, debility and bondage, these powers are reduced, in his whole being, - grief, shame, and sadness take hold of him to such a degree, that everything in him weeps, and all his essences become so many torrents of tears.

On these floods of tears, represented, materially, by the earthly rains, the Sun of Life sheds His vivifying rays, and, by the union of His powers, with the germs of our own, manifests to our inward being, the sign of the covenant He comes to make with us.

Then, O Man, you are made capable of feeling the Earth's pains, and those of all that composes the universe; then, by virtue of the enormous difference there is between the infirm state of the seven powers, concealed in the earth, and your own revived powers, you can relieve its sufferings, because you may then do for it, what has just been done for you. In short, it is only when you enjoy your own sabbath, or your own rest, that you can help it to keep sabbath in its turn.

It is only thus you become really master over Nature, and are able to help it to manifest the treasures shut up in its womb, and all those prodigies and marvellous deeds, with which mythologies and traditions, sacred and profane, are filled, some of which are attributable to imaginary Gods, but others, to the real rights of

Man, when revived in his faculties by the principle which gave him being.

In this way, you may, in some sort, subjugate the elements to your rule, dispose, at will, of the properties of Nature, and retain within their limits, all the powers of which it is composed, that they may act together in harmony.

It is only by their acting in their state of disorder and disharmony, that they produce those monstrosities which are met with in the different kingdoms of Nature; as well as those figures of beasts, and voices of animals, which are sometimes seen and heard in storms and tempests, and which it is not at all necessary to attribute to apparitions, or intervention of Spirits, as vulgar credulity is apt to do.

But, if, on the one hand, superstition exaggerates on this point; ignorance and philosophic haste, on the other, condemn this kind of facts too contemptuously. When the powers of Nature are in harmony, they restrain each other. In times of tempest, their curb is broken; and as they bear in themselves, the germs and principles of all forms, especially Sound or Mercury, it is not surprising, that some of them, then more reacted upon than others, should display definite figures, castles in the air, and such like, to our eyes, or voices of animals, to our ears.

Nor is it surprising, that these voices and figures have so ephemeral an existence; they can have neither the life, nor the substantial qualities which result from the harmonious union of all the generative powers.

Of course, I nowise exclude the general concurrence of a Higher Power, which may, and often does join its action to that of the powers of Nature, according to the designs of its Wisdom. Nevertheless, if this Higher Power may intervene in the great scenes, of which Space is the theatre, and we the witnesses, it is not the less true, that the elementary powers are habitually under their own law in this world, and, being always ready to come into play, according to the re-action they receive, they are susceptible of any figure, sound, or other sign, analogous to this reaction.

It is also true, that, when the Most High thus acts with the elementary powers, He then has Man more particularly for His aim, either to rouse and instruct him, if he is guilty; or to employ him as a mediator, if he is one of the Lord's workmen; for the Spiritual Ministry of revived Man, extends to every phenomenon that can be manifested in Nature.

How should it be otherwise? How should the Ministry of the Spirit-Man, raised to new life, not extend over every possible phenomenon in Nature, since our regeneration consists in our being restored to our primitive rights, and the Primitive rights of Man called him to be the intermediate Agent and representative of Divinity in the Universe?

SECOND PART - On Man

What is spirit?

To comprehend the sublimity of our rights, we must go back to our origin. But, before considering the nature of the Spirit-Man, we will enquire, in general, what may be called Spirit, in any, or all classes and orders; we will disclose the radical sources from which this expression is derived; and begin by taking the word Spirit in the different meanings, under which it may be viewed, in our languages.

The spirit of a thing may be considered to be the actual engendering, whether partial or complete, of the powers of its order.

Thus music is known to us for what it is, only by the actual emission of the sounds by which it reaches our ears, and which are nothing but the effective expression, or active spirit of the design or picture it would represent.

Thus, wind is the actual emission of air, compressed by the clouds or atmospheric powers. And, in the elementary order, as soon as the compression ceases, there is no more wind: now we know that the ancient languages used the same word to express wind, breath, and spirit.

Thus, the breath of Man, and other animals, is the actual emission of what results in them, from the union of the air, with their vital powers; and, when their vital powers cease, their breath, spirit, or expression of life, ceases also.

Thus, the jet (*jaillissement*) of our thoughts, and what the world calls wit (*esprit*), in man, is the actual emission of what is developed by a secret fermentation in the powers of our understanding, and this jet is consequently the fruit of their actual engendering: and, when this secret fermentation is suspended in us, we are as if we had no more thought, as if we had no more wit (*esprit*), although we still have in us, all the germs which may produce it.

Spirit, an emission of the Eternal Powers

According to this exposition, we may, without fear, consider Spirit to be the fruit which proceeds perpetually from the Supreme Eternal Powers, or from their Universal Unity, since, by the actual engendering, which produces this fruit without intermission, it ought, above all other emissions, to bear the name of Spirit, which we give to whatever has the character of an emission or actual expression.

And here, we must call to mind that the Eternal Generative Powers of this Universal Being, rest, like everything that exists, on two fundamental bases, which, in *'L'Esprit des Choses'*, we have indicated under the names of force and resistance; and which, Jacob Boehme, applying them to the Divinity, represents under the name of a double desire, - to remain in its own centre, and to develop there its universal splendours; also, under the names of harshness and meekness; darkness and light; and even under those of anguish and delight, anger and love; although he says continually, that, in God, there is neither harshness, nor darkness, nor anguish, nor anger, and that he uses these expressions only to designate powers which are distinct, but which, acting simultaneously, present, and will do so eternally, the most perfect unity, not only in and with themselves, but also with that Universal and Eternal Spirit, which they never ceased, and never will cease to engender.

Perpetual emission of Universal Unity, the Divine Being

It seems to me, moreover, that it is no barren or indifferent notion we here obtain of the character of this Perpetual Fruit of the actual engendering of Universal Unity, whose Powers are continually, necessarily, and exclusively dependent upon themselves; and if observers had thus considered this productive unity in its character of actual necessary emission, they would have derived greater profit from their researches on the Divine and Universal Being resulting from it, than by trying to scrutinize at first starting, the Nature of this Being, as they do, and that, without looking at His Action; whilst His Action is probably His whole Nature: and the consequence of their false tactics has been, that, not only they have not found that Universal Being whom they sought amiss, but they have gone so far as to persuade themselves, that what they had not found, did not exist.

If we had considered Universal Being, the spiritual, divine, and actual fruit of the powers of Eternal Unity, in His true character, we should have derived the following great advantage from it.

Spirit, the fruit of all the powers of Unity

As the fruit of every generation of which we have cognizance, repeats and represents everything that constituted the powers which engendered it; so, what we call Spirit, in the generative act of the Eternal Unity, can be nothing else than the actual and manifest expression of everything without exception, that belongs to that Eternal Unity: thus, it is for this Universal Spirit to make that Unity known to us, to describe it to us entirely, as Man reproduces tempo-rarily, all the properties of his father and mother, whose complete living image he is.

Yes, if we look with our understanding attentively, at this actual perpetual fruit of Eternal Unity, we feel that, since the powers of this Unity are perpetually, necessarily, and exclusively dependent on each other, and the fruit of their union is an actual engendering, as boundless as it is endless, this fruit must really be the actual and complete expression of their mutual union; it must have within it, and actually and universally represent, all that can serve as ground to the mutual attraction of these powers, one towards another.

Thus, it is necessary that the fruit of this engendering, this Universal Being, should disclose and present to us, without ceasing, at all points, such an abundance and continuity of love, life, strength, power, beauty, justness, harmony, measure, order, and all other qualities whatsoever, that our thought should everywhere find the living effect of their plenitude, and never want means to recognize the supremacy of their universal unity; above all, it is necessary, that this fruit which it engenders, should likewise make but one with itself, since it must have and be all that this Unity contains, and since it can neither admit any interval, nor any diversity of degrees, between the love of these powers, and the act of their engendering, nor is it possible to perceive any difference between their essential being, and their constituent nature.

The Spirit alone can reveal itself

But, to this Universal Being, this actual perpetual emission of Eternal Unity, alone, it likewise belongs to afford us this knowledge, as it belongs alone to the fruit of the natural generations before our eyes, to afford that of the powers which generated them.

Hence, those who have disowned this necessary Being, this actual perpetual fruit of the engendering of Eternal Unity, have naturally ended in no more recognising the Eternal Unity itself, since absolutely nothing but this actual fruit could represent it to them with all its constituent qualities and properties; in like manner, if we turned our eyes away from the fruits of the earth, we should soon lose knowledge of the virtual generative qualities of Nature; and if we considered man, mute and motionless only, we should soon lose the idea of his extraordinary activity of body, and the vast extent of his thought and intelligence.

Hidden generation and anastomosis of beings

If the powers of Eternal Unity are necessarily one in their engendering, and the Universal Being or Fruit which proceeds from their engendering, necessarily makes but one with them, this, doubtless, is a fundamental reason why His generation is concealed from us, since we cannot conceive Him separate from His generative Sources.

But if, on another hand, there must necessarily be a progressive and gradual union of the entire Universal Unity with every possible production which appears before our eyes, we ought no longer to feel surprised, that we have never been able to penetrate the generation of things, since, not only do the generative powers, in these partial generations, also follow the law of Unity, according to their order, but even their fruit also makes only one with them, after the pattern of Universal Unity, at least in the root, and the generative act, though, afterwards, the fruit detaches itself from its generative sources, as belonging to the region of successions.

Let us pause here, to contemplate what an admirable thing, and how impressive this profound law is, which hides the origin of all that is produced, even from those who receive or take this origin! Under this impenetrable veil, the roots of all engenderings are anastomosed with the Universal Source. And only when this secret anastomosis has taken place, and the beings' roots have received, in the mystery, their vivifying preparation, then substantiation commences, and things take ostensible forms, colours, and properties.

This anastomosis is insensible, even in time, and becomes lost in immensity, in the eternal, and the permanent, as if to teach us that time is only the region of the visible action of things, but that the region of their invisible action is infinite.

Yes, Eternal Wisdom and Love cherish their own glory, and our intelligence also; they seem afraid of allowing us to believe that anything had a beginning, and that there is anything which is not Eternal; since, truly, no creature, not even man, has any idea of his own beginning, unless as to his body; and he acquires even this knowledge as much from the weariness which this body occasions his spirit, as from the examples of his reproduction which he witnesses daily ; for, in fact, nothing can have a commencement (absolutely speaking) but evil and disorder. And, as Man belongs to Unity, or the Centre, which is the middle of all things, he may grow old in his body, and not the less believe himself to be in the midst of his days.

Thus the concealed origin of things is a speaking evidence of their eternal and invincible source, and we feel that there is nothing but death and evil which commence, but that life, perfection, happiness, could not be, if they had not always been.

The Universal Being everywhere engenders or reveals Itself, especially in us

And this confirms the principle we have established; if, in all the examples we have given, nothing can bear the name of Spirit, but by its presenting the phenomenon of an actual and always possible emission, it is very certain that the Universal Being must bear the same character, and thence develop to our intelligence, the actual and necessary plenitude of an uninterrupted existence, without beginning or principle.

Happy is he who can elevate his thought to this height, and maintain it there! He will thereby attain such clearness of intelligence, that the ground of all that exists, in the order of things invisible, as well as of those which are visible, will appear to him simple, active, permanent, and, so to speak, diaphanous; seeing that the Universal Being, by his continual living Actuality, must carry everywhere the Light and limpidity of which He is the perpetual focus.

But, if we can thus consider the living continual Actuality of this Supreme and Universal Focus, in all visible and invisible things, what will it be when we consider it in ourselves, and see what it works in our own being? For, we shall discover a remarkable difference, in regard to ourselves; that is, that we can, by reflection, readily observe this actuality in all individual things, but that we may feel it, in reality, and in nature, in ourselves.

Yes, if but for a moment, we would dive into the depths of our inward existence, we should soon feel, that all the divine Sources, with their Universal Spirit, abound and flow at the root of our being, that we are a constant and perpetual result of the engendering of our Principle, that it is continually in its actuality within us, and thus, after the definition we have given of Spirit, we may easily see, how a being, who is capable of feeling the ebullition of the Divine Spring within him, has a right to the name of Spirit-Man.

Man's origin

We may now arrive at a fixed idea of Man's origin. Man was and is continually born in the Eternal Source, which ceases not to be in the perpetual intoxication of its own wonders and delights. This is the reason we have so often said that Man can live only by admiration, since, as shown by the German author we have quoted, no creature can be nourished except by the substance or fruits of its own mother.

Desire and Will

But Man is also born in the Source of desire; for God is an Eternal Desire and Will to be manifested, that His Magism, or the sweet impression of His existence, may propagate and extend to all that is capable of receiving and feeling it. Man ought also to live by this desire and will; and he is charged to keep these sublime affections alive within him; for, in God, desire is always will, whilst in Man it rarely reaches this term, without which nothing is done. And it is by this power which is given to Man of bringing his desire up to the character of will, that he ought really to be an image of God.

Union of the Divine Will with Man's desire

In fact, he may obtain that the Divine Will itself come in him, to join his desire; he may then work and act in concert with Divinity, who thus condescends, in a manner, to share His work, His properties, and His powers with Man: and if, in giving him desire, which is as the root of the plant, He reserves the Will, which is as its bud or flower, it is not to the intent that he should remain deprived of this Divine Will, and not know it; but, on the contrary, His wish is that he should ask for it, know it, and do it himself; for, if Man is the plant, God is the sap, or life. And what would become of the tree if the sap did not run in its veins?

The Divine Covenant

It is in these deep, yet true and natural grounds, of the emanation of Man, that the divine contract is found, which binds the Supreme Source to Man; a contract by which this Supreme Source, in transmitting to Man all its own sacred germs, could plant them in him, only accompanied with all the fundamental irrefragable laws which constitute its own Eternal creative Essence, and from which it could not itself depart, without ceasing to be. And this contract changes not, as ours do, by the will of the parties.

In forming Man, the Supreme Source is supposed to have said to him: "With the eternal grounds or bases of my being, and the laws eternally inherent in them, I constitute thee Man; I have no rules to prescribe to thee but those which result naturally from my eternal harmony; I have no need even to impose any penalties upon thee, if thou shouldst infringe them; every clause of our contract is in the very basis of thy constitution; if thou observe them not to do them, thou wilt work thine own judgment and punishment; for, from that moment, thou wilt cease to be Man."

The Covenant extends through all Nature

And we may follow this principle through the whole chain of beings, in which we shall find that all productions whatsoever are bound, each according to its class, by a tacit compact with its generative source; that from these sources all their laws proceed; and that, by the fact itself, they fall into disharmony the moment those laws are infringed, which they carry in their essences and received from their generative sources at the instant they gave them life.

Weight, number, and measure in Nature

By paying attention to the fixed and regular laws, by which Nature produces and governs all its works, and following, step by step, carefully the tracks it leaves behind, we recognise everywhere a weight, a number, and a measure which are its inseparable ministers, which shows that these exist primitively in the Source above, and constitute the eternal Trinary, whose image we find in ourselves, and on which the divine contract rests. We see, moreover, that these three interior bases suffice the Almighty for laying the foundations of all the works of Nature, and characterising externally all the varieties of His productions; or those external developments of form, colour, duration, smell, essential properties, qualities, etc., things which are not numbers, though they have numbers for signs and index.

It is by these means that the Universal Trinary varies, ad infinitum, and so multiplies its operations that it keeps them as if always working in the infinite on which they depend, so that Man can never number them nor possess himself of them; and, in fact, it is sufficient for him to have the use of them; he is forbidden to possess them as his property, since, by that multiplicity of means which the All-Wise has of varying the manifestations of its Universal Trinary, He secures to Himself alone the right of property in this generative act ; never ceasing, however, at the same time to manifest this infinity outwardly to be admired.

The opposing power in Nature

Without the contrary power, which brought disorder into the Universe, Nature would know no disharmony, and never depart from the laws prescribed by the Eternal plans; but, notwithstanding its disorder, when we consider Nature as composed of so many various instruments and organs, serving as channels to life universally diffused, we perceive a gradation in its works, which fills us with admiration of that beneficent Wisdom which directs the harmonious course of things.

Steps in the knowledge of Nature, and plan, and Spirit

We shall, indeed, observe, that in the series of Nature's works everything serves as a step to arrive, not only at the next, but at the highest degree.

The play and harmony of the phenomena of Nature lead to the knowledge of its grounds and constituent elements.

The knowledge of its constituent elements leads to that of the immaterial temporal powers which create these phenomena.

The knowledge of these immaterial temporal powers leads to Spirit, for they do not in themselves possess the key of the general design.

The knowledge of Spirit leads to that of the communication between it and our thought, since we at once hold intercourse with it, and all intercourse supposes two or more analogous beings; it cannot take place when there is only one.

The knowledge of the communication of our thought with Spirit leads us to the Light of God, since this Light alone can be the central generative point of everything that is light and action.

The knowledge of the Light of God leads us to know our own wretchedness, through our awful privation of that Light, which alone can be our life.

The knowledge of our wretchedness shows us the necessity of a restorative power; since Love, which is eternal order, and the eternal desire of order, can never cease presenting this order and love to us, to enjoy them.

The knowledge of a restorative power leads us to the recovery of the holiness of our essence and origin, since it brings us again into the bosom of our primitive generative source, our eternal trinary. Thus everything in physical, as in spiritual nature, has an object of increase and improvement, which might serve as a thread in our labyrinth, and help us to give value to the rights of our divine contract; for, independently of our finding in this divine covenant fresh nourishment for that insatiable need we have of admiring, we should learn besides to fulfil one of the noblest functions of the Spiritual Ministry of Man, that of being able to share this supreme happiness with our fellow-creatures.

"Thy will be done"

According to this, when, since the fall, we ask for the fulfilment of the divine will, this petition has a very profound, as well as a very natural meaning; since it is asking that the divine covenant may recover all its value; that all desire and will proceeding from God may arrive at its term, and, therefore, that man's soul may blossom again in its true desire and original will, which would make it participate in the development of the desire and will of God; so that we cannot ask of the Supreme Ruler that His will be done, without, by this prayer, asking that all the souls of men may be restored to the enjoyment of the primitive element, and placed in condition to be reinstated in the Spiritual Ministry of Man.

Observe here, that, in the prayers which God has recommended, He has not told men to ask for what may not be granted to all; He promises only what is compatible with His universal munificence, which refers, in its turn, to their universal wants and His universal glory. When we ask God for particular things which cannot be given to all our fellow-creatures alike, such as goods, employments, dignities, we depart essentially from our law.

What to pray for

This proves that we ought never to ask Him for anything belonging to this world, because all in it is counted and limited, so that it is impossible for everybody to have profit out of it; and if one is provided with a large share, another must necessarily be deprived of it. This shows how foreign to the primitive code estates were, and that the Gospel precept, as to relinquishment of goods, is intimately connected with the exact and fundamental grounds of true justice.

It shows that we ought, on the contrary, to ask incessantly for things of the real and infinite world in which we were born, because nothing can come upon a man from that world without thereby opening the way for it to descend upon all.

In the prayers recommended by God to men, the first thing asked for refers to God and His kingdom, that it may come; only after this is Man thought of.

What is asked for, for Man, nowise refers to earthly things; the daily bread spoken of is not our elementary food, for Man has his hands to labour with, and the earth to till, and we are forbidden to be careful about the wants of our bodies, as the heathen are. This daily bread, which must be gained by the sweat of the brow, is the bread of Life, which God distributes to His children daily, and which alone can help forward our work.

Finally, we ask forgiveness of our sins, and to be kept from temptation.

All in this prayer is Spirit, all is divine charity, because its object generally is that divine contract, to maintain which all have to contribute.

When we are told, in the Gospel, "Seek first the kingdom of God and His righteousness, and all other things shall be added unto you", we may believe that the temporal succours we have need of will, indeed, not fail us, if we make our abode in the spiritual riches; but it goes farther, and intimates that we should first seek the divine kingdom, and that the spiritual kingdom will be given to us also; that is, if we establish our dwelling in God, there will be nothing in the Light and the mighty gifts of the Spirit which will be refused to us.

This is the reason why those who seek only in the spiritual sciences, and do not go directly to God, take the longest road, and often lose themselves. Therefore it is said that one thing only is needful, because it embraces all others. It is, in fact, an indispensable law, that any region must embrace, rule, possess, and dispose of all that comes after it, or in a lower rank than itself. Thus the divine region, being above every region, it is not surprising that, on attaining it, we attain the supremacy over all things. Let us seek God, and nothing else, if we would have all things; for this, we were born in the source of Eternal Desire and Universal SPIRIT.

Animals and other things of Nature have also a desire; but the will that crowns this desire is quite foreign to them, and separate from them: for this reason they have not to pray, as man has; they have only to act.

Light is part of the Divine Covenant with Man

But Man took his origin not only in the Sources of admiration, and desire, and will, but in the Source of Light also, and, consequently, this Light also formed one of the bases of the divine contract with him.

For this cause, Man is the first term of the relation between himself and all the natural and spiritual objects around him. For this reason, if he cannot account to himself for his own existence, he will never account for that of any other production or emanated being.

Man is the scale of measurement for all creatures

In fact, if Man had his origin in the real source of admiration, desire, will, and light - in a word, in the source of reality - he becomes, in his quality of a real being, the scale of every object and creature that approaches him, and he can measure their existence, laws, and action, only by what they differ from him: a profound and important truth, which many seem to distrust, but which they reject from indolence only, when they flatter themselves they do it from modesty.

This truth is, moreover, proved by the daily experience of what passes amongst men. For, how do men become judges and arbitrators in sciences, laws, arts, and institutions - in short, in everything which fills up their fleeting life? Is it not by beginning to master, as far as they can, the principles which relate to their subject? And when they have thoroughly penetrated these principles, and made them their own personally, then they take them for ground of comparison for everything that is offered to them for examination: the more they are filled with the knowledge of these fundamental principles, the more they are supposed to be able to judge correctly, and determine the value and nature of the subjects submitted to their tribunal.

The holy race of Man, engendered in the Sources of admiration, desire, and intelligence, was, then, established in the region of boundless time, like a brilliant orb, that he might shed abroad a heavenly light: in short, Man was a being, placed between Divinity and the betrayer, who in the spiritual region could produce, at will, explosions of thunder and lightning, or the serenity of calms; load the guilty with chains, and cast him into darkness, or impress the signs of consolation and love upon the regions of peace.

Man and God, the extremes of the chain of beings

Man and God, are the two extremes of the chain of beings. And Man ought, even now, to have the executive word, here below. All things between these two beings, arc subject to them; to God, as His productions; to Man, as his subjects. And everything would bow down and tremble before us, if we left free access in our being, to the divine Substance: first, Nature, because it never knew, nor ever can know, this divine Substance; secondly, our implacable enemy, because he knows it no more but in the terror of its invincible powers.

Man responsible, as the dispenser of God's riches

No doubt, Man was born to penetrate the wondrous works of God, and repress disharmony; but it was, also, that he should always dwell near to God, and, from that eminence, continually overlook the whole circle of things, and distribute the divine riches, under the eye of Wisdom itself; and we find it to be so, in that we never feel at rest, and in our right measure, except when we attain this high position; though this be but at intervals, here below.

Think, then, O Man, of the holiness of your destination; you have this glory, that you were chosen to be, in some sort, the seat, sanctuary, and minister of the blessings of our God; and your heart may still be filled with these delicious treasures, whilst, at the same time, it sheds them abroad in the souls of your fellow-creatures; but, the more important your ministry is, the more just and right it is, that you should answer for your management.

The Earth, an example for Man

When the visible heavens send down their substances, or materials of daily work, that the Earth may bring them to maturity, they arc supposed to say to the Earth: These are our plans, these our desires, as well for the preservation of things, as for the expansion of the wonders of Nature; thou must account for all we confide to thee; suffer not one of thine essences to remain inactive; let all concur with us, in causing this universal death, which devours all things, to disappear.

The Earth, then, to escape from her own death, incubates, and cherishes the virtues which the heavens have just deposited in her; she develops her shut up, coagulated, powers, and, in her aspirations, adds others to them; then, she brings to the surface the faithful account which we witness, of all that was committed to her, with the countless increase from the exercise and concurrence of her own faculties.

The same law is laid down for you, O Spirit-Man, for the management of your domains as the officer of Truth. You are God's earth ; you are a divine functionary in the Universe. God sends you, every day, perhaps every moment, at least, every spiritual season, the task that He gives you to perform, according to the Counsels of His Wisdom, and your own age and strength. He sends you this task, wishing you not to spare yourself in pains for its accomplishment, and warning you that He will rigorously exact His returns, which consist in nothing less than the restoration of order, peace, and life, in the portion of His domains which He trusted to your care.

This work is the Magism of God, and the complement of prayer

This desire which God manifests, and the warning He gives you, ought not to appear a strange thing to you; you should see in it, nothing but God's own thirst for justice, and the annihilation of disorder; and, when He thus sends His desire or thirst into you, He does more than admit you into His council, for He brings His council into you; and insinuates within you, the sweetest and highest purposes of His Wisdom; and impregnates you with the same relations, which

He Himself has to all that is defective, and Himself provides you the needful, wherewith to work its rectification; that is, He provides you with funds out of His own glory, and seeks to stimulate your zeal, by the hope He gives you, of partaking of all the fruits, with Him.

This work is the very complement of prayer, since it is the very action, not to say, the living generation, of the divine order, which passes into you.

Theurgy, its shortcomings and dangers

This work is far above all those theurgic operations, in which the Spirit may attach itself to us, watch over us, pray even, for us, without our being either wise or virtuous; as that Spirit is then joined to us only externally, and works these things often unknown to us, which feeds our pride and encourages our false security, more dangerous to us, perhaps, than our weaknesses and faults, which recall us to humility.

The true work is central, and develops in action

Here, on the contrary, everything commences at the centre, and we are vivified before our works proceed from us; so that we have too much enjoyment to be drawn out of ourselves by our works, and make room for vanity; and, when a man is made to be truly God's servant, this mode of existence, this sublime condition, must appear so natural to him and so simple, that he cannot conceive any other.

For, what can the end or aim of action be, but to connect those who apply themselves to it, with the Universal Action? It is by acting, that we unite with action, and end in being nothing less than organs of constant continuous action; then, whatever is not this action is as nothing to us, and nothing but this action appears natural to us.

Man should be the continuation or recommencement of God

Man is a being, commissioned to continue God, where God is no longer known by Himself: not in His radical divine order; for, there, God ceases not to make Himself known by Himself; for, there, He works out His secret eternal generation. But he continues Him in manifestations, and the order of emanations; for, there, God makes Himself known only by His images and representatives.

He continues Him, or, in other words, recommences Him, as a bud or germ recommences a tree, by being born immediately from that tree - without intermedium.

He recommences Him as an heir recommences his predecessor, or a son his father; by entering into possession of all that belongs to that predecessor or father; otherwise he could not represent him; with this difference, that, in the order of

Spirit, life still remains in the source which transmits it, because that source is simple; whereas, in the material order, life does not remain in the engendering source, because this source is mixed, and it can engender only by dividing itself. In the material order, particularly in vegetation, the fruit, - which is life or germ, and the grain, which is death, are closely connected. In the grain, life is hidden in death; in the fruit, death is hidden in life.

The recommencing process reversed by the Fall

I have here described Man, in reference to his original state, only. Describing him according to what he has made himself, by the false and guilty use of his privileges, this high privilege which he had, of recommencing God, vanishes; and we are compelled to say, that, since that fatal epoch, God has, on the contrary, had to recommence Man; and that He recommences him daily.

For, not only at the moment of his fall, was God obliged to recommence Man, or renew His divine contract with him, but, at every epoch, at which He sent laws for our restoration; which epochs, rendered unavailing by our want of respect for His gifts, and the little fruit we derived from them, had each to be succeeded by another, always more important than its predecessor; but which, in its turn, was equally profaned by us, thereby throwing us so far back, instead of advancing us; and requiring the Divine Love to recommence us again.

Were it not so, this visible universe, in which we are imprisoned, would, long ago, have been buried again in the abyss, out of which Supreme Love took it.

Process of Man's escape: out of crime, through law, to vital action

Man passed out of crime, into darkness. Out of darkness, Supreme Goodness made him pass into Nature. Out of Nature, He made him pass under the ministry of Law. Out of the ministry of Law, he passed under that of prayer, or the law of grace which should have restored all things for him.

But, as the human priesthood has corrupted this law of grace, and made it void, it has to be suspended, in its turn, and replaced by violent vital action; as prayer, or the law of grace, replaced the law which was abused by the Jews; such is the Spirit of Wisdom and loving-kindness, in which Supreme Love directs, or permits, all these lamentable events to happen, at which the earthly man complains, forgetting that his own crimes bring them about, and turn the earth upside down, whereas be was born into the world to pacify and improve everything.

The French Revolution was probably designed by Providence, to prune, if not to suspend, this ministry of prayer; as the ministry of prayer, in its origin, was designed to suspend that of the Law. In this, the French may be considered to be the people of the new law, as the Hebrews were of the old. We need not be astonished at such an election, in spite of our crimes and brigandage. The elect Jews were, in their time, no better than the French.

There is, besides, a coincidence worth remarking; which is, that the Temple of Jerusalem was twice destroyed and burnt, once by Nebuchadnezzar, the second time by Titus; and that the days on which these events happened, were the same as that on which the temporal sceptre of France was broken ; i.e. the 10th August. 'When Titus withdrew into Antonia, he resolved to attack the Temple, the next day, the 10th of August, with all his army; they were on the eve of that fatal day on which God had, from long before, condemned this holy place to be burned, as it had been before on the same day, by Nebuchadnezzar, King of Babylon". (Fl. Josephus, ' Roman War,' lvi. ch. xxvi.)

And this vital action, which, according to all appearance, has to replace the ministry of prayer, will yet make but partial conquests amongst men, compared with the great majority, who will not profit by it; seeing the propensity to abuse everything, which man has exhibited from the beginning.

The process consummated in the last judgment

Therefore, God will again be obliged to recommence Man by the last judgment, or the end of time; but as, then, the whole circle will have been run, the work will be accomplished beyond recall; that is, without fear of any new delinquencies on Man's part, and consequently without God being obliged to recommence Man any more.

On the contrary, Man will then have recovered the sublime privilege of recommencing God, as he ought to have done from the beginning.

There is, however, this difference: In the beginning, Man was only under the eyes of the covenant (alliance), and he could deport himself as he chose: at the end, he will be in the alliance; so that he will be no more able to choose, because he will be swept onwards, eternally, in the divine stream.

The door of Light and Love in Man

In this earthly passage, which we are all condemned to make, and the various spiritual paths, in which Man may walk during this passage, there is a particular door for each of us, through which the Truth seeks to enter, and by which alone it can come into us. This door is distinct and independent of the general way of our origin, through which the life of our Root descends into us, and constitutes us Spirit; for this general door is common to us, and to the Wicked one as well.

The particular door or way alluded to, has for object to renew us in the fountain of Life, and the Eternal Light of Love; and this door is not given to the Wicked one.

So truly is it intended to enable us to recover the sources of Love and Light, that, without it, we pass our days in vain, even though it be in the contest for true knowledge; till the fountain of Life finds this door open in us, it waits outside, for us to open it.

Through this door alone, can we obtain our subsistence; if we fail to open it, we remain completely destitute; if we open it, it brings us abundant nourishment; and, if we were wise, we should commence no work till we had paid our debt ; that is, till we had opened this door, and completed the task it leads to.

But as this door is also ordained of God, to introduce us into our ministry, when we are of the number of those called to the work, storms and tempests may torment us, to delay the work, but the Fountain of Life will still find this door, in such as are fit to be employed, and the glory of God will triumph in them, to their great satisfaction.

All may open the door in themselves

Although God opens this door in those whom He employs, those who may not be employed must not repose on any pretended impossibility, on account of no door being opened in them; for, in all men, there is a door for desire and justice; and we are all obliged to open this door ourselves, which we can do, if we persevere.

Door of election

As to the other door, which leads to His work only, it is quite just that God alone should open it; but this door is no proof of our advancement, if the other remains closed through indolence or idleness. We may cast out devils in His name and He know us not.

As to why it is so hard for any thing acquired by outward means, to be really useful to us, it is because it conflicts with what ought to pass in and out of our true door. It is like a grafted plant, the juices of which are in conflict with the sap of the tree on which it is grafted; and the conflict lasts till the sap of the tree takes its natural course, and draws the new juices with it. But, sometimes the sap of the wild plant is conqueror.

The sap of the Tree of Life

What is the true sap that ought to carry all things with it in its course? You who aspire to be admitted into the rank of the Lord's workmen, you know what it is.

You know that it ought to animate your own essences, and that it flows from the eternal Divine Generation.

You know that it cannot circulate in you, without retracing in you this same eternal Divine Generation.

You know that the smallest branches of your being may be vivified by this sap.

You know that its power vivifies and rules all spiritual regions, as well as the stars, animals, plants, and all elements, visible and invisible.

You know that what it does for all these, it has the right to do for you, if you did not oppose it.

Present yourself therefore to the eternal Principle of this fecund sap, and say: "O Supreme Author of all things, leave no longer thine image degraded and lost in vanity. All Nature experiences continually, and directly, the effects of thy sap, and is not for an instant deprived of its vivifying action; Suffer not Man, thine image, to be less favoured than Nature, and other creatures which thou hast made; make him to be partaker of the same favour; suffer him to be reconciled with thy universal Unity, and, thenceforward, like thee, he will never move, but the visible and invisible universe will move with him; he will never stir without being surrounded with agents who will make him a participator in thy glory and power".

This, O man of desire, is the aim to which all your efforts should tend. You have within yourself, the door by which this sap should enter. If you perceive that, whether as regards human spiritual help, or on account of circumstances, all other doors are closed against you, rejoice thereat, for it proves that the Sovereign Father would thereby force you to look towards that sacred door, where He is waiting for you, and through which He will give you access to the wonders prepared for you.

Now these wonders embrace the universal circle of All, which was once the seat of your empire; and, a proof that all powers, visible and invisible, were present at our primitive birth, is, that they are sensibly present at our regeneration, and each performs a part in it. So then, if God wills that all secrets shall penetrate to man, what is there that can remain hidden from us? As soon as we look at the God within us, we see into all regions, in Him.

All inward infection must be exhausted

God, no doubt, knows our inward state; He knows all the corrosive substances we accumulate in ourselves daily; yet He allows us to go on, and even leads us into situations to realise this our inward state sensibly, and cause us to bring to the surface all these injurious substances, and show them outwardly.

In thus allowing these false influences to run out their complete circle, divine glory shines, no doubt, all the brighter; for this circle of false influences may go round as it will, it ends not the less in nothing; and the elect, who has undergone the trial to the utmost, is all the firmer for it, and more on his guard against the enemy.

It is even more for our purification, than for His own glory, that God allows us to go through these painful and humiliating stages; it is, that hypocrisy may one day cease; for it reigns universally, here below.

106

Where wickedness is, hypocrisy reigns

If man were careful of his ways, he might produce the same result, or come out of himself, another way ; this would be, when he felt attracted to what was false, to try not to forget that the true has not therefore ceased to be; it would be, to say to God, in his inmost being, that more has yet to be done for the improvement of Nature and the human soul, and for the advancement of the Divine work of Wisdom. It would be, to represent to Him how urgent that work was, and ask to be employed in it, and not left idle, or given up to any other work, till this was finished.

It is certain that man would be greatly preserved thereby. But this salutary caution can only be the fruit of long and habitual labour; it can be only, so to say, the reward of wisdom. He must first have expelled from himself all wickedness and deformity; for, while there is a vestige of these, hypocrisy is near, and ever ready to cover this deformity: because, to be preserved from all hypocrisy, there is but one means, and that is, to keep from all wickedness.

On the other hand, by keeping from all wickedness, man facilitates the development of the holy oil within him. Now when this is so, the holy oil within us approaches the fire, and, in doing so, it cannot fail to inflame. And then, all our ways are illuminated, and there is no more room for hypocrisy.

Different Hells

It is, unhappily, but too true, that Man may, by illguided acts, and false contemplations, kindle a fire within himself, which will be injurious to every region in which he has to exercise his ministry, as well as to himself; for, all is power, and it is the respective strength of the different powers, that makes all the danger, suffering, and frightful opposition of all creatures which combat each other here below.

At first, when we cease to live our true life, that is, as soon as we cease to rest on the fundamental ground of our primitive contract, we at once learn by experience that there is a sort of passive hell, which may, however, be called a divine hell, since, to us, it is like the struggle of real life against the inertia or void into which we descend through indolence.

But, if we go further, and, instead of resting on the ground of our primitive contract, if we rest upon, or unite with disorderly or vicious grounds, we soon come to a more active hell, which has two degrees: In one of these degrees, we must rank all those passions which bind us more or less to the service of our enemy; the other, is the very portion or estate of the devil himself, and those who identify themselves with him.

The first degree of this active hell embraces, so to say, the whole human family, and, in this point of view, there is perhaps not a single man who does not daily the devil's work, and perhaps that of many devils at once; though, in this degree, men do this work without suspecting it, unknown to themselves. For, it shows no little address on the part of this demon, thus to keep all men in his service, and make them play whatever parts may suit him, and yet feign so well, and by keeping behind the curtain, that, in making them so act at his pleasure, he persuades them that he himself does not exist.

This enemy, being spirit, drives all thought of an end out of man's mind, by leading him from illusion to illusion, for he really works man in spirit, while he seems to be acting only in the outward order of things, and because man, who is spirit, naturally gives the colour of his own boundless existence to every thing he approaches.

This is the way the enemy whom he blindly serves, leads him on, even to the grave, with projects and passions to which he can see no end, deceiving him alike in his real and in his transient being; this is also the reason why Eternal Wisdom, with whom we ought always to dwell, is obliged to withdraw so far from the infected abode of man. How, indeed, could Eternal Wisdom dwell amongst them? Seeing how they serve a master whom they do not know, and in whom they do not believe; and seeing that, in their blindness, they judge each ether, corrupt each other, rob each other, fight and kill each other. All these turbulent movements fill Her with fright, who was ordained solely to watch and dwell with peace, order, and harmony.

In the second degree of this active hell, men also serve the devil, but not unknowingly, as in the preceding degree; they are no longer in doubt or ignorance of his existence; they participate, knowingly, and actively, in his iniquities. Happily, this class of traitors is the minority, otherwise the world would, long since, have sunk under the weight of the enemy's abominations.

The divine, or passive hell, comprises every region of sorrow, except that of iniquity. Therefore, anguish succeeds anguish there, like waves of the sea. But there, also, one wave swallows up another, so that none has entire dominion. On this account, hope is still, from time to time, known in this hell.

In the first degree of the active hell, there is, at first, spiritually, neither anguish nor hope; there is nothing but illusion; but under this illusion is the abyss, which soon makes the sharpness of its bitter sting to be felt.

In the second degree of this active hell, there is nothing but iniquity, there is neither hope nor illusion; the unity of evil is unbroken there.

Although, to sojourn in the painful ways of the divine hell is a sore thing, it is, nevertheless, a mercy of Divine Wisdom, to allow men who plunge themselves into it, to dwell there a little while. If they were not detained there, they would never know, or they would forget that, even there, the powers are still divine. Yes, this hell becomes one of the springs of our salvation, teaching us to tremble before the power of God, and rejoice, so much the more, when we come to compare it with His love.

Supreme Wisdom permits, also, that nothing concerning this hell, nor even the two degrees of the active hell, should be concealed from the man of desire; seeing that he ought to be instructed in every branch connected with his ministry, since he, afterwards, has to come to the assistance of others; even of those who, though still living, may have sunk into, and, as it were, naturalized themselves in this abyss, or active hell.

For, the existence of these walking associates of the devil is one of the frightful horrors which the Lord's workman has to know; and this is the most painful part of his ministry. But, for the prophet to be installed, must he not, like Ezekiel, swallow the book written within and without; which means that he must be filled to overflowing with lamentations?

Yes, God allows even His prophets to be tried by the Wicked one, that they may learn to feel for their brethren in captivity, and redouble their zeal for the promulgation of the law.

Thus, for the Lord's workman to fulfil his destination, which calls him to be useful spiritually to his fellow-creatures, above all things it is necessary for him to beware of falling into the active hell; but, besides this, he must labour to escape out of the passive or divine hell, if he has carelessly approached it; for, so long as he is there, he cannot be employed in the work at all.

It is only accordingly as he delivers himself from this passive hell, that the riches of the divine covenant enter in him, thence to come forth again to vivify other men, both living and dead. Hereby, man becomes not only the organ of praise (admiration), but, even, in some sort, its object, when he manifests those inexhaustible wonders with which his heart may expand to overflowing; which, in fact, may come out of him, just as we see all manners of brilliant prodigies disclosed by, or come out of light, as it flashes out of its fire-source.

Different elections attainable by Man. The Always

Let this man have courage and perseverance, not to limit himself to a mere election of purification; let him aspire to obtain an election of vocation and teaching; thence, to an election of intention and will ; which, even yet, is not the last term; for Man is still nothing, if he is not transported in an election of action and operation; and because this last election itself, should not count till it become like the ALWAYS.

For the ALWAYS is the denomination which best characterizes Him who Is, as it describes Him in the imperturbable activity of His action; whilst the title of He who Is, describes Him in His existence.

The Action of God, a vivifying focus in Man

Now, His existence is farther from us than His action ; and His action is what serves as His intermedium. And we are nothing, we fall into annihilation, if the divine movement and action are not constant and universal in us.

Do we not see that our blood continually dissolves, purifies, subtilizes, all the gross matter with which we overcharge it? - without which, their weight and corruption would put an end to our existence? Do we not see that, if Nature had not, within, a living basis, which performed for it the functions of our blood, it would long since have succumbed to the corrosive forces which counteract and infect it?

So, in our spiritual region, there must be an active, vivifying Focus, to decompose and rectify, without ceasing, all the false and poisonous substances with which we are filled daily, whether of ourselves, or by contact with our fellow-creatures. Otherwise, we should all, long since, have been in complete spiritual death.

This Focus is that universal principle of real and eternal life in Man, which continually renews the divine contract in us; this is He who never leaves us orphans, if we accept His presence: but this is also that vivifying power, which we disregard, and pass by every minute, though it never ceases to be in close company with us. And it might say of us, as it is said in St. John (xiii. 8): "He that eateth bread with me, hath lifted up his heel against me".

The Focus of action creates mirrors of Wisdom around us

Thus, then, our junction with this vital and vivifying action, is a radical necessity of our being; moreover, this same living and life-giving action alone, can satisfy this urgent want of ours; it is also what contributes most to our true joys, by putting us in position to make, so to say, so many wisdoms spring up around us, which reflect the fruit of our works; and, as Eternal Wisdom does to God, give us the happiness to see that they are good.

For, all spiritual and divine beings need these wisdoms, to serve as mirrors to their own spirits, as themselves serve to the Spirit of the Divinity; and, only the animal material class has no need of these mirrors, for this class has no works of wisdom to produce.

Its power over our brethren and all things

Now, the power of the divine living action in us, extends to nothing short of making us open the inmost centre of the souls of all our brethren, past, present, and future, that all may sign the divine contract together; of enabling us to open the interior centre of all spiritual and natural treasures, disseminated throughout all regions; and rendering us, as it is itself, so to say, the action of all things. This is the reason there are so many men devoid of intelligence in this world; for there are none who really labour to become the action of things: "There is not one that doeth good; no, not one".

How we may attain this action: through Spirit, and the spiritual voice of Man

It is by the irruption of the Spirit in us, and the fervid aspiration of our own spirit, that we can attain to be the action of things; because, by this aspiration, we disengage each principle from its coverings, and enable it to manifest its properties; an aspiration which effects in us, what breathing does in animals, or the air in Nature.

Strictly speaking, we may say, that every thing, in all the *minutim* of every order of things, is done by spirit and air; in elementary Nature, the air only is open, and opens every thing, as, in spiritual Nature, here below, man's spirit alone has this double privilege; and it is because the air is open, that the voice of the Spirit-Man has such extensive rights over all regions.

For, in his musical concerts, in which he tries to develop all the marvels of music, the accompaniments represent the play of the natural, spiritual, celestial, and infernal correspondences with the voice of Man, who has the right to move all regions as he will, and make them partake of his affections.

Divine magism, the principle of this action

But, as the Spirit of Man penetrates even to the Universal Centre, we must also not be surprised, if we see men so fascinated and carried away with their respective gifts, talents, and occupations, to which they devote themselves. All these things point to one and the same term, the Divine Magism, which embraces all things, fills all things, penetrates all things.

If men direct their aspiration with never so little constancy, in any direction where this Magism is likely to be found - and this, from the fecundity of the divine fountains, is almost every where, in both the spiritual and the natural orders, - they are not long in arriving at one of these springs, which all have the same Magism for principle, and they soon get intoxicated with delights, which, though coming through different channels, all have the same foundation in God.

Men should be brethren in enjoyments, all which have but one basis

Therefore, men would be all one in their enthusiasm, if they looked to the unity of this basis and term of all their enjoyments, which is nothing else than the movement of eternal Life and Light in them; and they would soon banish all those rivalries, jealousies, and preferences, which all regard merely the form or mode in which these joys affect them.

Men of letters have, without knowing it, endeavoured to subject the fine arts to this principle; and, to the same principle, must all sciences, discoveries, inventions, and secrets be brought, as well as all the sublimities of men's genius, and all the charm and enjoyment they communicate to us, here below; because, if the Lord's Spirit fills the earth, we cannot stir without coming in contact with it.

Now, do we not derive happiness from even our smallest approaches to the Lord's Spirit? And, as there is but one Spirit of the Lord, must not all our felicities rest on the same foundation, and be radically one?

The enemy's breath or Spirit

The enemy also has an aspiration of his own spirit, a breath, by means of which, instead of making us triumph, he tries to subject us to his false dominion. But, this breath of the enemy's, his spirit, in short, is not opened, like that of man. While we are watchful, therefore, he can do nothing, either in the spiritual order, or even in the order of Nature, for he has then no access to the air, which, though open in itself, is, nevertheless, shut for him.

Thus, the false and figurative means which he employs, may represent designs and principles, and exhibit them to us; but he cannot give them, for he has them not; nor realize them, because he has power only to destroy, not to generate.

The enemy, thereby, proves that his primitive crime was that he wished to master the root of things, and the thought of God; since he continually wishes to master man's soul, which is the thought of God.

O monster! Sated with blood, how couldst thou become the enemy of God's thought? ... But you, O Man! Were not you also a thought of the Lord? And yet you sinned! Here the man of desire exclaims: O sorrow! Let me be flooded with tears; cover me, hide me from the face of the Lord, till I am permitted to see Man, the thought of the Lord, cleansed of his stains.

God, the clarifier of His thought, the human soul

Our mind (*esprit*) is sealed with seven seals ; and men, by reacting upon each other, use indeed the keys, reciprocally, by which means they open each other's spiritual seals: but, for our thought to be pure, God Himself must clarify it; since we can live only on our mother.

And, when God admits a man to the first rank, in the Spiritual Ministry of Man, it is to transform him into a living penetrating agent, whose action shall be universal and permanent; God's ways are not thus made manifest for trifling or transient objects. Therefore, the whole universe should be as nothing in value in our eyes, compared with such an election, if we were happy enough for it to be offered to us; since we then might work successfully for the relief of the human soul.

Earthly tribulations

All is Spirit in the divine work. Therefore the tribulations of this world, wars, and catastrophes of Nature, which are not sent directly from God, do not occupy His attention like the care of souls; and, when men slaughter each other, or their bodies are victims to great calamities, He feels chiefly the evils which their souls suffer; for the soul is His thought, which is dear to Him, and calls forth His zeal and action.

It was only to the mature Man, the Spirit-Man; in short, to His ministers and elect, that it was said: all the hairs of their heads were numbered, and that not one should fall to the ground without His permission.

He leaves those who are in the regions of the inferior spiritual powers, to be ruled by those lower powers.

Those who are lower still; in thé regions of mere matter, fall under the class of oxen; and, according to Paul (1 Cor. ix. 9), God does not care for oxen; although the Spirit did care for them, in the time of the Levites, and in reference to the Jews, who were the figurative apostles; but not to other nations, who went after spirits of abomination in their sacrifices.

We will add, that God often makes no change in the painful and disastrous course of things, even for His elect, here below, but only gives them strength to endure: all which does not prevent His caring for their souls and spirits, in every case, and under all circumstances, with a care which our weak understandings could not conceive, nor our tongues express, so intent is He to preserve us from the only real dangers which surround us, and alone are to be feared, and so great is His desire to see us realize the divine covenant which attended our origin, as we shall observe, presently.

Man in infancy

I pause a moment, here, to consider Man at an age when he does not yet present any of those lamentable characteristics we have been noticing, or any of those bright rays of which we have announced him as the recipient and the organ.

When we contemplate the simple joys of children, how is it possible to imagine the extremes of virtue and vice of which the grown man is capable, and which may lie hid and shut up in this infantine envelope?

This creature, transported with a doll, bursting with laughter at a bubble in the air, or drowned in grief at the loss of a toy; this being may, I say, be one day so developed, as, on the one hand, to elevate his thoughts to heaven, or, on the other, to look into the abyss and understand the righteous execution of the supreme decrees upon the family of the wicked; he may become a living example to the world of the divine pattern; he may exhibit the greatest penetration in science, and the greatest heroism in virtue; in short, he may be, every way, a model of excellence.

But, alas, this very being may come to be a pattern of the contrary; and, steeped in ignorance and crime, he may become the enemy of the Principle which made him, the active focus of depravity and every abomination.

The contrast is so heart-rending, that it is impossible, without pain, to entertain the thought that these tender and innocent creatures may, under this interesting exterior, contain the seeds of every disease, and end in a shameful degradation of heart, soul, and spirit; that, in their feeble branches, they possibly nourish a pestilential sap, the explosion of which will be only the more deadly, because it is tardy and deferred to another time; in short, that they perhaps bear in their essences a juice, sweet and benign at present, but which may one day become the bitterest and most corrosive of poisons.

How can the thought be borne, that the ingenuousness of this infant, for whom the smallest trifle affords an innocent enjoyment now, may become, one day, the ferocity of a tiger; that he may turn into a persecutor of his fellow-creatures, and be the victim and tool of that enemy, whose servant, as I said before, we all are here below?

Hope in the Covenant

But what may assuage, if not remove the painfulness to the man of desire, of this lamentable prospect, and give him consolation and hope for the future, is, that the divine contract has also been again written in the essences of this tender plant, and brings with it a specific which can not only repress the disorderly germs, which perhaps already infect it, but cause the divine germs to flourish, of which it is also the depositary, by right of its origin.

Yes, we cannot too much adore the Supreme Wisdom, when we see the gentle progression by which He seeks continually to lead us to the exalted term for which we received life and being; and if intelligent eyes, lovers of what is good, watched carefully over the infancy of man, and concurred with the higher powers to bring the treasures, with which the divine contract has enriched the young plant, to maturity, there would be no kind of raptures and delights which it might not expect, at every stage of its existence.

All this man's steps would be peaceful, all his movements connected, all his degrees of progress would be united insensibly with each other, and divine joy would accompany them all, for this joy should be the term of the progression, as it was its beginning; in short, he would arrive, almost without pain or trouble or effort, at a height of perspicacity, intelligence, wisdom, virtue, and power, from which, in his tender age, he seemed so distant, that we must collect our thoughts before we can believe it may one day be possible.

Tuition of the young

Nevertheless, it would be well to teach this young plant a very useful lesson, of a more sombre colour. It is, alas, that Wisdom, which ought, of itself, to have brought us so much joy, is obliged to clothe itself, for us, here below, with garments of mourning and sadness; our wisdom must be to suffer now, instead of rejoicing, because crime has divided everything, and made two wisdoms. The second, or latter of these wisdoms, is not life, but it collects life in us, and pre-pares us to receive life, or the first Wisdom, the source of all joy; and it is this sublime first Wisdom which creates and maintains all things. Therefore it is always young.

This young plant should also be taught, as it advances in growth, that if Supreme Wisdom cannot permit us, here below, to look at the heavenly Jerusalem itself, such as it formerly existed in the soul of Man, it permits us, at least, sometimes to look over its plans, which suffices to fill us with the sweetest consolation.

It would be well to teach him, and persuade him to convince himself, by his own experience, that prayer ought to be a continual spiritual partnership; for we ought to pray only with God, and our prayer does not deserve even the name, but in so far as God prays in us, for only thus do they pray in God's kingdom.

It would be well to teach him that physicians are supposed to know the nature and properties of their medicines, and to have ascertained all the virtues of their remedies, thereby to be enabled to cure any disease; that this simple observation may enlighten him as to the original destination of Man, which ought, doubtless, to have been such as to enable him to cure all disorders, and to know the properties of every substance in Nature, for all were subject to Man. He should learn from this what a shameful degradation Man has undergone.

It would be well to tell him that the man of truth should be separate from the men of the stream; that he would lose too much in mixing with them, and moreover, that what he risked was not his own, but his Master's.

It would be well to warn him that there is more danger for a man off his guard, amongst men who are lost, than there would be amongst evil spirits; because men now combine two powers, which they abuse as they will, by disguising one under cover of the other, whilst the devil has only one; besides, the devil has no form of his own, and is obliged to create one every moment, to serve as a receptacle for his power; but man carries everywhere with him a form which is both the receptacle and the instrument of his double power.

On this subject it would be well to tell him that there are many wandering spirits, who seek to clothe themselves with us, whilst we ourselves are almost naked, in spite of our bodies, and have nothing else to do here below, but seek to clothe ourselves with our first body, in which the Divinity may dwell.

It would be well to tell him that chastity comprises, at once, purity of body, justness of spirit, warmth of heart, and activity of soul and love; for it embraces, generally, every virtue, and is the absence of every vice.

It would be well to tell him that the virtues we cultivate, and the intelligences we acquire, are so many lamps we light around us, which burn when we sleep.

It would be well to tell him that nearly every creature in Nature is a type humiliating to man; for they are active, vigilant, orderly, and he alone is passive, indifferent, cowardly, and, in some respects, a monstrosity.

It would be well to tell him that, although God rules all sensible things, He is so distant from them, that our earthly nature and material man cannot comprehend how we are to make His kingdom known amongst the Gentiles, since our spiritual words are unintelligible even to our own senses. And we must be completely renewed, and lifted out of our senses and all figurative things, before we can become spiritual witnesses of the Word, and enter upon the Spiritual Ministry of Man.

It would be well to tell him that, from their commencement, rivers flow to their destination, without knowing whether they traverse opulent cities, or poor hamlets, arid deserts, or fertile countries embellished by Nature and man's industry; and that, such should be the ardour of the man of desire, that he must, in like manner, tend towards the end which awaits him, without enquiring what borders upon his earthly route.

It would be well to tell him that, when a man of desire works on himself, he really works for all men, since he strives, and thereby contributes, to show them the image and likeness of God in purity; and, to know this image and likeness is all they want.

It would be well to tell him that, when Deists recognise the existence of a Supreme Being, and yet will not allow that He concerns Himself with the government of this world, nor with the men who inhabit it, their error comes from their having made themselves material and brutish; that, in fact, God does not meddle with matter nor with brutes, but has them ruled by His powers; that the Deists so deaden their souls, that God no longer comes near them to lead them, for He cannot be pleased with anything but His own image, nor concern Himself with anything else, and that is why they say God does not meddle with the government of mankind; for truly, in the state of degradation and darkness into which the Deists have allowed themselves to sink, He no longer meddles with them.

It would be well to tell him that a proof that true thoughts do not come from ourselves is, that, if we created them, we should be no longer dependent on God; that neither do false thoughts come from ourselves; but we are merely placed between the two, to distinguish between their divine and infernal sources; that men can communicate nothing to each other, but by making their thoughts sensible, by words or equivalent signs; that it therefore follows, that all thought coming to us from without is sensible, by the fact of its communication, and therefore spoken, though we may not always hear it materially; that infants are examples of this: we cannot deny that they have senses, but it would be in vain to attempt to convey our thoughts to them by word, we know they would not hear the sounds; in a little more advanced age they distinguish the sounds, but do not understand the meaning; at last, in a more perfect state, they both hear the sounds and understand their meaning, and thereby receive the inward communication of our thoughts; that, in fact, we act before infants rather than speak to them, but that they certainly neither see nor understand; movements and noise are equally lost upon them; at first, they are affected by the grossest senses only, the touch, the smell, the taste; to this incipient state and age succeeds the use of sight and hearing; at last comes speech, which, however, is subject to a very slow progression, for it begins only with cries; and, hereupon, man may take a lesson, and humble himself.

It would be well to tell him that the grand thoughts which God so often sends us in the painful course of our expiation, are so many witnesses we may bring before Him, when we pray: and nothing will please Him more than that we should make use of them, and remind Him of His promises and consolations.

It would be well to say to him that, as God was alone when He made Man, so He will also be alone to instruct him and lead him into His divine depths.

It would be well to caution him how prudently he should conduct himself, in the management of divine riches which may be confided to him by the Supreme bounty, as he will not have far to walk in the path of Truth before he will feel that there are some things which cannot be said, even to the Spirit, since they are higher even than Spirit.

It would be well to tell him that there is a line and order of instruction, from which he should never deviate, when he tries to direct the understanding of his fellow creatures, and that order is this: - our thought, a divine mirror; - existence of a superior Being, proved by this mirror when it is clean and pure; - our privations, proving that there is a Justice; - this Justice proving that there has been a free and voluntary corruption (alteration); - Supreme Love, awaking; - laws of generation, given under different covenants (alliances); - time of return; - spiritual life; - light; - speech (*parole*); - union, entrance into rest: - such should be the course of teaching, if the teacher will not deceive, nor delay his disciples, nor lead them astray.

It would be well to tell him not to flatter himself that he can ever possess wisdom in his memory, or by the mere cultivation of his intelligence; that wisdom is like maternal love, which can be felt only after the fatigues of gestation, and the pains of child-birth.

Finally, it would be well to tell him that it is not enough for a man, that he should acquire the light of wisdom; he must keep it, when he gets it, which is incomparably more difficult.

The Fall

When we fall from a height, our heads get so turned in the fall, that we lose consciousness; only at the instant of the shock, the sharp sense of pain seizes us; and we often, even, remain motionless and insensible. Such was the history of the human soul when it sinned: it lost sight of the glorious region from which it fell, and Man was left, as it were, altogether dead, and deprived of the use of every faculty of his being.

The treatment

But our curative course of treatment, was also similar to our human practice. Just as, when a man meets with any grievous accident, the physician has him bled profusely, to prevent inflammation, so, after the terrible fall of the human family, Divine Wisdom took from Man nearly all his blood; that is, his strength and powers; otherwise, this blood, finding the organs no more in condition to concur in its action, would have destroyed them completely.

It is true that this indispensable precaution on the part of the physician, may curtail the patient's future life, which perhaps, might have been longer. For the same reason, God has shortened our days, as He shortens the duration of the World, in favour of what are called the elect; without which, no man could be saved.

Conformably also with the medicinal regimen, spirituous liquors are given to revive us; then, healing ointments are applied; and, finally, we are allowed substantial nourishment, to restore our strength.

When, in the tender effusion of Supreme Love, the first treatments were applied to the human soul, it recovered its motion, and this enabled it to profit, in the way of instruction, by the movement which ruled the Universe; for these two movements should be coordinate. We seek, in fact, every day, to regulate our thoughts with everything that moves in the universe; and it was a special favour to the human soul, that it was still allowed the means whereby it might contemplate the truth in the world's images, after being banished from the reality.

The soul becoming subject to the physical universe, its first law follows it

This human soul had known, in its glory, that it ought to have no other God but God; and, although it was not to know the fullness of its glory till it attained the complement of its work, yet, how little soever it may have tasted of the divine wonders and goodness, it knew perfectly well, that nothing else was to be compared with them.

Nevertheless, this soul submitted to be infected (*altérée*) by the power of an inferior principle, namely this universal physical world, in which the sun and stars exercise so imposing a part, so that it became corporeally subject to their rule. But, although it fell under this inferior rule, which was part of its degradation, the Source which produced this human soul, willing, in no wise, to lose sight of it, transmitted to it, in this new order of things, the fundamental precept of its first law: "Thou shalt have no other God before me".

The Sun a physical symbol of Divinity

Thus, the sun, in the physical world, is a material organ of that sublime revelation, which was far anterior to books; it prophesied this revelation from the beginning of the world, and will not cease to prophesy it, before all people, till the consummation of all things.

It is in the sun's absence, during the night, that the stars become visible ; then the reign of those gods of the Gentiles becomes manifest; then, notwithstanding the shining of the stars, the earth is in darkness, flowers lose their fragrance, vegetation is retarded, lugubrious cries of night-birds and beasts are heard, crimes and vices of evil doers are ripened, and wrongful designs and deeds of wickedness are perpetrated; then, in a word, those high places triumph, on which all people of the earth have offered sacrifices, at first in mere delusion, but which soon became abominably wicked, through the infections of the prince of darkness, as we shall see presently.

But, at the approach of day, the stars grow dim; and they vanish altogether, when day bursts forth in its fulness; and the sun, causing by its presence, the vain multiplicity of these false gods to disappear, seems to say to the universe, as it was said to the human soul, when it came forth from its glorious source: Thou shalt have none other Gods before me.

The human soul forgot this law, when, from its state of splendor, it wandered after a false attraction; but this law, which cannot be abrogated, followed it even into the earthly abyss; for the Principle of all things can produce nothing without imprinting its divine language in it.

Idolatry of the Sun

Yet, notwithstanding the force of the instruction conveyed in this symbol, the nations took the letter only of the phenomenon, instead of its spirit; and this is one of the causes in which the idolatry and worship of the sun originated.

Idolatry of fire

The idolatry of fire comes from a more remote source; it could only have been engendered, as a consequence of the primitive rights of Man, by some mortals having sensibly known the origin of fire, (which is not mere lightning,) for it is a fundamental truth, that everything must make its own revelation; and there is nothing done in the universe which does not prove it.

Motive for natural calamities

When Supreme Love saw you lose yourself still more, through the very means provided to enable you to find your way again; when He saw you exasperating your wounds with the sensible objects which He displayed before your eyes, to divert your pains, He could not help again proclaiming this important command in your ears: Thou shalt have none other Gods before me, by using means still more potent than before.

As the spectacle of Nature in her harmony, only produced in you a contrary effect to what He intended, He allowed her powers to act upon you in disharmony, to try to bring you, through tribulation and suffering, to where your intelligence had not sufficed to keep you; and this is the key to all those calamities related in the history of every nation of the earth.

Thus, a mother acts towards her child, a tutor towards his pupil, leaving them to bear for a time, the consequences of their weakness or levity, that they may learn to be more careful in future.

Direct Spiritual communications, Divine commandments

But, when these trials fail, when the danger is still more pressing, and the heedless one, instead of coming out of it, only goes further in, even to the risk of losing his life; then the teacher, or the mother, goes herself, and enforces authoritatively the important precepts she had inculcated before, so as to effect by fear, what gentleness had failed to accomplish; and this is a positive and natural explanation of all those divine and spiritual manifestations, of which the religious history of Man, written and unwritten, is full.

Yes, O human soul, this was assuredly the way of Supreme Love towards you, when He saw that the great calamities of Nature, which your carelessness had provoked, had not made you wiser. He came to you with discomposed looks, and, assuming a threatening tone, reminded you of those ancient commandments or regulations, on which your own origin and the divine covenant were based; regulations which He published before you, when He gave you being; which He caused Nature again to proclaim, when you subjected yourself to her figurative rule; and which may, any moment, resound in your inmost being, for you still are, from your origin, the organ of the divine Eternal Fountain, and what the Eternal has pronounced once, can never cease to be pronounced through all eternity.

The traditions of all nations afford traces of this watchful proceeding of Supreme Love towards you; from the beginning His way has been, with nations, as with individuals every day, bestirring Himself, by violent secret movements, to awaken them out of their lethargy, and snatch them out of the dangers to which their follies have exposed them; it was, in short, in and by this spirit that Moses represents the voice of the Most High, publishing in the midst of thunders and lightnings, to the Hebrews, this imperative and exclusive divine command, which the nations had so forgotten: Thou shalt have none other Gods before me.

Every thing must make its own revelation

Independently of innumerable other instructive lessons which Nature is commissioned by Supreme Love, to transmit daily and physically to the human soul, we are intimately convinced, that, were it for nothing but to have a name amongst men, everything must have made its own revelation. Thus the religious practices so universal amongst men, do not permit a doubt to remain, that a way was opened by Supreme Love through them, for the healing of the human soul; though these healing waters have become so choked with ruins, as to be hardly recognizable.

All human institutions derive from patterns on high Man's power

When we are fully convinced of the rigorous truth that everything must make its own revelation, without which, it could never be known, nor repeated, nor communicated, we shall perceive that there is nothing, even to human politics, and civil institutions, the patterns of which are not to be found without us, and above us. If there were no legions above, no different degrees of superiority, chiefs, and governments, on high, we should have had none of these institutions ourselves. Man himself, here below, walks under the eye and protection of invisible powers, to whom he owes everything, though he scarcely seeks to know them, and hardly believes in them, so taken up is he with his own power; yet, if he gets so intoxicated with his own power, it shows that he ought to have power really; he ought to have an empire, and faithful, obedient subjects.

When a sovereign, for instance, or a general, sees himself surrounded with his armies, and holds brilliant reviews of them, and feels a secret joy and glory in having before him, so many soldiers grandly equipped, and devoted to his orders; when he seems to say to all spectators: "Not only do all these forces which I command, depend upon me, but for me they were created, and to me they owe all they have", - they merely repeat, in a conventional apparent order, what, with the primitive Man, ought to have been real, and positive, and permanent.

This primitive Man would also have had legions, over which he would have had absolute authority, by communicating his spirit to them, as we see a general, so to speak, pass his will into the hundred thousand men he commands, making them one with himself, and taking from them, in a manner, their own wills, to give them his only; otherwise, his control over them would be impossible, and inexplicable.

This primitive Man would likewise have contemplated himself in his legions, and reaped thereby a real glory, because he himself would have counted for something in whatever they had; the beauty of their arms; their courage in defending the cause of justice; all marvels which he could in fact cause to proceed out of himself, and spring up in all his subordinates at will. Instead of this, here below, his legions come before him already clothed, armed, and drilled; here, he has not himself always sown what he reaps, since most of those he inspects he perhaps never saw, and knows not even their names; a species of knowledge which would have constituted the real strength of the primitive Man, as regards his cohorts.

Now, what we here say in respect to the military order, may be said of all our other institutions, political and social; we might even say it in respect of Nature, for Man might have concurred with every region, and all their powers, in every order, to produce those marvellous pictures, those ravishing sights, which would have every where enchanted his eyes, and filled his heart with a justly acquired and merited glory, whereas, in his present limited estate, he often counts for very little in all that surrounds him, and in all he glories in.

But, if it is from on high, that man first had, and still receives all that is best for the government of his fellow-creatures, the more he reads on high, the more good things he will discover for his own benefit, and that of human nature; as it is from on high that all the healing processes, sent by Supreme Love for his recovery, have come*.

---

*Jacob Boehme's MYSTERIUM MAGNUM.

On the subject of the religious media opened to man by Supreme Love, I would engage the reader to draw, if he can, from the well of one of Jacob Boehme's works, The Mysterium Magnum, 'The Great Mystery.' He would there find numerous ramifications of the tree of the covenant which this Supreme Love has renewed with Man since his degradation. He will there see the sap of this tree, showing itself, first of all in the roots, then developing itself in the different buds as they grow, and, at length, in the flowers and fruits of the tree, deploying all the properties contained in its germ, and brought to light through its channels. He will there see the true line of descent under cover of the figurative, and yet one only sap running through both these lineages simultaneously, and distinguishable, notwithstanding the diversity of characters it takes; and thus harmonizing all the epochs it embraces in its course. But he will, also, there see an opposing sap, likewise circulating through the earth, ever since we have been imprisoned in it, and presenting since that first epoch down to our

Religious institutions: Sacrifices

Amongst the religious institutions once generally established over the earth, but of which we have now almost lost all traces, the sacrifice of animals and other productions of Nature holds a prominent place, and deserves to be considered in detail, inasmuch as neither tradition nor observation has given us any thing satisfactory, and even Boehme is incomplete, on this point; although he has opened some very beautiful views, in regard to it.

No, it cannot be denied, that sacrifices, in such general use all over the globe, must, notwithstanding their abuse, and, perhaps even through their abuse, be classed amongst our privileges, and included in the succours granted to us since the Fall, by Divine Wisdom, for the revival, as far as possible, of our divine contract; and, as such, they come within the cognizance of the Spirit-Man.

Man, a King subjugated by his own subjects; in bondage under blood, as a means to his recovery. Spirit-of sacrifices

In spite of the ceaseless efforts of false philosophy to extinguish the sublime nature of man, it is too late now to question his having been born to a high destination; and the inestimable value of the gifts which he can still discover within himself, even in his wretchedness, is an indication of what he may formerly have possessed in freedom and abundance.

We need not then be afraid of erring much, if we consider Man, in the bosom of the Universe, as a guilty King, subjected to the power of his own subjects, whom he himself led into disorder and anarchy, by the injustice of his government; but, above this agitated sea, we may discern the eternal reason of things, tending by the immutable weight of its wisdom, to make all our disharmonized faculties recover their calm and equilibrium.

Perhaps we may even recognize that, in his primitive state, before the Fall, man may also have had a ministry of sacrifice to fulfil; not expiatory, for he was pure, but sacrifices of glory to his Principle; not bloody sacrifices, but sacrifices of the divine wonders which are comprised in all creatures, and which he would have had power to develop before God, who entrusted this ministry to him; Man being, as it were, established in the centre of the universal creation.

But while we are occupied with the sacrifices in use upon the earth, and their particular signification, spiritual or physical, we shall see Man fast bound to blood, which seems to be the organ and resort, or abode, of all his enemies here

---

own days, a sanctuary of abomination, along side of the sanctuary of holiness. The descriptions he will find in this author, will instruct him fully on the course of those different institutions of religion which have spread over the earth ; and I must be satisfied with indicating this debt to him, which otherwise, I should have had to transcribe or translate, almost entirely.

below, the sepulchre of bondage, in which this idolatrous king is buried alive for having sought to oppose the decrees of Providence, and worshipped strange gods.

The law which condemns man to bondage, has for aim, to keep him in privation, that privation may lead him to repentance, and repentance to confession of his faults; that confession may put him in the way that leads to pardon; and, as the zealous care of Supreme Wisdom, for this unhappy exile, is inexhaustible, it provided him with means to cure the evils he is daily exposed to from the hands of his enemies, and to preserve himself from their attacks; and, lastly, it provided him with means of consolation in his misery; and we will here endeavour to show that this was the spirit of the institution of sacrifices, how absurd or impious soever those ceremonies may have become in passing through the hands of men, and falling under the control of the very enemy they were intended to expel.

Unities of action in the Universe and Nature

A positive and well-known law, which I here retrace to the friends of wisdom, as one of the most useful lights in their course, is, that, notwithstanding the innumerable diversities of creatures and classes which compose the universe, there are certain unities of action which embrace entire classes, and act upon the individuals of those classes, by natural analogy.

This is why, in all productions of Nature, there are genera, species, families, all bearing the impress of this unity of action, each according to its class.

The powers and faculties of our minds may be said to present the same law, showing a sort of uniformity in the movements of men's thoughts, and reducing all their systems to a limited number of theorems and axioms, and all their institutions to fundamental formulas, which hardly vary from each other. The medicinal art, morals, politics, deliberative and scientific assemblies, things belonging to the religious order, and, if I may say so, even to the infernal order, all testify in favour of this principle.

By this law of unity of action, the same physical action which rules in the blood of man, rules in that of animals also, because the bodies of both are of the same order.

But, if the same physical action governs the blood of man and that of animals, this action is, doubtless, exposed to the contractions and disorders to which both are liable; and this physical law, although not based upon liberty, as the moral laws are, may therefore suffer derangements, from the obstacles and opposition which surround and menace every thing that exists in Nature.

If these different individuals, men and animals, are subject to the same laws, in the disorders to which they are exposed, they also participate in the perfections of the unity of the regular action which governs them; and, if derangement is common to both, restoration must be so equally, from whence both the spirit and the use of sacrifices may be presumed; but this would not be sufficient, if we could not also find out, how these sacrifices operate in themselves, and how their results can affect man.

Reason of Sacrifices; their spiritual operation

The Hebrew law tells us that there are animals which are clean, and others which are unclean. Jacob Boehme gives a positive reason for this, in the two tinctures, which were in harmony before crime, and were subdivided in the great change. Nature is not opposed to this, since we recognize a distinction in animals, some being useful, others mischievous. So that even in a mere physical sense, the meaning of Scripture would be borne out.

But, what if it had a spiritual meaning? And, in truth, as matter has only a life of dependence, and it has existence, virtues, and properties, only through the different spirituous actions or influences, by which it is engendered, combined, constituted, and characterized; being, moreover, the continual receptacle of powers opposed to order, which tend only to stamp their mark of irregularity and confusion everywhere; it is not surprising that this matter should present the types and play of all these diverse and opposite actions or influences, of which we see melancholy evidences in ourselves.

Thus, when man has fallen under some disorderly influence, the clean animal might be a means of delivering him from it; the disorderly action being attracted by the basis here presented to it, over which it may have certain rights and power.

But, for this attraction not to prolong the consequences and effects of this disorderly influence, it is necessary, in the first place, that the animal's blood be shed; secondly, that this animal, though clean by nature, should receive some extra preservative influence, because it is composed of mixed elements, and exposed to the disorganizing influence of the enemy, like every thing else that is matter. Now the preservative action, in this case, was represented, among the Hebrews, by the imposition of the priest's hands, on the head of the victim, the priest himself representing Man reinstated in his first rights; and such is the spirit of these two laws.

By the shedding of the animal's blood, the disorderly action attached to man's matter, is more forcibly attracted outwards, than by the mere bodily presence of the animal, because, the nearer we come to the principle, the more energetic and efficacious are all its relations, in any order whatever.

But, through the sacerdotal preparation, or that of Man, enjoying the virtuality of his rights, this blood, and this victim, are placed beyond the reach of this disorderly action; which thus abandons man's matter, drawn by the attraction of the animal's blood; but, being repelled by the powerful virtue which the priest communicated to the blood, it is forced to cast itself out, to be engulfed in the regions of disorder, out of which it came.

This, it seems to me, gives a general view of the spirit of the institution of sacrifices.

This view of the subject may help us to discover the particular spirit which ordered the details of all the Hebrew sacrifices; those, for instance, for sin and expiation; those called peace offerings; and even those of atonement, or reconciliation, and man's union with God, confirmed by the sensible signs of their alliance.

Sacrifice for sin

This simple law of transposition, of which we have been speaking, is sufficient to give us an idea of the spirit of the sacrifice for sin, - casting out defilement into the regions of disorder, and upon the enemy who caused it.

Peace offering

The object of the sacrifice for peace, would seem to be to give strength to man to resist that enemy, and even to prevent his attacks. The preparation of the victim, by the imposition of the priest's hands, makes this intelligible, since it places a pure blood which is in conjunction with regular influences, in proximity with a blood which is surrounded with destructive and maleficent influences, and is thereby able to restore calm and repose. A great many of the details of the sacrificial ceremonies warrant our confidence in these conjectures. The blood poured round the altar, and applied to the four corners, the sprinklings of blood, the eating the victim, etc., all strikingly refer to a work of peace and preservation.

The perpetual, and the consecration sacrifices

As to the perpetual sacrifices, and those ordained for the consecration of priests - the spiritual purport of which was, to unite the pontiff with God, - their law will enable us to arrive at its own meaning; but this kind of sacrifice was not instituted for all men, but only for those called by God, by a particular election, to His own service.

Such men, prepared by their very election, were in connection with the higher virtues ; these higher virtues, embracing all things, are always united with those regular actions which watch over our blood, to clear it from disorder. The immolated victim, after these preparations, presented a blood on which these influences developed their power, and enabled the higher virtues to develop theirs in their turn, because all that is harmonious partakes more or less of the properties of the divine contract, even amongst animals.

It is not surprising, then, that these same higher virtues should act upon the chosen man, and produce for him all those sensible manifestations which he feels he so much requires, to direct him in his darkness; he can receive the evidences of truth only through an intermedium.

All that happened to Abraham, when he sacrificed the animals divided in two; what happened to Aaron, on the eighth day of his consecration; to David, on the threshing-floor of Ornan; what took place in the Temple, after the high priest's sacrifices, sufficiently indicate the object, and the power which the really sacred sacrifices had, when performed by the Lord's elect, who exercised, in a measure, suitable to the epoch, the Spiritual Ministry of Man.

From these few observations on the sacrifices of blood in general, it follows that their object was to develop certain pure and regular influences (actions) which, uniting with man, might help him to rise out of his abyss, to the regions of regularity and order.

Anathemas and exterminations, their reasons and operation

In an opposite direction, but tending to the same end, the interdict or anathema operated, spoken of in the last chapter of Leviticus. What was consigned, by this sort of consecration, to the justice of the Lord, was, apparently, the seat of what was most irregular and abominable, which, therefore, might be most fatal to the chosen people. Thus, all these subjects of anathema had to be exterminated, that the irregular influence or action which was in them, finding no more to rest upon, should be compelled to depart, and be no more able to injure the people.

We may here learn not to find fault with the punishment of Achan, the execution of Agag by Samuel, and the rejection of Saul, who wished to save this condemned and impious king; and even all those ordained massacres related in Scripture, of entire cities, with all their inhabitants, which appear so revolting to those who are not prepared, or are little familiar with profound truths, and especially those with whom the material body is every thing, whereas God counts souls only.

Why the innocent fall with the guilty; extermination of animals

This class of persons are far from suspecting the great secret, spoken of in "L'Esprit des Choses", by which the Divinity frequently permits the innocent to fall with the guilty, in plagues, or catastrophes of Nature, that they may, by their purity, preserve them from greater corruption, as we cover with salt the meats we would preserve, which, otherwise, would putrefy.

In a word, it is in this intent of removing the bases of poison, that we may discover the reason why, in the conquest of the Promised Land, the Jews were so frequently ordered to exterminate, even to the animals, because, in this case, the death of animals infected with the impure influences of those nations, preserved the chosen people from the poison; whereas, in the sacrifices, the death of clean animals attracted wholesome and preservative influences.

To have destroyed these nations too soon, would have exposed the children of Israel to the impure influences of those beasts of the earth, because those nations were their receptacles and bases of action; therefore, Moses said to the people: "The Lord thy God will put out those rations before thee, little by little; thou mayest not consume them at once, lest the beasts of the field increase upon thee". (Deut. vii. 22.)

Blood of clean animals, the seat of good influences in bondage

This does not mean that the pure and regular virtues are shut up and buried in the blood of animals, as some have thought, who, like the Hindoos, believe that all kinds of spirits lodge and abide there; it presumes simply that those pure and regular influences are attached to certain classes and individuals of these animals, and that, by breaking the bases in which they are fixed, they may become useful to man; it is in this sense we should read the passage "It is the blood that maketh atonement for the soul" (Lev. xvii. 11); for we must not confound the fleshly soul, and, therefore, the soul of animals, with the regular external actions by which they are governed.

But from this species of bondage or constraint, in which this kind of actions or influences is, there results another consequence, justified beforehand by the painful state or sort of reprobation under which man is, and which announces him to be a criminal. This consequence is, that if man requires all these actions to be set free, before he can begin to recover his own liberty; if, in a word, he is the object for whom this law is put in operation, he must himself have been for something in the revolution which enthralled them.

Man brought these Virtues *or influences under bondage*

The knowledge of Man, which the reader will, by this time, have gained, will make this appear quite natural to him. If we have considered him as a King; if he had his origin in' the very Source of Light; if we acknowledge him to have been made in the image and likeness of the Divinity, and intended for His representative in the universe, he must have been superior to all these actions which are now employed for the preservation of Nature.

Now, if these divers actions looked to him to keep them in their order, and their first employment, that is, if he ought to have developed and manifested in them the divine wonders of which they were depositaries, and which should serve as sacrifices for glory; it is clear that, when man lost himself, his fall may have brought these actions or powers into a state of subjection and violence, for which they were not made, and which, to them, is a sort of death.

Thus we see in the Hebrew traditions, the Jews being, as it were, the firstborn of people, that Pharaoh's prevarications and hardness of heart compelled Justice to strike, not him only, but all the firstborn of his kingdom, of beasts as well as of men; the son of the slave, as well as the son of him that sat upon the throne.

Dedication of the firstborn

After this terrible vengeance, executed upon Egypt, we see the Hebrews ordered to consecrate all their firstborn to God, from the firstborn of man to that of beasts. This coincidence is a further indication of what we have advanced, as to the aim and spirit of the sacrifices; for, the consecration of the priest, which seems to combine in itself the meaning of all other consecrations, was not made without the sacrifice of a ram.

If we followed up this comparison, we should see that, by man's crime, all the firstborn, all produced principles of every kind, were buried with him in his abyss; but that, through the never-failing love of Supreme Wisdom, he received power to restore them successively to their rank, and then his fellow creatures, in their turn ; and make souls enjoy their sabbaths, as he had power to make Nature enjoy hers.

We should see, in a word, that the bloody sacrifices tended to that double object, whether by restoring their original liberty to all those pure and regular actions, which sin had attached to the different classes of animals and created things, or thereby enabling them to bring relief to man, and deliver him from the thraldom in which he languishes.

The Exodus, a double type, founded on the nature of Man

For, in the example we have just quoted, we must always consider that its object was Man; only we must observe that its double types apply to two distinct nations, the Egyptians and the Hebrews, one of which represents Man in his fall and state of reprobation, and the other under his law of deliverance and return towards the sublime post from which he descended.

We do not, however, take the Hebrew laws and customs for the ground and foundation on which this theory rests. It rests, in the first place, on the nature of Man as he was in his origin, and as he is at present, that is, on our greatness and our wretchedness; and when, afterwards, it finds on earth testimonies which support and confirm it, it makes use of them, not as proofs, but as confirmations.

Therefore, we need not refer to the sacred writings, to find out the time when sacrifices originated. The sacrifices of glory date from an epoch anterior to the fall of man: as for the bloody and expiatory sacrifices, they commenced as soon as guilty man began to see the way of deliverance open before him, and that was when he was permitted to come to inhabit the earth; since, being previously swallowed up like an infant, in an abyss, he could have no matter for sacrifice at his disposal, not having the use of his faculties.

Man's relations (Rapports) with Nature and Animals

Man's first destiny was to be connected with all Nature, till the work was ended which he would have had to perform if he had kept his post. Notwithstanding his fall, he was still connected with this Nature, out of which he could not get, and its oppressive weight was still further increased by the dominion which he allowed his enemy to acquire over it, and over himself. Thus, man's connection with Nature was nothing but suffering, and his being, himself, so to say, identified with the power of darkness. At length, when the way to return was opened to him, these salutary means (sacrifices) could operate only through the organ or channel of Nature, in which he was buried, instead of being its ruler.

Thus the relations (rapports) he has with animals will not end, till Nature have fulfilled her course; but these relations vary in their character, according to the different epochs in which man is placed. In his time of glory, he reigned as a sovereign over animals; and, if we may presume that there were sacrifices in that epoch, their object could not have been man's restoration, for he was not guilty.

When he fell he became the victim of these animals, and of all Nature.

At the time of his deliverance, he was permitted and enabled to employ them for his advancement: this cannot be doubted, after what has been said.

Now, these foundations being thus laid on a firm basis, it is satisfactory to find them fully confirmed in the sacred writings.

Spiritual signification and correspondence of Mosaic Sacrifices

The first man, in his state of glory, is, in the Scriptures, shown to have been invested with entire authority over Nature, particularly over animals; since it was given to him to apply to them their essential and constituent names; after his fall the earth was cursed, and enmity was placed between the woman and the serpent; but we hardly see man sent to till the ground, before we find sacrifices of animals in use in his family, a strong indication that he practised them himself, and that he transmitted the practice to his children, from whom it afterwards spread over the whole earth.

It is easy to see how advantageous this institution, so salutary in its principle and in its object, would have been to man, if he had observed it in its true spirit; we have only to look at the sacrifices restored in the time of Moses, to acknowledge that, if the people had observed them faithfully, they would never have been abandoned, but would have drawn upon themselves every good thing they were then capable of receiving, since divine light and power would have surrounded them always.

The first thing to remark, in the rules relating to these sacrifices, is, that they were, by far, most numerous and important at the three great Hebrew festivals: the Passover, the Feast of Weeks, and the Feast of Tabernacles. These three solemn epochs, so instructive from the facts which they recall, the fixed periods at which they were held, and the connection they have with the spiritual history and regeneration of man, clearly show how important the sacrifices then celebrated must have been, since it is natural to suppose they had to concur in the development of those great objects.

The better to perceive the connection of these three principal festivals with the spiritual history of the regeneration of man, we must look continually at our own nature, and observe that, as we are characterized spiritually by three kingdoms, or eminent constituent faculties, which require as many developments in each of the three orders, earthly, spiritual, and divine, through which we pass, it is certain that all the means and laws which cooperate for our regeneration, must follow a course conformable with this number, and analogous to the kind of assistance we require, according to our states of development and the work of their respective epochs.

Digression on numbers

But, lest the word number should alarm the reader, I will stop an instant to observe to him that numbers, though fixed in the natural order, are nothing in themselves, and serve only to express the properties of things. Just as, in our languages, words serve only to express ideas, and have essentially no value in themselves.

But some have thought that, as numbers expressed the properties of things, they really contained these properties themselves: this has been the cause of so much delusive credit, and so much discredit, attaching to the science of numbers, in which, as in a thousand other instances, the form has swallowed up the substance; whereas numbers can no more have existence or value, without the properties they represent, than a word can be worth anything, without the idea of which it is the sign.

But here there is a difference, namely, that our ideas, being variable, the words we employ to express them may vary also; whereas, the properties of things being fixed, numbers, or the figures which represent them, cannot be liable to change.

Mathematics, although far from recognizing and employing these fixed numbers, give an idea of them in the free or arbitrary numbers which they make use of; for they continually apply these arbitrary numbers to the values of what they speculate upon, and when they are so applied, they are nothing more than their signs and representatives; separate them, and they are nothing. But pure mathematics, abstractedly of all application, is an invention of our own.

Nature knows nothing of this sort of mathematics. Nature is the continual union of geometrical laws, with fixed, though unknown numbers. Man may, in his mind, consider these laws independently of their fixed numbers; but Nature is the effective execution of these laws, and knows no abstractions.

Now, as mathematicians concern themselves only with external movements and dimensions of things, and not with their inward properties, it is certain that they need not be troubled about the fixed numbers, which are only signs of these properties. And, in fact, as they have merely to do with the visible dimensions of things, or at most, their approximate weight, velocity, and attraction, it is clear that, to attain their object, the ordinary numeration suffices.

What I have just said on numbers is sufficient to remove the prejudice that generally waits upon this order of knowledge, and I return to our subject, sacrifice.

The Exodus, a correspondence of Man's regeneration

The first step of our regeneration is our call out of the earth of oblivion, the kingdom of darkness and death. This first step is as indispensable, that we may walk afterwards in the path of life, as it is that a grain should first ferment in the earth, to pursue afterwards its course of vegetation and bear fruit. We accordingly see that the regeneration of the Hebrew people commenced with the mighty work which brought them out of Egypt, and put them in the way to the promised land. But what is remarkable is, that the season itself brings its tribute of correspondence to this marvellous work, in that it took place in the first month of the Hebrew holy year, which, beginning in spring, expressed, temporally, the passage which Nature then makes out of the languor and death of winter, to life and fertility.

The Hebrews did not, it is true, at that time offer sacrifices; for, like man, in the first act of his deliverance, they were still in a state of impotence, and ignorant that their law was acting upon them unknown to themselves, as it acts on an infant when it is just born into the world.

Nevertheless, they killed a lamb in every house; and though this was not done according to the form of sacrifice which was instituted afterwards, there was in this ceremony an efficacious virtue initiatory of what was to follow; thus, at that great epoch, we see four important things come to the front at once, namely, Man's call to terrestrial life, the deliverance of the chosen people, the birth of Nature in spring, and the shedding of blood of animals; and these four things could not coincide in so remarkable a way without having an inward correspondence.

The lamb

It must be observed that the slaughter of the lamb was the preparatory act, anterior to the delivery of the Hebrews; and from this we may presume how pure and regular were the influences attached to this species of animal, when set free by its slaughter, since they were respected by the destroying angel, and became the means of protection ordained by God to preserve the Hebrews from the sword of justice.

This brings us, with sufficient evidence, to what we said before, that blood is man's sepulchre, from which he must necessarily be delivered, to take the first step in the great line of Life. It shows likewise that, of all animals, the lamb has the widest and most useful rapports to man's deliverance and regeneration, and that its sacrifice was the one from which he might derive the greatest advantage, by its disposing him, by the secret virtues of the sacrifice, the more surely and gloriously, to go out of his own blood.

We may find some evidences of this truth, even in the mere material order, in which we observe that the species of cattle to which the lamb belongs is the one most useful to our bodies, and sufficing of itself for all our first wants, providing us with food, clothing, and light. And it will not be superfluous to add, that this species of cattle provides, nevertheless, for our passive wants only, wants which may be compared to those of our infancy, or of man in privation; but that it renders us none of those active services which we need at a later age, and which are supplied by other kinds of animals.

And here we see why the lamb only was sacrificed at the departure out of Egypt, in that, at that epoch, the chosen people were only just born, and represented temporally the bodily and spiritual infancies of man, as the spring-time represented the birth and infancy of Nature.

The Passover, its threefold character: first epoch

This first epoch presented three characters at once: it was commemorative of the call of the first man to terrestrial life; it was the actual call of the chosen people to the spiritual law; and it was a prophetic sign of our future new-birth in the law of God; and this threefold character will be found in all the epochs we shall review, for all are connected in fulfilling their respective numbers, and thus become, successively, 1st, commemorative; 2ndly, actual, or effective; 3rdly, figurative, or prophetic.

The Law, its spiritual correspondence: second epoch

We see this first epoch followed by a second, in which the Hebrews received the Law, on Mount Sinai. All the relations named above will be found also in this epoch.

After we are called into terrestrial life, there is an age at which the spirit first joins us, and communicates its first rays to us. After the first man was plucked out of the abyss into which crime had plunged him, and he had obtained, through the death of Abel and repentance, an entrance into the ways of justice, he received consolation, indicated by the advent of his son Seth, who drew down upon his family the first deposit of those gifts, which Supreme Mercy still deigns to grant to mankind.

Even supposing we know nothing about the epoch when the first man, who never was a child, first received the succours of grace, we know that for the individual man the first germs of the spirit show themselves at about his seventh year, and the fruits of these germs would naturally be developed at epochs corresponding to multiples of this number.

We know that the Law was given to the Hebrew people, forty-nine days after the passage of the Red Sea; we know that this epoch falls at the time of the first fruits, and that the festival which was instituted in reference to it was called the Feast of Weeks, and of First Fruits.

Finally, we know that this law was sprinkled with the blood of sacrifices and peace offerings, taken from the large cattle, or calves (Exod. xxiv. 5). It is easy to carry out the comparisons which result from all this, according to the principles we have laid down.

Seven forms or spiritual powers: Second epoch continued

Recalling here to mind the universal ground of the seven forms of Eternal Nature, the number seven contained in forty-nine will show the play and operation of the seven spiritual powers, opening the way of living works to the chosen people, as this process is also shown at this epoch, by the production of the first-fruits of the earth; and there ought to be no doubt that this law acted, by the powers of the same number, on the first man, as it does still on the individual man, and would assuredly do so more positively and sensibly, if we did not cram ourselves daily with false substances, which hold us in false measures, and prevent those which are true from acting on us. In this epoch, the blood of calves was shed; in the first, it was only that of lambs.

In the first epoch, which was that of deliverance only, the blood of the lamb served as organ in the work of mercy, which was wrought upon the people, and was indicated by the meekness of which this animal is the symbol; for, in the apparent characters of the animals, we may obtain glimpses of the influences which rule in them, and of the works in which they have to take part, in the designs of Wisdom.

In the second epoch, the people being in the wilderness, on the way back to their country, required more strength to resist their enemies; and everything leads us to believe that the blood of large cattle, shed on this occasion, indicates that this was the object of the sacrifice of this class of victims.

In the first epoch, the people had nothing to do; they had merely to follow the spirit which did everything for them, as a mother or a nurse does for a child in its tender age: and there was no law then.

In the second epoch, the people are considered as being able to act for themselves; and then the law was given to them; then its precepts were taught, by which to regulate their conduct through the arduous journeys that were before them.

It was natural, therefore, that the same wisdom, which dictated the laws, should also communicate the strength needful for their observance, and the sacrifice of calves points to this; to say nothing, here, of the spiritual strength derived from witnessing the prodigies wrought before them on the mountain, nor that which they might expect from the ordination of their priests, which was subsequent to the promulgation of the law, and the emancipation of the people, and may be regarded as completing and consolidating this second epoch: Moses was ordained directly, without intervention of any man's ministry; for he was to be as God to Pharaoh, and take Aaron for his prophet (Ex. vii.).

It is certain that this second epoch is at once commemorative, real, and figurative, as the first was; but we must observe that each of these relations ascends a degree, as the second epoch starts from a degree higher than the first; a remark which must be borne in mind, when we come to consider the following epochs, which, always advancing by degrees, elevate their operation continually, without losing their character.

Feast of Tabernacles: Third Epoch

The third epoch, in the restricted sense to which we limit ourselves for the present, is not marked by any historical event, in the sacred writings. It was indicated only by the solemnity of the festival ordained for its celebration, the feast of Tabernacles. This feast, not having any actual events to consecrate, is given in Scripture (Lev. xxiii. 43) only as commemorative of a previous fact, which was, to remind the people that God had made them to dwell in tents, after He had delivered them from the Egyptian bondage.

But it will not be amiss to add, that the process of regeneration was not then sufficiently advanced, for this epoch to offer to the minds of the people all it conveyed; particularly in regard to the station which man is compelled to make for a time, in the middle regions, between his first and his present abodes, when he puts off his corporeal envelope, his land of Egypt, in which his blood reigns a veritable Pharaoh over him.

The Feast of Tabernacles prophetic of the future advent of the Spiritual Kingdom

Now this festival, the most important of all, from the number of victims offered, was the figurative and prophetic expression of the benefits which awaited the people in the times to come, but of which they could have no idea, because those times had not yet arrived.

We may judge bow great these benefits would be, from the time of year in which the festival was held; it was in the seventh month; it was after the ingathering of all the harvests; it was at the renewal of the civil year, though at the half of the holy year.

We may, then, confidently, see in this festival, the end of the circle of temporal things, the advent of the reign of Spirit, and the unspeakable gifts and riches which follow the development of its powers, through all the consecutive and intermediate epochs, from the first institution of this festival, to the complement of the great circle.

I need not recall the characteristic properties of the septenary, to confirm this view; to name it will suffice, to convince us that this festival was prophetic, rather than commemorative-for the enlightened men of those days; though, to the people, it may have been commemorative, rather than prophetic. Let us only add, for the information of those who are acquainted with the principles of which numbers are signs, that this septenary acts, at this third epoch, more amply than it did at the second; the second was only an initiation to the law, whereas, the third was the fulfilment of its time.

At the second epoch, the septenary yet acted, only, so to speak, within itself, and its own circle; whilst in the third, it penetrated the whole circle of things, by means of the six lunar months through which it extended and developed its powers; and this points to the six primitive operations of creation, terminating in the sabbath, and to the great sabbatic Epoch, by which the great circle of the duration of the Universe will arrive at its term, and restore liberty to all creatures.

Law of Sacrifices continued

A second fundamental truth, connected with what we have said above, may be stated here; namely, that under the law of sacrifices, everything was done by transpositions, because man was too far from the truth for it to unite with him directly.

The brazen serpent, the oblations, the sacrifices, even the journeyings of the Hebrew people, are sufficient evidences that such was the character of that law; this becomes manifest, when it is seen that man being connected, through crime, with divided, though analogous influences (actions), could be delivered from this painful division, only by the re-union of these analogies.

But this law, as it advances, seems to become more and more profitable to the chosen people, who must be recognized as the type of Man. Accordingly, as we have before observed, we see a progression of favours, activity, and grace, succeeds that of festivals and epochs; and the perpetual sacrifice, whilst serving as a commemoration of the deliverance out of Egypt, showed at the same time, the continual watchfulness of Supreme Love over His people, whom He will never forsake.

The extraordinary holocausts which were added at the three great festivals, were to bring down upon the people, such active virtues as corresponded with the plans of these different epochs; for we there see bulls, rams, seven lambs - independently of all the other offerings which were always added to the burnt sacrifices.

Thus, germs were planted in this people, which should begin to give their first-fruits at the following epoch, and which could not have been so planted in Egypt, because it was necessary this people should first be purified; the abode of death is not capable of receiving the seed of life.

The primitive names of animals would disclose their nature and influence in Sacrifices

No doubt, if there were not a veil spread over all Nature, and the properties of animals, we should see plainly the final positive reason why rams, and bulls, and lambs were employed in preference to other animals, in all these sacrifices. We could justify, by particular details, the fundamental and general principle, that by their connection with external influences, these victims were, by the shedding of their blood, to bring upon the people the influences of which they were respectively the emblems or types; and that powers were thereby approximated, representatives of those they would one day receive from the spirit itself, from which they were still far off.

But we have lost those animals' primitive names, and nothing short of knowing them could shed a living and clear light on the different kinds of animals admitted into the rank of victims, as well as on the different kinds of vegetable productions which served for offerings at the sacrifices; for, if true numbers express the properties of things, their real names express them still more forcibly, for they are their active organs. This is what once characterized the pre-eminence of the first man, and ought still to characterize, at any rate, partially, the true sage, and real dispenser of divine things, for him, usefully, and efficiently, to fulfil the Lord's Ministry.

The Hebrew names do not help to throw much light on this great subject. These names are active only when applied to men, to the generations of the chosen people, and their ministers, as we see by the characteristic names of the patriarchs and prophets, because Man was the chief object of this process of election and restoration; whereas, the time for Nature's great restoration not being yet come, the names of plants and animals proceed no further in Hebrew, than in other languages, and their true names are still buried in what Jacob Boehme calls the language of Nature till the seals be opened.

We might enlarge upon the general idea we have expressed above, namely, that in the frightful overthrow of Nature, on the occasion of the criminal lapse of Man, some substances, mineral, vegetable, or animal, were better preserved than others; that is, they retained a greater proportion of the living and powerful properties of their first estate; and that, doubtless, these will have been what were used in preference in the sacrifices and other ceremonials of worship, as being best able to render service to man, seeing that they remained nearest to the primitive covenant: but this would require a more extensive knowledge on our part, of the primitive state of things; and we merely allude to it.

Circumcision, its reason and effects

Let us now consider an objection that may be raised, to the key we offer for the explanation of the sacrifices.

If sacrifices operated for man, by means of their correspondences; if the shedding of the blood of victims was the established means for effecting this object; it may be asked how it happens that circumcision would not answer instead of sacrifice? For, the blood of man himself being shed, it might be supposed it would operate more efficaciously for him, than that of any other victims, by reason of the superiority of its correspondences. We may reply as follows:

The Virtue of sacrifices derived through faith

If the bloody sacrifices acted through their correspondences, still they derived their virtue, radically, through the desire of the minister, and that of the believer who joined him; for then, the divine desire itself united with theirs. Now, as this desire, which is real faith, cannot, under any circumstances, do without a ground or basis, the blood of animals served for this, and assisted it to reach a higher ground, till it could rest on the perfect basis, the Divine Heart, which ruled, in secret, all the sacrifices, and would crown them in the end.

One faith; diversity of forms

We may remark, *en passant*, that the necessity of a basis on which to rest our true faith or desire, is the key to all the diversities of sacrifices, whether bloody or otherwise, as well as to idol worship, and every other kind of worship in honour on the earth; in all of which we see that nations have the same faith, and are mistaken only on the basis; but, the choice of this basis being so important, - since it should have fixed correspondences with a true centre, natural, spiritual, or divine, - and nations err so greatly in this respect, it is not surprising that their darkness should be so universal.

Circumcision, not a basis of faith; only an initiation

Now circumcision could not serve as basis for this faith or desire, since it was performed only a few days after birth; and if, on Abraham, it was performed at mature age, it was only because this patriarch would not have been chosen as a child, to be the chief of the elect race, and he had moreover, to enter freely into the alliance. Besides, he therein represented only the first degrees of his reconciliation.

However, though a child can have no true faith or desire, man's blood, shed at the circumcision of infants, had no doubt an effect; but this was limited, so to speak, to performing in them a sort of ablution, like cutting them off, in some sort, from this system of blood into which man's crime plunged us, and initiating them thereby into the active and efficacious work in which their faith or desire would some day employ them voluntarily. It was, moreover, rather a figurative effect of the great circumcision, their corporeal deliverance, than possessing in itself any vivifying regenerative power, like the holocausts in which faith had at least some influence, in which a pure victim was slain, and in which the entire development of all correspondences of regular influences acted in restoring man, partially at least, to his rights and enjoyments.

Moreover, we have seen that man's death was the only bloody sacrifice which could restore him to the fullness of his relations, and perfect way of return to his relations, and perfect way of return to his Principle. Therefore, as the principle of animal life was not cut off by circumcision, the observance of this law could not, in itself, bring down upon him any powerful restorative influences ; and, if the blood of animals (slain) had not been substituted for his (in circumcision), he would have remained through life in the same privation and bondage.

At the same time, as we have said, this circumcision was not useless, since it was a sort of initiation into degrees which man could not yet enjoy. But, precisely because it was an initiation, it was necessary it should make him capable of receiving its progressive fruits, and it really accomplished this for him, by opening his blood to all the regular influences which the sacrifices of animals could bring to him.

Therefore, when divine authority consecrated this principle, which was, perhaps, already in use amongst other people, - but not applied by them to its true object - and ordained it as one of the holy laws of the Jewish people, this ceremony was then so strictly prescribed. Then, all who were uncircumcised were excluded from the sacrifices because the regular influences, which those sacrifices attracted, finding no way open to reach their principle of life, would have acted forcibly and with violence against these breakers of the law, and exterminated them in the midst of the people.

Before and after the Deluge

It would follow from this, that, as circumcision seems to have been practiced only subsequently to the Deluge, all sacrifices, made previously to that event, must have been fruitless. Now, if we have no proofs that this practice was in use before the Deluge, neither have we any to the contrary; and, admitting that it began after the Deluge, all difficulty disappears, when we reflect on the difference of states in which mankind were at these different epochs: a reflection which applies to animals as well.

Before the Deluge, Man enjoyed all the powers of his animal corporeal nature; this temporary covering given to him as an organ for the higher influences and virtues which are so needful to him, was more in accordance with the plan appointed for his restoration; and, being consequently more open to the healing influences, he might not require circumcision for them to gain access to him.

On the other hand, as animals then enjoyed a greater amount of life than they have since, their blood would be more efficacious, and this would render the assistance of circumcision less necessary than it became at the second epoch.

At this second epoch, everything was changed. All Nature had been tortured and altered by the calamity of the Deluge. Mankind, whose crimes had drawn down this Deluge, became much more bound by the chains of matter; the animals themselves lost virtuality in the renewal of their species, which brought them lower than they were before this explosion of the vengeance of Supreme Justice. In short, what reflections do not those enormous mammoth skeletons lead to?

If Wisdom had not provided for man, means to remedy these fatal results of justice, he would have continued without any way of return to his Principle, and the plan of divine Love in favour of mankind would have been unfulfilled, since the first initiation into this path could not have taken place. Now, from all that we have seen, circumcision appears to have been the means, which, after the Deluge, supplied the advantages which men and animals had enjoyed before that catastrophe.

Perhaps, even, if the people had faithfully observed the laws and instruction which Noah, as the elect and chosen of God, transmitted to them, they might have continued under sufficiently powerful conditions, for this new medium to have been unnecessary.

But, by the offence of Ham and Canaan, and the abominations committed in the plains of Shinar, they added more chains to those which the Deluge had put upon them, and aggravated the obstacles which already opposed their re-union with their Source. It would not, then, be astonishing if the unquenchable love which created them, followed them even into the abyss into which they sank, and offered them a new route whereby to return to Him.

Let us return to the three epochs, and we shall see them retraced in miniature, in the account given of circumcision amongst the Hebrews.

Jewish circumcision: first period, under Abraham

It is under Abraham that we first hear of circumcision in the Scriptures; the Lord confirming thereby His alliance with him and his posterity. Under what circumstances was this circumcision commanded by the Lord? It was when He gave a new name to Abraham, and one also to his wife, by adding to their old names, a single letter of the sacred name by which He first made himself known to Moses. It was when he was ninety-nine years old, just after he had made a covenant with him, promising him the land of Canaan; in short, it was when He first chose to Himself a people, in whom all generations should be blessed.

All these things, again, taken together, show that circumcision had an initiatory virtue into all the benefits which God prepared for His people, all which would have been without effect if He had not opened this way to their fulfilment. Abraham had received, however, divine favours previously to this ceremony; he had been taken out of his own country, where iniquity had entered; he had built altars to the Lord at Bethel, and invoked His name; he had been blessed by Melchizedek; and, in the bloody sacrifice which he offered by God's command, he had received evidences of the Spirit's presence; but this nowise contradicts the principles we have established.

Abraham was the elect of the Lord, although he was born amongst idolaters, and some accuse him of having traded in idols. His heart may have remained pure, even though his spirit may have been given up to the same darkness which covered his contemporaries. Thus the divine favours may have found access to him, without the secondary means of circumcision.

Besides, we must make an essential distinction between the means employed by God to manifest an election, and those used for bringing that election to its term. We shall see them always forming two classes in all subsequent elections and epochs; we have a positive proof of this in Abraham's election, since, notwithstanding all the favours of which he was recipient, before his circumcision, it was only after he and all his household had been obedient to this law, that he received three angels as guests; that the time for the birth of Isaac was clearly fixed; and that, at the end of the year, he received this promised Son, through whom the covenant, which began with Abraham, was to be realized and fulfilled.

Nothing more is needed to convince us that, at the time we first hear circumcision mentioned, it was intended as an initiation into all the benefits promised in the election; and as such, it bears a sensible relation to what we have said of the Passover, or the first epoch of the Hebrews' return to the promised land.

Second period; under Moses

The second time circumcision is mentioned in Scripture is under Moses (Ex. iv. 25), where it is to be presumed this ceremony bad been neglected, and that this was the cause of the angel's anger, inasmuch as circumcision was again prescribed, with all the other laws and ordinances, on the mountain (Lev. xii. 3); which leads us to consider this law of circumcision, given on the mountain, and that performed on Moses' son, as constituting but one and the same epoch.

The time when this law reappeared is remarkable for its conformity with what passed under Abraham. It was after Moses saw the burning bush and received God's promise that the people should be delivered; it was after he had been himself chosen to be the instrument of this deliverance, and received the most extraordinary signs of his mission, that the divine vengeance, about to fall upon his son, was arrested by Zipporah's submission; lastly, it was at the moment of Moses' return to Egypt to commence his mission, that this ceremony was performed on his son.

This comparison shows clearly that this ceremony was to serve as an initiation to the fruits of the promised deliverance, as it did, under Abraham, to the fruits of his election; and that neither of them could be attained without shedding of blood. We must pay no attention to the difference that the son's blood, in Moses' case, was shed, and not that of the patriarch himself; for, although the two individuals were distinct, their blood may be considered as one; there are besides, under this veil, innumerable relations of other truths, which penetrating eyes will discover without difficulty.

Thus, without my undertaking to expose these truths, there will be seen therein a middle epoch, a double circumcision, a commemoration of the sacrifice of Abraham's son, and a prophecy of another sacrifice, of which it is not time to speak yet. We must, then, be content with observing that this election of Moses, and the circumcision which attended it, aiming at the living firstfruits of the promise made to Abraham, connect themselves quite naturally with the second epoch, or second of the Hebrew festivals, in which the earth rendered her first produce, and the people received the first-fruits of the Spirit, which are the Law; because, in these comparisons, it should never be forgotten that every trinary of epochs makes a circle, and that every preceding circle is a degree less elevated than its successor.

Circumcision, third period, under Joshua: its correspondences

Finally, the third time the ordinance of circumcision appears in Scripture, is under Joshua, when the people are about to enter the promised land (Josh. v. 2). This ordinance had not been kept during the forty years the people journeyed in the wilderness; and those who had been circumcised in Egypt had all perished; so God revived it for all who remained uncircumcised, in order "that the reproach of Egypt should be taken from off the people"; and all the people were circumcised in Gilgal.

We cannot help remarking the moment at which this circumcision appears again, and the numerous marvels which followed it The time was that of the entrance into the promised land, as the circumcision of Abraham was on the occasion of his entrance into the covenant of election, and as that of Moses' son was at the moment of his entering the path of law and work; and, in this respect, this epoch is connected with the third of the Hebrew festivals, which was that of abundance, of harvest-home, the term of all their labours.

It is only so connected, and that commemoratively, in the temporal and earthly order, for it represents the future rest which the people should enjoy after they had destroyed or subjugated the inhabitants of Canaan, prophetically only, because their entrance into the land of promise admitted them only to the battles they would have to fight there; and the victories which would follow had been indicated by those they had gained over the people of the desert.

Nor is it superfluous to observe that it was on the first month that this entrance into the promised land took place; as it was on the first month that the Exodus out of Egypt, or the deliverance, happened; because here the two circles return to the same point, although the second here relates to a far grander and more active order of things than the former.

But what shows how advantageous circumcision was on this occasion is, that after that ceremony manna ceased to fall, and the people began to eat of the fruits of the country; that Joshua entered under the direct protection of the visible Prince of the Lord's hosts; that the trumpets of jubilee became the chief weapons of the people, and at their sound, accompanied with that of the Word, or speech (*parole*) the walls of Jericho were overthrown, and every man was able to enter straight before him into the city; all figures of what was in reserve for man at subsequent epochs, and what awaits us when we are out of our mixed and earthly circle.

Efficacy of Sacrifices down to the destruction of Jerusalem

Here it is, especially, that the power and efficacy of sacrifices are seen; for all the wonders we have mentioned were preceded, not by circumcision only, but also by the burnt sacrifices of Passover which the people celebrated at Gilgal, and probably also those which Moses and the elders recommended when they should enter into the land of promise (Deut. xxvii), and which the book of Joshua does not mention till after the con of Ai (viii. 30), but which, it may be presumed, were offered after the passage of Jordan, as Moses had commanded.

We will not recapitulate what we have said of the efficacy of these sacrifices, confirmed by the wonderful successes which followed them; it is sufficient to have once established as a principle the relation which blood has with the orderly influences (actions), and that which these have with the higher influences, to understand the advantage which man, or the chosen people, might derive from these ceremonies, in respect to their deliverance and progress towards the term of their true liberty.

We should view in the same spirit all the sacrifices offered by the Hebrews, from their entrance into the promised land to the destruction of their last Temple by the Romans; and it is unnecessary to follow the thread and the epochs, because they all come within the recognized principle, and it is particularly with the principle, or the universal key, that we have to do; fully persuaded that, if this is derived from the truth, it will solve all difficulties.

We shall, therefore, pass to another sort of observations in reference to these sacrifices, namely, how it is that this institution came to be established all over the world, and that under such various forms, and often so contrary to reason, and even criminal.

Practice of Sacrifice amongst other nations; its corruption

It is evident that the use of these ceremonies amongst other nations is not to be attributed to the Jewish religion, nor to the sacrifices on which it was grounded, because the Jews were an exclusive and isolated people, who held no intercourse with other nations; because they have ceased to exist as a people only under our era, and since then only have they lost the use of their ceremonies and sacrifices; moreover, sacrifices, having been in use from the beginning of the world, when the world was renewed after the Deluge, their revival among all nations is no more to be wondered at than the dispersion of these nations, who will have carried with them the customs and ceremonies of their fathers.

It is not, therefore, the universal prevalence of sacrifices which should now surprise and occupy us, for, as they are known to originate on natural grounds, all their ramifications can have no other origin; but the changes which these streams or branches have undergone in their course are what must now be the object of our reflection and researches.

This corrupt change could never have happened if there had been no pure spring to begin with; and those who have attributed the use of sacrifices to mere ignorance and superstition, have confounded the abuse and the consequences with the principle, and thereby precluded themselves from knowing either the principle or the consequences. Let us never forget the unhappy situation of man in this world of sorrow and darkness, exemplified by the sufferings of all mortals, and the tears of all ages. Let us not forget that, if we are surrounded by regular influences, of which clean animals are mediums, we are also surrounded by disorderly influences, which incessantly tend to introduce disorder into everything that approaches us, that it may invade and enter ourselves, and delay our return towards the light.

This picture, unhappily too true already, to our cost, becomes still more so when we call to mind the sacerdotal preparations which the victims underwent, according to the Jewish law; and especially when we remember the fowls which came down upon the carcases, on the occasion of Abraham's sacrifice, and that this patriarch drove them away.

It is not to be supposed that, in the multitude of sacrifices that were offered, whether in the family of Noah, or under his descendants who peopled the earth, nothing of these sacerdotal preparations was ever wanting, and that the fowls were always driven away from the victims; this, I say, cannot be supposed, when we see abomination make its appearance in the bosom of the family of Noah himself, and his posterity enveloped in darkness to such a degree, as to oblige Supreme Wisdom to make a new election. Yet it needed but one single act of negligence, in these important ceremonies, to give access to this disorderly influence, and all its consequences.

Judge, then, what the consequences must have been, if the sacrificer to negligence added pollution, to pollution impiety, and to impiety a criminal purpose; in short, if he himself opened the way for the disorderly influence, and acted in concert with it, instead of resisting it. Nothing more could surely be wanting, for a flood of horrors and abominations to arise from it, which, increasing daily, in a ratio that cannot be estimated, must have inundated the world with its foul waters, and covered it with iniquity.

The disorderly influence or action to which the sacrificer gave access in himself, will have led him wrong in many ways; at one time, it will have suggested the idea of changing the victim, and have replaced the clean victims with such as best suited its abominable designs; from whence, it is no longer surprising that we should see on the earth so many kinds of animals used in sacrifices.

At another time, without interfering with the victims, it will have urged the sacrificer to address to itself the spirit and intention of his worship, leading him to hope for greater profit thereby than he could expect from a severe and jealous Being, who withdrew all His favour for the slightest negligence in the ceremonies which He had instituted; and, by flattering his cupidity in every way, this disorderly influence will have attached him to itself, and drawn him into the most fatal abuses and monstrous abominations.

At another time, employing all these iniquities together, and colouring them with an apparent piety, to insure success, it will, under this mask, have led man into the most revolting and inhuman practices, persuading him that the higher the price, and the greater the number of his victims, the more he would be beloved by the Divinity; besides, as this disorderly power was, as well as the orderly, connected with all the substances and materials of the sacrifice, it will have been able to strengthen and confirm all these false insinuations, by visible manifestations, all the more efficacious because they agreed with the inward feelings and secret movements which the sacrificer had already received.

Let us then consider the human race under the yoke of an ingenious and watchful enemy, who breathes only to lead Man from error to error, and has made him everywhere bend the knee before him, by the very means which were given to Man to repel him.

Three classes or degrees of disorder or abominations

These errors may be divided into three classes; First, abominations of the first degree, in which all the faculties of Man were corrupted. Secondly, pious abominations, which, no doubt, commenced, like the preceding, in his own corruption; but which have since ruled over him only through his weakness. Thirdly, the mere superstitions of idolatry, which, though descending from the two first kinds, have not the same effect and consequences.

We may even believe that the puerile superstitions and secondary abuses, into which man has often been led by his weakness and credulity, may have preserved him, and saved him from more essential crimes, as much so as if he had possessed more light, or more power.

And, in truth, it is not the idols which have mouths, and speak not, that he has to shun, so much as those which have mouths, and which do speak; which have ears, and do hear; eyes, and do see; etc.

The first degree of abominations ; swallowed up by the elements

The abominations connected with this kind of idols, wounding justice in its centre, must be classed in the first degree; and these have drawn down innumerable calamities, both known and unknown, upon the guilty for, how many crimes have sunk into the abyss with those who committed them! We may judge from all the abominations handed down to us in Scripture, of the others on which it is silent.

Call to mind the sin of the first man, which wrought an absolute change in him, and made him pass out of light, into the darkness in which we live; remember the abominations committed by his offspring, down to the Deluge, and, from the immense number of the guilty swallowed up in it, judge what an enormous amount of crime must have been thereby obliterated from our sight; think of the abominations of the Egyptians, and of the inhabitants of Palestine, which drew down the wrath of God upon those regions, compelling Him to arm the elements, and powers of Nature, and even the fire of heaven, to destroy them.

In short, we have only to look at our globe, where we shall perhaps not find a single spot which does not still show signs of the wrath of heaven poured out upon the unfortunates who were insane and guilty enough to join the enemy against Divinity; and this picture of our globe will be a speaking history, more convincing than any contained in books, and demonstrate the universal prevalence of crime, not mentioned in books, or alluded to only in abridgment, or incidentally.

Since these calamities, abominations of the first degree seem to have diminished ; and, if they have not ceased altogether, they are at least no longer in the bulk of the nations, but practiced only by individuals. The second order of abominations have taken their place, and their origin was this:

*Second order; pious abominations, Satanic delusions,
occult sciences, etc*

In the pure observance of the legitimate sacrifices, the faithful officiator and his people received visible evidences of the approval of the Sovereign Power; they received instructions for their conduct in the path of holiness, and answers to questions, in wisdom and justice; but, as soon as negligence or corruption invaded these sacrifices, then, disorderly influence entered into them, showing itself visibly under whatever form it chose; it made the responses, and established itself as the oracle, and the veritable ark of the covenant.

How many officiators have been dupes and victims of these lying apparitions; and how many, after first submitting to be ruled over by them, themselves have ruled the nations by these attractive seductions! This disorderly influence could communicate some truths which it got to know through the imprudence of men; it predicted events which should come to pass, and frequently answered questions correctly; that was enough to make the people prostrate themselves before it, whatever form it assumed, or whatever orders it prescribed.

Such is, beyond doubt, the origin of many religions and forms of worship in the world, as well as of the atrocities with which they have been piously accompanied; for, we must carefully distinguish these secondary abominations from those of the first degree, which wilfully attacked Divinity itself; whilst the effect of the second seems to have been only to lead men astray, and deprive them of the benefit of the divine purposes; which is attacking Divinity only indirectly. But they seem to make up in number and extent what they want in importance.

For, in this class we must rank all those professors of occult sciences, whom the ignorant have called illuminati; all those who have, or have had, Pythonic spirits, who consult familiar spirits, and receive answers from them.

In this class must rank all those oracles with which mythologies are full, all those ambiguous sibylline answers which poets have made the groundwork and knot of their poems, trying to raise our interest in their heroes by representing them as the victims of fate, or even as victims of a word of two meanings, whereby they have been led into paths of error and trouble, instead of marching under the banners of truth and wisdom.

In this class must be ranked most of those prodigies performed in the suspension of our bodily senses [mesmeric sleep, somnambulism, etc.], which thus deliver men over to every dominion that presents itself; the more so, that we have reason to believe that Man's crime commenced with sleep, and that, for having once allowed his true senses to become torpid, he sank into illusion and darkness.

In this class must be ranked all those illegitimate and false practices, in all ages, which, under the appearance of truth, separate men from the only one Truth which ought to be their guide. I say all those abusive practices; for, notwithstanding the cessation of sacrifices over a great part of the earth, it is enough that these abuses originated in a former corruption of those sacrifices, for them to be propagated from age to age, and produce new errors down to our own days, seeing that the criminal source from which they spring is a living one, which seizes every opportunity that men afford it to extend its kingdom, and realize its designs.

We are compelled, moreover, to believe that if most men live under the yoke of these iniquities and illusions, in good faith, and through ignorance, many also bring their passions and selfish cupidity into them, instead of virtue; who, thereby approaching the abominations of the first degree, show too well on what the lamentations of the prophets have been and ever will be founded.

Third class of disorder; superstition, idolatry, worship of saints, images, etc

Finally, the third class of these abominations is that of all kinds of idolatry and superstition. The manifold forms which the disorderly influence was able to assume, in order to alter the sacrifices and lead Man astray, were the chief source of material idolatry, the officiators who received such manifestations being led, by a natural proclivity, to honour animals or other natural substances to which those forms, assumed by the disorderly power, had any relation; and this was the origin of the worship offered by so many nations to different creatures.

From this to figurative idolatry, or the worship of images, there is but a step; innumerable causes often leading to the substitution of the image of the idol, for the idol itself; the people easily transferred their veneration from the idol to the image.

Apotheosis has a similar origin; the officiator himself having often been taken for the object of the worship. Thus, in nearly all nations, we find a visible Divinity, and an invisible; in the North, two Odins, one a supreme God, the other a conqueror; we find two Jupiters amongst the Greeks; two Zoroasters amongst the Persians; two Zamolxis amongst the Thracians, etc.

It is not more difficult to discover the source of popular superstitions. It was not the fault of the prophets that the Jews fell into all kinds of idolatry, since, in their writings, particularly the Psalms, the Supreme God is so clearly distinguished from whatever man has ever taken for God. But on approaching the sacrifices, whether corrupted or not, and on witnessing the ceremonies of those secondary abominations alluded to, men will have seen that, under certain circumstances, preparations of victims, or arrangements of substances, such or such results followed; they will soon have lost sight of the spirit which ought to direct all these formalities, and give them value, and looked to the empty form, substance, or isolated ceremony alone, to give them what they had done when. their animating spirit was in them.

Here we see how people came to consult the entrails of victims, even to the smallest movements of the slaughtered animal; the flight of birds; talismans; ciphers; amulets; meeting such or such an object; in short, those innumerable natural signs to which opinion, disquiet of men's minds, and cupidity have everywhere attached an importance and value which they no longer possessed.

These sad pictures arc enough to show to what aberrations the mind of man is exposed, when be ceases to watch against the disorderly influence, which, after having led him astray in the time of his glory, did so again when sacrifices were instituted for his regeneration; and has now so propagated disorder, that man can know no peace till his dwelling is entirely renewed.

We must just remark, on the presents which were always offered to the Seer, in imitation of those made to the temple through the sacrificer, that these presents and offerings partook, at first, of the virtue of the sacrifice; then they became inferior organs of correspondence; and, at last, the mere object of speculation, avarice, and fraud.

Laws, progressive in their order, and their object

All laws given to Man since his sin, have had his advancement for object. For this reason the law is always below the term to which it points, and to which it would lead Man, though it is superior to that in which it found him: for this reason also, these different laws would have been always progressive, if Man had not so often arrested their course by his errors; but, having continually multiplied his own falls, and increased his own darkness, he brought down laws of rigour and constraint, when he ought to have received those of gentleness and consolation.

The law given to Adam

After the first expiation of the first guilty man, he received a law certainly more vast and luminous than that which was afterwards given to the Israelites; we may judge of this by the difference of the names by which these laws were governed. It was the Proper Name of God which directed the first; it was only the representative name which governed the second. See Paul to the Galatians, (iii. 19,) where he says, "this law was ordained by angels in the hand of a mediator".

Besides, Adam, though guilty, was only under due privation of his primitive enjoyments; he was no longer under the pollution of sin, which had been washed out by his baptism of deliverance out of his enemy's hands, or what may be called his great, or spiritual circumcision.

The corporeal covering he had received, was a pure extract from all the most vital substances of Nature, which had not yet undergone the secondary catastrophes which have since befallen it; it is not surprising then, that, under these circumstances, the law of return given to Adam, should have been more powerful and virtual than the Judaical law. We will content ourselves with a single example to show the difference.

It was forbidden to the Hebrews to ally themselves with the nations they were going to make war with, in the promised land; and the transgression of this law led to the several special bondages they suffered. As for Adam, and his posterity, the whole earth was given to him to cultivate it, and to root out the thorns and briars from it; and it is for having, ou the contrary, filled it with wickedness, that the Lord withdraws his spirit from men, and pours out the Deluge upon them. From the extent of the crime, we may judge of its power; from its power, we may judge the extent of the law.

This law could not be given to Adam while he was still in the abyss, under the absolute yoke of his seducer. It was free grace only which operated in that terrible moment, to snatch out of eternal death him who was the image and likeness of the God of all being; man was then incapable of profiting by any law; but, this first step surmounted, he became susceptible of a law for his restoration. Now, the law he received, bore, no doubt, the three characters we have mentioned; or, to speak distinctly, it was a judgment upon the enemy, by whom he had been overthrown; it was a warning to man, to recognize the dangers which surrounded him, and preserve himself from more falls; lastly, it was a means for his sanctification, through the way marked out for his return, and the sacrifices, which, as we see his first-born used them, we may suppose he will have used them as well.

The law under Noah

That restorative law having been made void, by the frightful conduct of his posterity, Man, now doubly guilty, was again cast into the abyss, one only shoot being preserved. Noah remained faithful to the Lord's ordinances; and when, after the Deluge, we see him offering a sacrifice of sweet savour, we must not therefore conclude that he was the founder of sacrifices, but consider him as the preserver and minister of a law as old as the very beginning of things ; which, in fact, indicates that sacrifice was offered by the first man.

If Noah's offspring had continued in that patriarch's wisdom and holiness, the work would have advanced towards its term, without its being necessary to institute a new law, and elect a peculiar people; because, all sinners having been cut off by the Deluge, the family which escaped, and their descendants, would have been the living image of the first man on his way back, and in the law which favoured their return.

But Noah's offspring, having given themselves to commit all wickedness, rendered that restorative law of no effect, and it then became necessary for Man, to repeat what had passed at the beginning, since all tongues were confounded, and there remained not, as in the days of Noah, a single family who retained the pure language.

Abraham, not under the law

In this state of universal darkness, Abraham was chosen to be the chief of an Elect People; everything was given to him in principle, revealed, so to speak, prophetically, even to the history of his own people, which he saw in a dream: but nothing was given in development; he possessed not the land that was shown to him; he was obliged to buy even the cave in the field of Ephron to bury Sarah in. He saw not the numerous progeny which was promised to him; he saw only the promised son, not even the sons of this promised son, for he died before the birth of Jacob and Esau; he was not charged with any ceremonial worship, for the sacrifice which he was commanded to offer, was ordained only to serve as a witness to the covenant; God did not give it to him as an institution.

In telling us that the measure of the iniquity of the Amorites was not full, the Scriptures certainly give a sort of reason why the law was not given to Abraham, but a more direct reason may be found; which is, that the law which was to be given, was intended for a people, and not for an individual, as in Adam's case, and this people was not yet born. It had to come to a people, because it was the peoples or nations that had corrupted themselves and departed from the law; because the ceremonies of this law required a larger number of ministers; because this law was to be grounded on the lost number, the old numbering of nations, to restore it to them; and, lastly, because it required a receptacle which might be connected in its subdivisions with every ramification of the law, whereas in Adam, who, corporeally, is the root and trunk of all Mankind, all these branches were in one.

The election of Abraham could not attain its complement, till the twelve children of Jacob were able, by their number, to offer a receptacle, capable of receiving the healing influence corresponding to this number. And even they received it only in principle, in their father's blessings; and, only at Sinai, did the twelve tribes receive the necessary development of this law, of which their ancestors had received the first-fruits.

The Mosaic law, preparatory to the spiritual or prophetic law

This law even was, as yet, only preparatory to the spiritual law which awaited them, after the law of forms and ceremonies should fulfil its course. It was needful that this law of forms should develop the spirituous grounds and essences which were in them, that they might, in their turn, present to the spirit a receptacle after its kind, on which it might come and rest.

The spiritual or prophetic law, preparatory to the divine law

Lastly, this spiritual law itself was to be only preparatory to the divine law, the only true term of Man, seeing that he is a divine creature. Now, it is in this slow and gentle progression of succours sent from God, that we can say, of all laws in general, what St. Paul said of the Hebrew law in particular;... "that the law was our schoolmaster to bring us, children, to Christ", (Gal. iii. 24-26); for there is not one of those temporal laws which may not be regarded as a tutor or conductor to what it leads to, and in respect to which, we really are children, till we are admitted into it, and acquire strength to practice it.

This has been the divine economy in all these epochs. Under the Levitical rule, or that of bloody sacrifices, the priest being yet only in the natural regions, received his subsistence from the people, and the law appointed cities and tithes for his spiritual wants. Under the prophetic rule, God fed His servants by special means, but through natural agency, as we see in Elijah and Daniel. Under the law of grace, the founder's intention was that the priests should be careful for nothing; nourishment was to be given them from heaven, as shown to St. Peter, and in the description and promised advantages of the living waters.

But it is only for tractable and submissive children, that these laws retain this character ; and they show rather what man ought to be, than what he actually is. And the hand which administers these salutary laws, is often obliged to let them work for man's punishment rather than for his reward.

This, we have seen, was the case, from the lapse of Man, to the law of Moses ; whilst, if Adam's posterity had been faithful to the assistance they received in the different epochs we have reviewed, they would have greatly facilitated their return to the Truth, and would have known only the pleasantness of the Divine Ways, instead of almost always experiencing their rigours and bitterness.

Such will again be the case with the children of Israel, in the epoch which we are now going to consider, that is, the prophetic epoch or rule.

The prophetic epoch, or rule ; menaces and promises;
their spiritual aim

If the people had faithfully observed the Lord's ordinances committed to the chiefs of the princely race, the same favours which had accompanied them through the wilderness, would not have abandoned them in the promised land; and the law of animal sacrifices would have led them to the spiritual law, under which they would have received directly, the succours which they received only indirectly, under the law of sacrifices.

But, as people, rulers, and priests, ceased not to add abomination to abomination, and, having violated all the laws of sacrifice, - as, witness the sons of Eli; having abandoned the theocratic government, to substitute one like that of other nations from whom their election separated them entirely, it is not surprising that this people should be delayed in their course; or, according to the language of Scripture, that the word of God should have become so scarce amongst them.

But, if man is arrested in his course by his iniquities, time is not stayed ; and, as the hour of the spiritual law had arrived for the Jews, it could but be carried out before their eyes, even though they should be found unprepared. Only, it then took a double character, in conformity with the double type of mercy and justice which it has to perform on the earth; and, as the light which was kindled at the election of the Jews cannot be extinguished, it then displayed, both the first rays of its brightness, and the terrors of divine wrath.

This is the reason why we clearly distinguish two kinds of prophecy, one terrifying the people with threats, the other promising days of consolation and comfort to the lovers of peace. We also observe how much the aim of prophecy is enlarged at this epoch; we see how it approaches the regeneration of the human soul, which, though aimed at in all previous divine manifestations, was there concealed under symbolical ordinances.

It is in the Prophets, that we see the chosen man deploy his character as priest and sacrificer of the Lord; there, we see the sacrifice of our sins substituted for that of animals, and the circumcision of the heart and spirit recommended as the true way of man's reconciliation to God; there, we see the false prophets and bad shepherds reproached with having first deceived the souls of their flocks, and then assured them that they were alive; there, in short, we see the dawn of that spiritual and divine day which then began to break, never to decline again; and Man saw, though still only by glimpses, that he was born in the region of spirit and holiness, and his true law, and true resting place, could only be found in this region of spirit and holiness.

We say that these truths were shown to him only in glimpses, because, besides mankind in general, whom the prophets came to awake, they had to act for, and prophesy to a certain people, in particular, who had not yet got beyond signs and figures. But, in every respect, the prophet may always be considered as a victim, whether by reason of the violent deaths which most of them suffered, or still more on account of the spiritual labours they underwent.

Prophetic sacrifies, their reason and operation

In fact, the extinct virtue of sacrifices then passed into the prophets' voices, and they took, in the eyes of the Spirit, the place of victims, which were now offered as a mere formality, and without faith on the sacrificers' part. The blood of these prophets became the holocaust of propitiation, on which the action of the Spirit operated both more terribly and more savingly, than it did on the blood of animals.

It operated more terribly, because this blood being unjustly shed, was a crying witness of the crimes and blindness of the people. This blood, however, attracted the most disorderly of the spiritual influences, with which this lost and guilty people were polluted, according to the laws of transposition that we have stated above.

The spirits of the prophets bore also, in their sufferings and travail, the iniquities of Israel, so that, by dispersing these irregular disorderly influences that clung to the people, the communication of regular and ordinary ones was rendered more easy and profitable. If the people had profited by all these succours which Supreme Love and Wisdom sent them, they would in their turn have relieved the blood and spirit of the prophets, of the oppression of those disorderly influences, by communicating to them again, and partaking with them, the effect of those virtues and orderly influences, which the prophets' sacrifice, bodily and spiritual, had brought down upon them.

But, hardening themselves more and more, they prolonged to the prophets, even after their death, the pains and labours they caused them during their lives; they made heavier by their resistance, the weight of their own iniquities, which, in their divine charity, the prophets had taken upon themselves; thereby bringing upon themselves the double reproach, of not having listened to the voice of Wisdom, and keeping in painful durance those whom Wisdom took for its organs; and, for this, all the blood of the prophets shed by them, from Abel to Zacharias, will be required of them; for it must not be forgotten that the Hebrew people were nothing less than the representatives of Man, of the whole posterity of Adam.

On the other hand, the blood of the prophets operated on the people more savingly than that of the Levitical victims, because, as man's blood and life are the seat of the very image of the Divinity, it could not be shed without releasing, or bringing to light, the holy influences which the souls of the righteous naturally diffused around them; and, if the sacrifices of animals could open the spiritual region to the Hebrew people, the blood and voices of the prophets opened to them the avenues of the divine.

End of the prophetic epoch. Continuous chain of divine guidance and mercy

By this two-fold power, the, prophets accomplished upon the Hebrew people what the Spirit sent them to perform. When this was accomplished, prophecies ceased amongst the Jews; for, although there is no time for the Spirit itself, the mixed abode which we inhabit subjects its action to intervals and parts; so, after the Babylonian captivity, which confirmed and realized the threats of the prophets, the work of the prophets seems to have ended; and, thenceforward, they give very little light, and this little only to urge the building of the second temple; and the people are then left to themselves, that they may have time to acknowledge the justice of the severities through which they have passed.

But, in thus leaving them to themselves, the Spirit left for their guidance, both the words of the prophets, and the memory of the events just accomplished; as, after their election, and their Exodus from Egypt, they had the Levitical law, and the history of their deliverance, and of their arduous journeys in the wilderness; as, after the Deluge, the children of Noah still had their father's instructions, and the tradition of all that had they filled the measure of their iniquities, by considering Him as their enemy, and, the veil which was rent for all the children of Adam, they made only thicker for themselves.

The 'Tableau Naturel', in showing the necessity of a Redeemer (*Réparateur*), who should be God-Man, exposed the high mystery of this sacrifice, in which the victim offered itself without committing suicide, and in which the blind sacrificers, believing that they executed a criminal, gave the world, without knowing it, an universal electron, which would work out its renovation; "L'Homme de Désir" has shown that the blood of this victim was spirit and life, so that when the Jews asked that it should fall upon them and their children, they could not separate the mercy from the justice which were both in it together; - We merely recall, in passing, these comforting and profound truths, which the spirit of man cannot have too constantly before him.

Man delivered from the prison of his blood

We have seen that, after the fall, blood became the barrier and prison for man, and that it was necessary that it should be poured out for him to recover his freedom progressively, through the transpositions which this blood-shedding wrought in his favour. But we have seen, at the same time, that each of the laws given for his regeneration, was only a sort of initiation into a higher one which should follow; and the aim of all these preparatory laws was to lead Man to make a free and voluntary sacrifice of himself; and no anterior sacrifice could supply the place of this, since, without the shedding of his own blood, he could not be said to be really delivered out of the prison in which his blood enclosed him.

Now what could teach him this profound and beautiful truth? Not the sacrifice of animals, for these animals, being destitute of morality, gave him no idea of a voluntary sacrifice; and as they brought nothing but their bodies to the altar, they could loosen nothing but their corporeal chains.

Nor could the sacrifice and death of the prophets teach it, because they went not voluntarily to death, though it may be, with resignation; and this death was, for those who suffered it, only an uncertain consequence of their mission and not their mission itself; - because they were sent to announce only the dawn of the eternal day of man's deliverance; lastly, because they themselves desired to look into that eternal day which they proclaimed without knowing it, and which they got sight of only partially, and at intervals, and by flashes of the spirit.

Conditions required in the victim, in the sacrifice
that should deliver mankind

Thus, though the voice and blood of the prophets may have been more profitable for Man than the victims of the Levitical law, though they may have passed from Adam down to themselves; and, lastly, as Adam, after his fall, had the remembrance of his crime, and of the sacrifice of Love which the Supreme Goodness had willingly made in his favour, to pluck him out of the abyss.

Thus, from the first divine contract, and the pure region where truth abides, a continuous chain of mercies and light extends to man, through every epoch, and will be prolonged to the end of time, till it returns to the abode from whence it descends, taking with it all the peaceful souls it shall have collected in its course; that Man may know that it was Love which opened, directed, and closed, the circle of all things.

Transition from the prophetic epoch, to that of the glad tidings
of universal deliverance

The blood and the voice of the prophets led the Hebrew people only to the avenues of the temple of the divine region, because the time was not yet come when man might enter the temple itself. Many prophets were employed in this preparatory work, and the hand that led them in the wilderness traced out different paths for them which they had never travelled before. For this reason, each prophet, walking in his own particular path, did not always know the final term to which his prophecies pointed; this was unveiled to him only in parts, and as afar off.

And the people, who had not recognized the law of the Spirit in the Levitical ceremonies, though it was in them, neither did they recognize the divine law which was contained in the law of the Spirit, or the prophecies; and, still continuing to walk in darkness, they reached the epoch of universal deliverance, which had never ceased to be spoken of by the prophets, by each according to what it was given him to know; and which was also pointed at in the books of Moses, particularly in the blessings which Jacob pronounced upon his children; for, if they had really made a careful study of those books, they would have found something to arrest their thoughts, when they saw the temporal power of Judah pass into the hands of Herod the Idumean.

Secret union of all divine laws

The intimate union of all these laws, one within the other, is one of the sublimest secrets of Holy Wisdom, which thereby shows itself to be always One, notwithstanding the diversity and the intervals of its operations.

The Jewish people were too gross to penetrate this simple and profound truth. Burdened, moreover, with all the iniquities they had committed, in neglecting the laws and ordinances of Moses, and in shedding the blood of the prophets, - the law of grace, the time for which, for all mankind, had arrived, came as a reprobation upon this people, who had so failed as its representative; and, instead of washing out their crimes by faith in the new victim, who came to offer Himself, carried him a step higher, by unbinding his mind; they did not lead him to that sublime idea of a submissive and voluntary sacrifice, founded on the knowledge of the abyss in which our blood retains us, and on the lively hope of our absolute deliverance, when this sacrifice is made under the eye of the Light, and in the true movement of our eternal Nature.

Another victim therefore was requisite, uniting in itself the properties of the preceding victims, and teaching man, by precept and example, the real sacrifice which he had still to make, to satisfy fully the spirit of the law.

This victim should teach man that, to attain the essential object of sacrifice, it is not sufficient that he should die like rams and bulls, without participation of the spirit, of which they are deprived; that it is not even enough, that he should die bodily, like the prophets, who were unjustly slain by the passions of the people to whom they preached the truth, for they believed that they might escape from this wrong, as Elijah did, without failing in their mission, when they were able.

It had to teach him that he should, of his own will, knowingly, and in perfect serenity, enter upon the sacrifice of his physical and animal being, as the only one that could separate him from the abyss in which he is confined by his blood, which, for him, is the organ and minister of sin; in short, that he should meet death as a triumph, which raised him out of the rank of a slave and a criminal, and gave him possession of his own inheritance.

These conditions fulfilled in the shedding of the Redeemer's blood

This was the sublime secret which the Redeemer came to reveal to mortals; this was the shining light he enabled them to discover in their own souls, by sacrificing himself voluntarily for them, allowing himself to be seized by those whom he came to overthrow by the breath of his word; and by praying for those who killed his body; and the shedding of his blood accomplished all these marvels, because, by plunging into our dark abyss, the Redeemer followed all the laws of transposition by which this region is constituted and governed.

In fact, the shedding of a victim's blood must operate according to the rank and properties of the victim; and, if the blood of animals could only loosen the corporeal chains of sin in man, which are altogether elementary; if the blood of prophets loosened the chains of man's spirit, by enabling him to discern the rays of the star of Jacob; the shedding of the Redeemer's blood was to loosen the chains of our divine soul, since the Redeemer was himself the principle of the human soul, and open its eyes sufficiently for it to see the very source of its existence, and to feel that it is only by the inward voluntary sacrifice of all that swims in or belongs to our blood, that we can ever satisfy the desire and essential want we feel of re-uniting ourselves with our divine source.

The Spirit-Man may now attain his regeneration, even in this world

It is not surprising that a revelation like this, should have abrogated all other sacrifices and victims, since the one now offered placed man in the only rank made for him: thus, from this time, the Spirit-Man is raised to the rank of a true sacrificer, and it rests with himself to re-enter the ways of regeneration, and to attain, at least by his understanding, its fulfilment, even in this world, if he unites himself in heart, mind, and work, with him who has opened the way and reached the goal before him.

Revelation of the Man-God compared with all that came before him

Nor is it surprising that, like all previous revelations, this also should come to us through a man, since Man was its object; but, what eminently distinguishes it from all others, is, that it was preached, proved, and entirely accomplished in a Man-God, a God-Man, whilst, amongst all the others, not one bears this universal character.

The death of Abel was not voluntary: it may have been useful for Adam's advancement, in the transposition of the disorderly influences which had attached to the guilty father of mankind, effected through this blood which was shed; but it did not complete the work of alliance with God; for Abel was but a man conceived in sin; and his brother Seth was appointed in his place, to transmit to man the continuation and course of the spiritual graces which his death had arrested.

The revelation of justice made to Noah, and poured out under his eyes, on the posterity of man, placed him, no doubt, in the first rank of those chosen by the Lord, for the execution of the plans of his divine Wisdom; but he appears, in this great catastrophe, rather as an exterminating angel, than as a liberator of mankind; and, besides, the victims he offered in sacrifice were of a different nature from himself, which could procure succours for man only after their kind.

Abraham shed his blood in circumcision, as a sign of his alliance with God, and evidence of his election but he did not pour out the principle itself of this blood, in which his animal life resided; we need add no more to what we have already said of this patriarch.

His son Isaac came very near, but did not consummate the sacrifice, because man was still only in the time of figures, and his father's faith sufficed to consolidate the alliance, without staining it by the atrocity of infanticide.

Moses served as organ for the election of the Hebrew people; he was even its minister, as man, and as a man chosen to operate upon Man or his representatives [the Hebrews]; but as he acted only on the representatives of Man in general, he was only called upon to employ outward sacrifices, and figurative victims, for this permanent reason, that, as Man was yet only at the age of symbols and figures, the law of transpositions could operate upon him only in that way, and could rise no higher.

The Prophets came to give their blood and their word to cooperate in Man's deliverance. If it had been necessary that men should come to execute the decrees of justice, and trace figuratively the ways of regeneration, it was still more needful that men should come to open the entrances of the real ways of the Spirit; and the prophets were the organ, tongue, and very speech of the Spirit; whilst Moses had received the law, and transmitted it only on stones; in short, Moses, before Pharaoh's magicians, took the serpent only by the tail; it required one more powerful than Moses to take it by the head, otherwise the victory would not have been complete.

Everything in the prophets shows what they wanted, for them to be able to introduce Man into the revelation of his own greatness; and we may add a simple and striking reason, to what we have said, which is, that those highly favoured men were not Man's Principle.

We may here find a partial explanation of the passage in St. John (x. 8): "All that ever came before me are thieves and robbers, but the sheep did not hear them"; though this passage applies much more directly to the high priests than to the prophets. It shows clearly that all those chiefs and envoys were unable to bring the people into the kingdom, since they walked only in the spirit, and the kingdom is divine ; but it also shows that they were not true shepherds, since they did not give their lives voluntarily for the people; and, instead of protecting them from the enemy, they were often the first to give them up to his rage.

This is what God so strongly reproaches them with, in Ezekiel, (xxii. 24-31), where, after marking the crimes of the princes, and the sins of the prophets, he says "I sought for a man amongst them, that should be as a hedge, and stand in the gap before me, for the land, that I should not destroy it ; and I found none".

Conditions required for a true deliverer, all fulfilled in Christ. "It is finished"

It was, then, reserved for Him who was Man's Principle, to fulfil all these conditions for Man. None but this creative, vital, and life-giving Principle could be his true deliverer, because the voluntary shedding of his blood, to which no blood upon earth could be compared, could alone accomplish the entire displacement of the foreign substances which swam in Man's blood.

And when this was done, nothing but this divine Principle could draw the human soul out of its abyss, and identify itself with it, so as to enable it to taste of the joys of its true nature; He only, who, being the depositary of the key of David, could, on the one hand, shut the abyss, could, on the other, open the Kingdom of Light, and restore Man to the post which he should always have occupied.

And it is to know nothing of this Redeemer, to look at him only in an external and temporal point of view; without rising, by a progression of the understanding, to the divine centre to which he belonged. Let us then draw from the diversity of characters with which he was clothed, some means of appropriating to our feeble faculties his spiritual homofication, which long preceded his corporeal advent.

As the Eternal Principle of Love, it was, first of all, necessary, that he should take the character of immaterial Man, his Son ; and to accomplish such a task, it was sufficient for him to look at himself in the mirror of the Eternal Virgin, or SOPHIA, in which his Mind (*pensée*) has, from all Eternity, engraved the pattern of all things.

After having made himself immaterial Man, by the simple act of his Mind's contemplation in the mirror of the Eternal Virgin, or SOPHIA, he had to clothe himself with the pure element, that glorious body, which is swallowed up in our matter, since the Fall.

After being clothed with the pure element, he had to constitute himself the principle of corporeal life, by uniting himself to the Spirit of the Great World or Universe. After having become the principle of corporeal life, he had to become earthly element, by uniting himself with the elementary region; and then he had to make himself flesh, in the womb of an earthly virgin, clothing himself with the flesh proceeding from the sin of the first man; since it was from the flesh, elements, and spirit of the Universe (*Grand Monde*) that he came to deliver us. And, on this, I can but refer the reader to Jacob Boehme, who has shed so great and profound a light on these subjects.

We now see why the sacrifice which the Redeemer thus made at every step, descending from the height from which we fell, was necessarily appropriate to all our wants, and all our sufferings.

So it is the only sacrifice that ever ended with those comforting, yet terrible words, It is finished; comforting, from the certainty they give us that the work is accomplished, and that our enemies will be put under our feet, whenever we walk in the steps of him who conquered them; terrible, in that, if we make them void by our ingratitude and indifference, no resource is then left for us, because we have no other God to expect, no other deliverer to hope for.

It is no time now, to expiate our faults and wash away our stains, by the sacrifice of animals, since he himself drove the sheep, and oxen, and doves, out of the Temple. It is no time now, when prophets may come to open for us the ways of the Spirit, for they have laid those ways already open, and the Spirit watches over us continually.

Lastly, it is no longer time to expect the Saviour of nations to come to us, for he has come already; and, being himself both the beginning and the end, we cannot, without insulting him, act as if there were another God after him, and refuse to give him whom we have known, a boundless faith, an universal confidence, which, indeed, can repose really and physically on none besides, for he alone is universality. It is finished.

Henceforth, we have no other work, no other task, but to strive to enter into the finished work, and, to banish from ourselves everything that may prevent our profiting by it, to the utmost.

Origin and nature of moral evil, a transposition, its rectification

If the Redeemer, by virtue of the simple but fruitful law of transpositions, restored all our essences to their places, and caused darkness and disorder to disappear for man, by reinstating him in his post, it is easy to recognize that evil is not an eternal essential principle, opposed, by the necessity of its nature, to the Principle of Good, as the Manicheans believed; it is easy, I say, to perceive, that, as liberty is the distinguishing character which places the moral being between God and matter, it suffices to leave him the use of this liberty, which the Author of all cannot give and take away at the same time, to conceive both the origin of evil in moral creatures, and its inferior nature.

According to this explanation of evil, as resting only on displacements (transpositions) of substances, it is equally easy to perceive the various properties and uses of the sacrifices, the process and effects of which we have endeavoured to explain.

Lastly, it is easy to perceive how vastly superior the sacrifice of the Redeemer was to all that preceded it; since the very prince of iniquity which ruled over man, had to be transposed into the abyss; and it was for the supreme and divine Chief of Light, and Strength, and Authority, himself, to obtain such a victory.

It may not be superfluous here, to observe, that, although the bloody sacrifices of the Jews continued after this great sacrifice, down to the destruction of their city, they had long retained nothing but the form; the spirit was entirely lost; and, since the sacrifice of the divine Victim, it was farther from them than ever.

Therefore they could but degenerate, more and more; and the period which ended in the great outpouring of vengeance upon this guilty people, shows, at once, the withdrawal of the protective influence (action) of the Spirit, and the terrible effects of justice of the avenging Spirit; a severe judgment, which could not be executed at the same time as the Redeemer's work, for He came to fulfill His work of love and mercy only.

Institution of the Eucharist

Although the sacrifice of the Redeemer placed men in a position to fulfil, as far as possible here below, their sublime task of regeneration, by uniting with him and serving him in spirit and in truth; he left, besides, when he departed from the earth, a sign of alliance, which might bring his presence and devotedness daily before us; as we have seen signs and witnesses left after the various manifestations of the laws of justice, the Levitical ordinances, and the prophetic revelations, which have been promulgated ever since the world began.

He intended this sign of alliance as a development of that divine seed which he came to sow upon our sterile and corrupt earth; and, as we are composite beings, he composed this sign of various operative substances, so that all the substances of which we are now constituted, might be nourished, preserved, and supported, each according to its necessities and its class. But, at the same time, he intended that this institution should derive all its value from the Spirit, from which all things proceed, and are sanctified; and, in this aspect, we shall see what great advantages this institution may afford us, when we rise to the sublime meaning which its founder gave it.

There are no mysteries for the Spirit-Man

If it is written that we must be holy, to approach what is holy; so also must we be spirit, to approach what is Spirit; this is the reason why the earthly man can see only with eyes of darkness and profaneness; whilst the Spirit-Man accounts for everything that is given for his use, and offered to his reflection.

And the ministers of holy things have thrown back the human mind on the subject of the Eucharist, by inserting, as they have done, in what they call the sacramental service, the words mysterium fidei, (holy mysteries), which are not in the Gospel, and were far from the Founder's mind; since, if we employed ourselves in our true regeneration, as he never ceased to exhort us to do, there would be no mystery for us; for we are, on the contrary, made to bring all mysteries to light, as ministers of the Eternal Source of Light.

How the Spirit works in the symbol

Let us remember, that the Spirit rested on the lamb, at the deliverance out of Egypt; and that is what gave all the value to that sacrifice. Then, let us remember that the divine life rested, and still rests, on the substances of the sacrifice of the new covenant; since the Spirit of Truth was not poured out in vain, and cannot be mistaken in its plans and effects; so that ever since the new covenant, (and perhaps from the beginning,) we may regard bread and wine as marked by the spirit of life which has been poured out upon them.

We ought never, at any time, to eat our bread and drink our wine, without calling to mind the sacred sign with which they have been invested; instead of allowing them to fall directly under the elementary powers which are not holy.

These substances are united with the pure element; the pure element is united with the Spirit; the Spirit with the Word; the Word with the first Eternal Source; and, by this harmonical order, the institution of the new alliance works for the profit of all the principles of which we are composed. It works, in fact, in spirit and in truth, on our whole being; the unleavened bread, for the purification of our matter; the wine, for the purification of our animal life principle; the glorious body, or pure element, to restore to us the primitive clothing which we lost through sin; the Spirit works on our understanding; the Word, on the root of our words; the Life, on our divine essence; and that, by raising every order of our being, to which its action extends, one degree higher.

Moreover, this institution of the new covenant has for signs, four great efficacious unities, namely:

The twofold elementary relation, which is communicated to us in the two substances;

The correspondence of all the elect, who have assisted at the sacrifice, since the beginning of the world ; who are seated at the holy table, and from thence cause to flow into our hearts, the sacred words they hear; superior, perhaps, to those known in the consecration;

The pure element, or the true flesh and blood, which strengthen all our faculties of intelligence, and our activity in the work;

Lastly, the Divine Agent himself, who, under the Father's eye, pours out sanctification everywhere, the seal and character of which he has received; and who, being at once the author, Designer, and founder of this sign of his alliance, thereby restores our weight, number, and measure.

Now, why is it, that this Divine Ruler alone can give this universal baptism? Why is he the lamb that taketh away the sin of the world, if it is not that his presence alone restores all principles to their places, there being no disorder but in transposition?

But, being subject to the law of time, which has divided everything for us, He caused his virtuality to rest on the material signs of his alliance, in a passive manner only, which waits for a reaction from the renewed man; thus, during the course of his work on earth, He himself waited for the reaction of his Father's word, to develop his own powers.

For this reason, He committed this institution to men whom He had regenerated, whilst He himself ascended to his source, there to drink the new juice of the heavenly vine, and pronounce incessantly, in the invisible kingdom, words of life corresponding to those of the sacrament. Thereby, the regenerate men, who ought to administer this ordinance, are in sympathetic relation (*rapport*) with Him, and His regenerative work, and are able to connect with this regenerative work all who wish to participate in it, and join in it in spirit and in truth.

Let us remember that we were dead, and that the Redeemer had to enter into our death, to make himself like us; but as, in entering into our death, he did not cease to be in life, so, in making himself like us, he was still our only principle ; thus he could not die without rising again, and raising us with him, that we might be like him; this resurrection was necessary, that we might taste, and extol, and celebrate Life, which was, and will be eternally, the end of the existence of every spiritual being, formed after the image of the Sovereign Author of all beings.

The institution of the Supper had, then, for object, to retrace this death and resurrection in us, even before the dissolution of our bodily essences; that is, to teach us both to die with the Redeemer, and, with him, to rise again. Thus, this religious ceremony, considered in all its sublimity, may become in us, in reality, an emanation, a creation, and a regeneration, or an universal and perpetual resurrection; it may, I say, transform us into a kingdom of God, and make us to be one with God.

Man's part in the Supper; confession and faith

At the same time, it is quite essential that the minister should incessantly repeat to the faithful, these words of the Founder: "The flesh profiteth nothing: my words are spirit and life"; for, alas, how many spirits have been slain by the letter of the other words! All thought of flesh and blood must be banished, both in the minister and in us; that is, we must mount, like the Redeemer, to the region of the pure element, which was our primitive body, and which contains the Eternal SOPHIA, the two tinctures, the spirit and the word. It is only at this price that things that pass in the kingdom of God, can pass also in us.

If we rise not to this sublime unity, which would embrace all things by our thoughts; if we confound the institution with the work we have to accomplish in ourselves; and, lastly, if we confound the end with the means, the subsidiary with the essential, we are far from fulfilling the spirit of the institution.

For this spirit requires that we should confess the death of Christ -to our own iniquities, to drive them away from us; to men of God of all ages, that they may be actively present in our work; to the Divinity, to remind Him that we are bought into life, since He stamped His own seal and character on the Deliverer whom He chose; lastly, it requires that we - should confess that death to the enemy, everywhere, to make him flee from us; for that was the object of the Redeemer's corporeal death.

Now, the institution of the Supper was given to us only to help us to labour effectively at this living work, which we have each to accomplish individually. For, it is in this living work that all transpositions disappear, that everything returns to its own rank, and we recover that pure element, or primitive body, which can only be restored to us in so far as we become again likenesses of God;

because the true likeness of God can inhabit only such a body.

The human form divine

And here we may discover the natural source of all those anthropomorphitic representations with which the world is so full.

If sculptors represent to us all the heavenly and earthly virtues, under human forms, masculine or feminine; if poets personify all the gods and goddesses of the Empyrean, and all the powers of Nature and the elements; if religious sects fill their temples with human statues; the principle from which all these practices derive, is nowise a delusion, as the results are.

The primitive human form ought, in fact, to show itself and rule in every region. Man being the image and extract of the generative centre of all that is, his form was the seat where all the powers of every region came to exercise and manifest their action; in a word, it was the point of correspondence for all the properties and virtues of all things.

Thus every representation which he makes of himself, merely reproduces the picture of what he is and ought to be, and replaces him, figuratively, in the position (*mesures*) in which he no longer is.

Let us observe, in passing, that, when savans compare the human body with that of beasts, and call it comparative anatomy, our real body is for nothing in this comparative anatomy, which, in fact, teaches us nothing more than that we are like other animals.

They would do better to compare our superior body, which is not animal, with our own animal body, if they would have our veritable comparative anatomy; because it is not enough to observe things in their similitudes, it is essential to observe them also in their differences.

From this comparison of our actual, with our primitive forms, we might obtain useful results, on the subject of our original destination; but, in default of this important comparison, which, indeed, would be in the reach of few, we may at least draw luminous inductions as to our ancient state, from the wonderful works of industry which we still produce through our corporeal organs; things which, notwithstanding our fallen condition, and the artificial means to - which we are restricted, ought to open our eyes to the natural marvels we should have engendered, if we had preserved the rights belonging to our primitive form.

Religious images, their origin

As to the abuse of religious anthropomorphism which fills the temples with human images, so readily turned into objects of adoration and idolatry by the simple, it comes of the very movement of God's heart for the restoration of mankind, at the moment of our fall, by which that divine heart became Spirit-

Man.

Now, as this covenant of restoration is planted in all men through successive generations, they are ever ready to see it germinate in them, and to look upon human idols which are presented to them, as the expression and fulfilment of this covenant, the need of which they feel so much, though it be confusedly. Still more, they are ever ready to form for themselves, both inwardly and outwardly, sensible models, according to which they would have the work to be done for them.

Thus, the necessity of having the God-man near them, and their readiness to believe according to their wishes, have been the origin of human idols, and their worship. It was easy, afterwards, for fraud, operating upon weakness and ignorance, to propagate superstition, whether absurd only, or criminal also; - without its being necessary, even in this case, to exclude the active spiritual origin of anthropomorphism, as indicated above.

Work of perfect regeneration after death; power of the enemy; the Virgin in the soul

Nothing but the renewal of our being, here below, can procure for men, what they look for in vain from their superstitions and idols; and, even this renewal is but preparatory to our perfect regeneration, which, as we have seen, takes place only at the separation of our corporeal principles, or the shedding of our blood. Moreover, after our death, we are, as it were, suspended to the Great Trinary, or the universal Triangle, which extends from the First Being down to Nature; each of the three actions of which draws to itself all our constituent principles, divine, spiritual, and elementary, to reinstate them, if we are pure, and restore liberty to our souls, that they may ascend again to their source. And this is what the Christ permitted to be done, physically, to himself, by his death and burial.

But, if we are not pure, the enemy, who does not oppose the separation of the corporeal parts, which are of mere form, opposes the renovation of the principles over which he had obtained rule, and retains all under his dominion, to the great detriment of the unfortunate soul which has become his victim.

Now, we can assist this renovation of our principles, only in so far as we have an Eternal Virgin born again in our souls, in whom the Son of Man may come in the flesh, with all his virtues and powers; and we can only get this new birth of this Eternal Virgin in us by reviving our primitive body, or the pure element within us. And, here we shall see written in man, all the laws of the symbolical sacrifices we have spoken of, and of which man is really the object, even when he seems to be merely their organ or instrument.

Man, a microcosm, in which sacrifice is offered

Man being in himself a miniature of the two worlds, physical and divine, it is certain that his body contains the essences of everything that there is in Nature, as his soul contains those of everything that there is in the Divinity. Thus, there must be in his body, a correspondence with every substance of the universe, consequently, with animals, both clean and unclean, and with everything comprehended in the sacrifices; and, though we may not discern these essences within us, we may believe in their external correspondence, by the sensible pictures and forms which they present to our mind, and by the symbols and images which good and evil spirits assume, daily, and physically, for our instruction or our trial.

Without its being necessary, therefore, in order to sacrifice, that we should know all these things physically, our intention should be pure and lively, for these first degrees of the material law to be accomplished in us; it suffices that, by the rectitude of our natural spiritual sense, we allow the Principle of Truth which animates us, to act, because He has under Him, sacrificers, who will sacrifice. within us, clean animals, the offering of which may be useful to us, and separate from us the unclean animals, which ought not to enter into the sacrifices.

This is the law which works in us, so to say, unknown to ourselves; which requires from us the legal purity commanded to the Hebrew people; but does not require more knowledge than they had when they approached the sacrifices; this is the law of our childhood, which will take us safely into the pure law of our manhood.

Let it not be doubted, that the sacrifice of these pure animals in us opens a way of salutary correspondences to us, as happened with the Hebrews, when they celebrated their outward sacrifices.

The effect would be even more certain and positive, for each man individually, if we were not continually disturbed by the strange nations whom we admit to the sacrifice, and the impure animals we allow to get under the sacrificer's knife, which open to us inverted correspondences; because, here, everything would act in man's principles, whereas in the Hebrew symbolic law everything acted outwardly.

But, this preliminary work being beyond man's strength, in his early age, it is the province of his temporal teachers to guide him, and direct it in him; they have to answer for him, when he arrives at the next epoch.

Progress of the individual man towards Canaan. The Decalogue

When, with the preparation we have named, he arrives at that epoch, then the spiritual law in him combines with the sensible, till it entirely takes its place. This spiritual law announces itself to us in a terrible lightning, as it did to the Hebrews at Mount Sinai; it proclaims with a loud voice within us, the first commandment of the Decalogue: "I am the Lord thy God, which brought thee out of the land of Egypt thou shalt have none other god before me".

This voice resounds through our whole being: it not only makes all false gods flee away by the terror of these words, but it likewise destroys all the strange nations, the idolatrous affections in which we had been living amongst the Chaldeans, till called into the land of Canaan.

It afterwards proclaims all the other precepts of the Decalogue, which are but a necessary sequence to the first. Now, as this terrible yet salutary law is proclaimed, only when we are supposed to have come out of the land of Egypt, and enjoy our liberty, we are thenceforward engaged to the law of the Spirit, and responsible for our own conduct under the light of this law. Therefore we are enjoined to "engrave this law on our hearts, and write it on our foreheads": etc. (Deut. vi. 9, &c.)

Individual spiritual bondage, sacrifice, and deliverance, lead to individual prophetic age

In this state, the law of sacrifice is, no doubt, still necessary for us; but, now, we ourselves are the Levites and sacrificers, since we have access to the altar, and we ought, according to the Levitical rule, to sacrifice to the Lord daily, victims of His own choice, for offerings of sweet odour to Him.

We ought, I say, to offer this sacrifice for our own advantage, on the ground of correspondences; for, in making a holy use of our constituent principles, we unite ourselves to restorative influences (actions) of the same nature as those principles. We ought, moreover, to do it continually, to conform to the spirit which has established itself in us, because the act of this spirit ought never to be interrupted, but increase always.

To this high employment, what we may call the first age of the law of Spirit is consecrated; and this duty is so imperative, that, if we fail in it, we soon fall under different kinds of bondage, analogous to our faults; but when, oppressed with the yoke of our tyrants, we, on the other hand, cry to the Almighty, He sends deliverers to put us in the right way again.

The succours He sends are founded upon the sparks of life and light sown in us by our call to the spiritual law, which, not being extinguished, altogether, by our faults, rather ferment the more, under the constraint and torment of our different kinds of bondage, and thus emit some rays, which the Divinity recognizes as belonging to Himself, and induce Him to come down to the assistance of His miserable creatures.

Thus He dealt with the Hebrews, when the time came for their deliverance out of Egypt; for it must not be forgotten that they were the children of the promise, and carried within themselves the spirit of their father's election; thus He dealt with them under the Judges, when they represented Man emancipated, or under the law of liberty. Thus, under an almost uninterrupted alternation of falls and recoveries, we arrive at the second age of the spirit, that is the prophetical.

When the individual prophetic age is fully attained, then the man's spirit burns within him to propagate the Truth, and charity begins

It must be remembered that it was said to the father of the Jews, that all nations should be blessed in him. Now, until the prophetic age, the Hebrew people lived quite separate from all other nations; their only relation with them being to fight them; this law forbad their allying themselves with strangers, and ordered them to practise the worship and ceremonies of which they were depositaries, for their own advantage alone; which is a representation of what we have to do, in our first age of our spiritual law, when we ought to separate ourselves from whatever may prevent our growth, or our acquisition of the needful gifts, that the nations may one day be blessed in us.

But, when the prophetic age arrived, then the germs of charity were first sown in Israel, as the institution of sacrifices had planted in them the first germs of the Spirit. This people, who, up to the prophetic age, thought only of themselves, and despised all other people, began, through the souls of their prophets, to feel zealous for the return of other nations to the truth.

Then, the prophets became oppressed with grief for all the evils which threatened, not only Israel, but all the sinful nations round them. Then they were sent to declare the Lord's wrath in Nineveh, Egypt, and Babylon, and the Islands of the Gentiles.

The reason of this may be easily perceived; it was the moment when the promises of the alliance with Abraham began to be fulfilled; but, as the Hebrews were further advanced in the fulfilment of these promises than the other nations, they were the first to feel the pains of charity, whilst the others, so far, received only warnings. Thus, the individual man, when he has passed the first spiritual age, also begins to suffer for the darkness of his fellow-creatures, and is pressed with a desire to bring them to the truth.

In this new stage, the man continues, no doubt, to observe the law of sacrifices, which cannot be entirely fulfilled till he has shed his blood; but, a stronger influence (action) is established over him, than that of the first spiritual age, and this influence holds dominion over him and guides him, because it is the divine Action itself beginning to make its appearance in the world; still, it leaves him free, because it is only an initiatory law, and a warning.

We see several prophets, who resisted the orders they received; as we see men, who, in their second spiritual age, make no proper use of the succour it affords them; which is the cause that so many elect never arrive at the fulness of their election.

It is not the less true, however, that, in this second spiritual age, or, in other terms, this first divine age, the true spirit of sacrifice, the sole aim of which, originally, was charity, and the happiness of others, begins to be accomplished.

The divine Spirit, by descending upon the prophets, and laying upon them the burdens of the nations, relieved those nations of part of the weight which crushed them, and who were thereby, also, better enabled to receive the first rays of the light which should lead them into the right way; they were, in short, enabled, by the pains and anguish of the prophet, to see realized, on themselves, what we have seen was done sensibly, by means of the material sacrifices.

The individual man, arriving at this second spiritual age, has the same employment; and we may say that it is only then, that the age of manhood, or the true Spiritual Ministry of Man, really commences; since it is only then, that he really begins to be useful to his brethren, seeing that, in the previous ages, he was useful only to Nature and himself.

The divine age for the blessing of all people

When the great epoch of salvation had arrived, the true spirit of sacrifice acquired a still greater extension; it was no longer limited, as in the first spiritual age, to the advantage of a particular people; nor to mere warnings given to other nations, as in the time of the prophets; but it embraced the whole human family, attracting everything towards the fulfilment of the promise made to Abraham, that in him all people should be blessed.

This great divine epoch of the Redeemer places the man who is able to profit by it, in the way of his true recovery; giving him the means to release the slaves [within him] from the house of bondage; and to manifest to all regions, and every order of things, the glory, justice, and power of the Sovereign Being, with whose seal and character the Holy Redeemer invests him.

Here we see the true meaning of the words addressed to Jeremiah (i. 10): " I have this day set thee over the nations, and over the kingdoms, to root out, and to pull down, to destroy, and throw down, to build and to plant". For, Jeremiah was established as a prophet, over earthly kingdoms only, whilst the reign of Christ establishes Man over all spiritual kingdoms.

Peace and harmony under the new law of Love

We have seen that, when man first enters the law of the Spirit, he receives the precept of the Decalogue: "I am the Lord thy God": etc. When he enters the law of the Redeemer, he receives a new commandment, that he should "love his neighbour as himself"; and this is the key to the work of Christ; for, what man who is in bondage, would not make every effort to recover his liberty? He ought therefore to make every effort to procure his neighbour's liberty, if he loves him as himself; and, if he do not love him as himself, he is not initiated into the Redeemer's spirit, who carried love so far as to cast himself, with us, into the abyss we were in, to pluck us out with himself.

Although we can, in but a very limited way, perform towards our fellow-creatures the immeasurable work which the Redeemer performed upon the whole human family, by breaking the gates of their prison and of death before their eyes; still, it is by his spirit alone, that we are able to perform the part which devolves upon us; and if, by the sacrifice of animals, the law brought down regular temporal influences upon man; if, through the prophetic dispensation, Wisdom poured down regular spiritual influences upon the nations; we, through the voice of the Redeemer's love and holiness, may bring upon ourselves, and upon our brethren, even divine virtues, with peace, order, and sacred harmony, according to our capacity, here below.

The perfecting of our faculties hereafter, requires the sacrifice of all here

When our covering of a day is dissolved, when time is rolled away for us like a scroll, then we shall more fully enjoy the spirit of life, and drink, with the Redeemer, the fresh juice of the eternal vine, which will restore our faculties to their perfect fulness, to be employed as it may please Him to ordain.

But, in vain should we promise ourselves such enjoyment hereafter, if we have not faithfully performed all our sacrifices here below; not only those belonging to our personal renovation, but those which concern the voluntary offer of our whole earthly and mortal being, by a daily care, on our part, to become orderly victims, without spot and blameless. For, in that invisible region which we enter on leaving this world, we shall find no more earth to receive those different kinds of blood, which we must necessarily pour out, to recover our liberty; and, if we carry with us the corruption, which these different kinds of blood may contain, there would remain nothing for us but suffering and anguish, since the time and place for voluntary sacrifices would be past.

This life is our eleventh hour: work ye in it

Let us then think of our real life; and of that active work to which we owe every instant of our time, and we shall have no leisure to inquire whether there be any future anguish to dread or not; such will be our zeal, and such our hunger after righteousness.

Crime is the cause of these distressing thoughts, and inaction leads man into crime, through vacuity of mind; and vacuity of mind (*esprit*) throws him into discouragement, making him believe that the lost time cannot be redeemed. That indeed may be true, in respect of things done in and for time; but is it so for things of the spirit?

There being no time for the spirit, may not a single act, performed by and for the spirit, render to the soul all it failed to acquire, or even all it may have lost by neglect?

Here, especially, we must remember the "eleventh hour": - though we must also remark, that, if those who were called at that hour, received even more than their regular wages, it was because they at least worked during that hour, else they had received nothing; so we also should have nothing to expect, if, after having passed the previous hours fruitlessly, we fulfilled not our eleventh hour, doing the work of the Spirit.

Since the Fall, we can only be mere workmen of the eleventh hour, which, in fact, commenced the instant we forfeited our rights. The ten hours which preceded this epoch, are, as it were, far off, and lost to us; so that the whole of our earthly life is really, for us, but the eleventh hour of our true and eternal day, which embraces the universal circle of things. Judge from this, whether we have a moment to lose!

Obstacles and crosses are our stepping-stones: "I say unto you, watch"

At the same time, everything that is requisite, for us to acquit ourselves usefully and profitably, in the work of this eleventh hour, is provided for us abundantly; plans, materials, instruments, nothing is withheld from us. Even the obstacles and dangers we meet with in our work, and which become our crosses when we recede from them, are steps and means of rising, when we surmount them; Wisdom, in exposing us to them, meant that we should triumph.

Yes, if we kept our post faithfully, the enemy would never enter the fortress, how powerful soever he were. But, it is necessary to guard all entrances with so constant a watchfulness, that, wherever he present himself, he may find us alert, and in force to resist him. A single instant of negligence on our part, is sufficient for the enemy, who never sleeps, to make a breach, mount, and capture the citadel.

Let us take courage. If our spiritual restoration requires, in reality, all our care, we may at least consider it assured, if we only resolve to undertake it; for, the malady of the human soul is, if I may use the expression, only a sort of checked perspiration; and the All-Wise ceases not to administer to us wholesome and powerful sudorifics, which tend incessantly to restore order and circulation.

Death is comprehended in our work; how it is overcome

Death, even, which also is comprehended in our work, is directed and graduated with the same wisdom that governs all the divine operations. Our material ties are parted progressively, and almost imperceptibly. Children of tender age, being still entirely under their matter, have no idea of death, because matter knows not what death is, any more than what life and spirit are.

Young people, in whom this spirit, or Life, begins to penetrate through their matter, are more or less afraid of death, as they are more or less imbued with this spirit or Life, and as they feel the contrast between their spirit and their matter more or less.

Grown men, and old men, in whom their spirit or Life has been developed, and who have faithfully observed the law of their being, are so filled with fruit, when their course terminates, that they look upon the demolition of their material covering, not only without fear or regret, but even with joy.

And this material covering, having been perpetually impregnated with the fruit of their works, has meanwhile, almost imperceptibly undergone decomposition in its springs ; and if the restorative treatment were followed, it would commonly meet its final dissolution without even pain. What can be conceived more sweet and gentle than all these progressions, appointed by the Wisdom of the Most High, for the restoration of Man?

Powers of the human Soul after death

But, if such are the enjoyments afforded by devotion to the Spiritual Ministry of Man, even here below; what must it then not be, when the human soul shall have deposed its mortal spoils.

We see that our bodies, here below, are destined to enjoy all their faculties, and held communion with each other. When they do not enjoy their faculties, they communicate nothing, as we see with infants.

When some bodies enjoy their faculties, and others do not, those that enjoy them can communicate to those who do not, and have knowledge of them; whilst these know nothing of the former. Apply this to the law of souls.

Those souls which, here below, do not enjoy their faculties, are respectively in absolute nothingness; they may be near each other, they may dwell together, without transmitting any impression to each other. Such is the case of most people of the world, not to say, perhaps, of all mankind; for, during our journey on earth, our souls are to each other, as the bodies of infants; they really communicate nothing, compared with those active treasures with which they might have mutually enriched each other, if they had remained in their primitive harmony.

Released souls communicate with those in the flesh and with each other

When some of these souls leave their state of infancy, that is, when they leave their bodies, and, after having devoted themselves here to the true Spiritual Ministry of Man, they come to enjoy their faculties after death, it is not surprising that they should be able to communicate some of their treasures to souls still in the body, though these understand neither the reason nor the means of this communication, even while they experience its effects. Thus, an infant may feel the salutary impressions, which another body in possession of all its faculties may communicate to it, though it can neither see nor know the source from whence they come.

And, when several of these regenerate souls are in the enjoyment of their active faculties, after leaving their bodies, it is not surprising that they should then unfold all their relations (rapports) to each other; this seems so natural, that we need not seek evidence of it in the physical order.

Exquisite beauty of a regenerate soul, and its intercourse

Now, if, notwithstanding our degradation, and the little of value we can communicate to each other here on earth, we are still so transported, when, amongst the virtues of our fellow-creatures, we can only get sight of what the beauty of a soul is - one of those feeble branches which the tree of Man is still permitted to shoot forth at intervals - we may judge what joys await us in the true region, when our souls, harmonized and disengaged from their earthly bodies, shall be together, and communicate to each other all the wonders they may have acquired during their eleventh. hour, and those they will never cease to discover in the regions of the infinite.

God's love and Man's insensibility, two miracles

O Man! You who desire, even in this life, to enter the glorious Ministry of the Lord, think daily of those healing waters, which, ever since the crime, the goodness of the Most High has poured out, at every epoch of the human family; for you have seen enough of God's ways toward us to know that He cares, not merely for the whole human family, but for each man in particular, as if He had none other to care for.

Thus, a torch, in the midst of a circle of men, gives all its light to each; thus the sun shows its whole face to all who are in view of it; thus the Divine Source of our admiration is universal, and tries only to find an entrance into such souls as will open themselves to its Light.

But, after admiring this inexhaustible fountain, whose treasures were lavished upon Man at his origin, in the divine covenant; and, since the Fall, have continued to accumulate around us; - what a fearful reverse you will experience when you see that, notwithstanding these riches, Man languishes in such distress and privation, that his dark abode seems to be grounded on despair and death!

Man abused the high gifts that were granted to him in his glory; after his crime, he abused the love which came to seek him in his ignominy. The more favours he has received, the more his ingratitude has increased; and, when we survey these vast pictures, we discover two most amazing wonders: first, the miracle of God's

love for man, notwithstanding our crimes and injustice; second, our insensibility
and contempt for God, notwithstanding His love and devotion to us!

Consequences of man's insensibility; his body a sore, his clothing the dressing, his life is his death

No! nothing can surpass these wonders! And, what has been the result to man,
of his incomprehensible ingratitude? - (I may address these lamentations to all
my unhappy brethren). - Instead of that superiority of all kinds that should have
been our portion, and by aid of which we might go as witnesses into every part
of the Divine domains, what is the actual condition of the different worlds and
kingdoms of which we are composed.

It is superfluous to say that, since our degradation, our bodies are a daily
prey to the elements that consume them, like the vulture gnawing the entrails
of Prometheus. We know that man's body is like a sore, always in a state of
suppuration, and that his clothing is as a surgical dressing, which it is necessary
to remove and replace continually if the sore is to be prevented from becoming
a plague.

Even though this sore should not take that character outwardly, we know
that, since the crime, we bear in the bosom of our constituent substances a
corrupting poison which secretly consumes our flesh, from which man cannot
deliver himself; neither can he correct its malignity, nor arrest its progress a
single instant; for this venom is itself the consuming fire on which our existence
now rests; which is recognized in human sciences, at least by its effects, as the
principle of our destruction, when they confess that our animal respiration is but
a slow combustion.

Who knows not that every individual wandering on this surface, is but a
necessary instrument of his own death ; that he cannot enjoy a breath of life,
without purchasing it at the cost of life ; that the same act produces both his
existence and his destruction? And this is the clothing of death which man has
substituted for that pure immortal form which he might have drawn from the
divine treasury throughout eternity.

It is superfluous, also, to say that to contain this fire which devours us, we have
nothing at our disposal, but corrosive elements like itself, which daily deposit
their sediments in us, and, like it, give us life only in giving us death.

Then, our maladies and Infirmities, in addition to these natural defects, what
benefit do they derive from those who undertake to cure us? The medicinal
substances they employ are infected, just as our bodies and as all Nature are. They
can be useful only so far as they may be a degree less infected than ourselves.
Nothing is really living either in them or in us; or at most, what life and power
there are, are merely relative; it is death compromising with death.

Why is man ashamed of his state of Nature?

Independently of these overwhelming calamities, we are ashamed of our natural state, in that we are obliged to provide for our wants in a way which is contrary to the dignity of our being; in that our desire is no longer sufficient for this, and our effective (active) word is no more felt; in that all these temporal cares, and the ephemeral advantages which we incessantly seek after, are signs of our reprobation, and, at the same time, of our distrust in our Principle, whose vivifying creative help we have forfeited since the Fall; lastly, in that we thereby, in a manner, offend against the Supreme Truth, which we try to do without altogether, whereas the existence, movement, and life of whatever was created by it, and proceeded out of its universal generative focus, can be maintained by it, and its living power alone.

But, what is worse, though less observed, is, that we have allowed those destructive influences (actions), those germs of criminal disorganizing powers, to enter our essences through all our senses and pores, and take possession of all our organs, making our bodies the receptacles and instruments of every abomination, which is the case with nearly all mankind; and this is the more deplorable, because we possess both the right and the power to defend ourselves; whereas, over our frail essences in themselves, we have not the same power; we cannot prevent their dissolution; we cannot prevent their giving us death while they give us life.

The causes of our seduction, and lessons to be derived therefrom

Yet, what is the cause of this false prestige which begins by seducing us, and ends by plunging us into these fatal precipices? It is that, unhappily, it derives from a source which becomes baneful only because it ought to have constituted our glory, if we had kept it in its proper place. It comes from this, that it is still spirit, though of an inferior order, which works in us, when we listen to the voice or attraction of a false affection.

This spirit acts upon ours, and represents to us, sensibly, grounds on which we flatter ourselves we shall find all its promised delights. It thereby insinuates itself in our essences, and causes sensations which enchant and deceive us.

It is only because every thing herein is spirit that we find it so ravishing. But we do not allow ourselves time to discern what spirit it is. We are in haste to convey this lively image that enamours us to an earthly object, which is always found ready to combine with it. Here the action of the spirit vanishes, that of Nature takes its place; and, as this is limited, it soon makes us feel its limits, and its vanity. Hence, we may derive three lessons.

First, that the inferior spirit deceives us doubly, by showing us, spiritually, delights which we can no longer know except by matter, naturally; and, in that this matter disappoints us of the delights which were shown to us spiritually. Now, none but a disordered spirit can concur to produce these discordances and incongruities. A well-regulated spirit would show us, though under images, what amount of enjoyment properly belongs to our spirit in our earthly relations; and, at the same time, the illusory nature of the delights of matter; by which means neither of our two beings would be abused, and order would reign in both.

The second lesson shows the reason why men of advanced age, who have made themselves the slaves or playthings of their senses, still enjoy, in their depraved spirits, the delights which their matter can no longer realize; it is but a prolongation of their first affection, the action of the inferior spirit.

The third lesson teaches the cause of the disgust which succeeds our illusions; that it is not through matter that we ought to enjoy.

Man's mind and central being enslaved ; he has become his own enemy

If we view man in respect to his knowledge, and his mind, we find fresh matter for lamentation; we shall see him a slave to system and conjecture; to continual efforts at the composition of a mere nomenclature of his sciences; to clouds of conflicting ideas, which render his mind a thousand times more stormy than our atmosphere in the most violent tempests.

What, then, will it be if we look into his inmost being? We shall find him sunk, not merely in the divine hell, but, often, in a more active one, and looking forward only to the rapture of his earthly ties, to effect his complete junction with that hell of which he is visibly the organ and minister on earth.

Lastly, what will it be when he is surrounded with empirics of all kinds, who, never opening his eyes to the fountain of his evil, prevent his seeking the remedy? What do I say! Who even neutralize for him the most specific remedies, substituting mere palliatives, which are either ineffectual, or positively injurious? And man can be insensible of his misery, still, and careless of the dangers that surround him!

But, what else, what other result could he expect, after repaying, as he has, with ingratitude, all the rich gifts which he has received from the Eternal Bounty?

And this man, who was made to appease the wrath of God, is the very one to provoke it continually, by his substituting darkness for light, and innumerable false influences for the true which he carries within him. He had no nearer friend, here below, than his own inward being, on which to lean, to hear of God, and partake of the fruit and marvels of admiration. Instead of carefully husbanding this resource, he has made himself his own nearest and most mortal enemy; he has thought it a proof of wisdom to confound himself with beasts, to commit all the atrocities which are the consequence of such a doctrine, and thereby creating for himself the active hell, a mere perception of which is all that he ought to have had, and that only during this time of probation.

For, temporally, he is surrounded by nothing but helps: Nature affords him her abundant harvests; the elements their wholesome reaction; the Spirit of the universe its breath and light; domestic animals their gifts and services; he has even the means to disinfect poisons, and subdue wild beasts, and he labours only to infect himself.

Behold yourself then, O king of the world, in so abject and infernal a state, that you are not even king of yourself; and, of all that composes your empire, the only thing you have to shudder at is yourself, and you cannot look at yourself without horror! For it is the transposition of your will which has upset everything; and things suffer so universally only because men continually put their false and changeable wills in place of the true and eternal law; and because, not only would they rule universal things in their own way, but they even undertake to compose them for themselves, instead of simply receiving their influences.

Sorrow, the strait gate through which the man of desire must now enter

If, under these circumstances, a man of faith (*désir*) aspired to become one of the Lord's workmen, what means could he find to help his fellow-creatures in this spiritual distress, and awful danger, which constantly menace their inward being? He would have nothing but tears to offer; he would be reduced to shudder at their lamentable condition, and could help them only with sobs.

Remember, O man of desire, that if the fundamental essence of Man were brought back to its primitive elements, it would naturally pronounce, and continually feed upon, one sublime word, HOLY, HOLY, HOLY, to the glory of its Principle, without interruption, through all eternities.

In our day, man's language, like man himself, has undergone a frightful change; and now, before that primitive language, the language of holiness and happiness, can be recovered, man's essences are reduced to speaking no word but that of sorrow (*douleur*), this being their prevailing sensation, and the one of which they are most susceptible.

Listen very attentively to this word sorrow, when it speaks within you; listen to it as the first helping voice that can make itself heard in the wilderness: gather carefully this precious specific, as the only balm that can cure the nations.

Since the great change, the life of Nature rests only on this basis. Since Man's degradation, we have no other means of feeling our spiritual and divine existence; nor have we any other whereby to make our fellow-creatures feel it. This sorrow is different from the pains of the mystics, who have carried love so far as to take delight in afflictions: therein they regarded only their own salvation and happiness. Here, you will have no time to think of your own holiness, since you will be constantly vexed, and, as it were, crushed under the weight of this cross of powers, which makes life burst forth in all creatures.

The work of the man of faith re-acts on the first man, or the whole tree of Man

No doubt, this simple picture might suffice to excite your devotion, and inflame your courage; for, what higher motive can there be than to labour for the sabbath of rest for the human soul? But this motive will become still stronger and more effective, when you reflect that your work is not restricted to the posterity, past, present, and to come, of the first man; but that it may extend even to that first man himself, through the relationship which still exists between him and his posterity; for he has suffered so much by contact with our discordant atmosphere, that he would not have been able to bear it so long, if the hand of the Most High had not tempered its first attacks.

The promised seed, destined to revive the tree of Man

In fact, when the first Man allowed the glorious privileges, which, by his birthright, he ought to have possessed eternally, to fade and vanish, the Eternal Word came to his assistance in that place of bliss in which the Most High had placed him, and promised him that the woman's seed should crush the serpent's head.

By this promise alone He planted in Adam the germ of his restoration. He never ceased to water this seed with the spiritual favours he sent into the world through the ministry of His elect, until He came Himself to water it with His own blood. But Man, the tree, still remains charged to produce his fruits, in, by, and through his descendants. The Word could but give Himself for man; He could not cancel the law by which the tree must, itself, freely manifest what it had received in its essences.

So it is allowed to advance each day towards the final epoch, when, supposing all its branches had fulfilled the beneficent intention of their redeeming Source, they would have been destined to show the majestic tree of Man, as he appeared in the garden of Eden; and adorned, besides, with the resplendent branches of all his posterity, who ought to second all his efforts, seeing that the work is common to both the children and the father.

But, instead of this concurrence on the part of the posterity of the first man, which is so essential, what an accumulation of crime and disorder do they not pour upon the roots of this ancient tree, which they ought to hold so sacred! With such heterogeneous and destructive substances, what progress can the posterity of the first man make in spiritual growth? What branches or flowers can it produce? What fruits can be expected from it, at the time of harvest?

The primitive Man on his bed of suffering, neglected by his offspring

Here, O workmen of the Lord, whatever your feeling of desolation may be, it is quite legitimate; but here, also, you will find the most touching inducements to animate your zeal, in the noble character and importance of your work, which amounts to nothing short of contributing to the repose of the chief of the human family, by announcing to all his children how sublime is the Spiritual Ministry of Man!

Behold, then, the primitive Man, extended on his bed of suffering, suffering more for us than for himself; behold him contemplating the sufferings of every member of his family, past, present, and future; hear him, through the course of long ages, imploring them to, at least, not exasperate his wounds by their crimes, if they cannot help to cure them by their virtues.

Try to form an idea of his affliction, when, of all this numerous posterity whom he addresses, you will not see one who heeds his complaints; not one who seeks to partake in his work; not one who weeps over the sorrowful condition in which he languishes: what do I say? Perhaps not one who does not daily pour out gall and poison in his wounds.

Go to his relief, through the inward being of these your brethren

Depressed by your own sorrows, you will withdraw within yourself; but, from the centre of your secret asylum, your zeal will carry you to your lost brethren, who are insensible alike to their own ills and to those they bring upon the venerable trunk of the human family. There you will take your station, close to their inward being, like Jeremiah at the gate of the Temple of Jerusalem. You will importune them to apply their minds incessantly to the exercise of their sublime powers, and the importance of justice.

How to gain your brother, and present him
an acceptable sacrifice to God

You will tell this inward being that the fruits of his field are required to keep up the supplies; that if he remain idle, and provide not his share of the provisions, the general sustenance will suffer; that the field, allowed to run to waste, will soon be covered with thorns and briars, which can but wound the hand, or with poisonous weeds which will spread infection; that it will then, ere long, give shelter to venomous reptiles, or wild beasts, always ready to devour their own master.

You will tell him that, if the thread which connected us with God be broken, it is always ready to be retied and to prove that in the Divine alliance alone, life and light, and all that can satisfy our longing to admire, are to be found; likewise, that all fruits must be brought back to the Most High, for God alone affords receptacles capable of receiving and containing His own crops.

You will tell him that, as soon as we descended into the abyss, God deployed around us His great Rainbow, or those innumerable septenary degrees or steps which are ever ready to help us to ascend again out of the pit; that God himself arms his soldiers with these powerful aids, requiring them each to serve according to his arm; and employing them according to their light, their strength, and their acquirements.

You will urge him to join the army of the Lord, persuading him that His mighty hand will never expose us to more danger or severer work than we are able to bear.

If he resists, you will redouble your efforts; you will even make use of the rights which belong to your ministry to subdue him, and drive away, by the power of your word, all the enemies which daily strive to seduce him and lead him astray; you will take no rest till you are able to bring him back to the path of justice, and present him as a sweet smelling sacrifice to the Sovereign of all, the Friend of the pure.

It is not, then, for your brother's sake alone, that you will thus devote yourself to the sacred work of making souls keep Sabbath, but for the sake of the Most High God, whose minister you aspire to be.

In fact, those are the best beloved of His servants, who labour to fill the ranks of the Lord's army with souls which will spread His glory by signalizing themselves in His service.

God seeking an entrance into man's soul

It will also be for the sake of the triste abode of man. For, when God cannot find a human soul, here below, in which to enter, and by which He can act, disorders are hatched, and succeed each other on earth, in a way to rend the hearts of all who love God; and this proves that the crime of the first man was, that he emptied himself to God, to follow his own dark spirit. But the abuses to which his posterity have given themselves are the cause that, if man's spirit leans all on one side, the Divine Power bears itself entirely on the other, and, by its great weight, penetrates at last into some human souls, from which it afterwards proceeds, to contain the excesses of evil and arrest disorder; otherwise the universe would have been long since overthrown.

The burden and reward of those who give
themselves to second God's work

The human souls which second the zeal of the Divinity, then, have heavy burdens to bear, and great labours to undergo; but they have also high wages to expect, and powerful assistance to count upon in their work; for they are strengthened by a great word of command, which, when issued to them, brings all their strength and powers into play and activity: this ought to be the daily life, light, and support of Man, as, in the military order, the word of command constitutes the safety of the whole army.

Besides, are not these souls abundantly rewarded by the happiness of giving their testimony? For those who have borne witness will be acknowledged as faithful servants hereafter; and it is particularly in the souls of men that we have to give our testimony. This testimony, which we may sow in men's souls, will resuscitate with them, and serve, in its turn, as evidence in our favour, not only that our own debts may be blotted out, but that we may receive wages.

O workmen of the Lord, use every effort that you may be sent as witnesses, and not remain without consolation and hope for the future. Happy will you be if, each day, you are able to say: I have not lost the day; I have borne witness in a man's soul (and this in your most secret being, even without the man's material eyes knowing it); and I have thereby added something to my credit for the future!

You may even expect that God will pay you for this testimony in this world, not only with joys which He will pour into your soul, but even by the manifest assistance He will send you, and the divine and wonderful works which He will cause to come out of your hands, as a sort of recompense, or return, or exchange, for the services you may have rendered Him in the Spiritual Ministry of Man.

The Lord's workman's pay: Relief to the Chief of the human family

Yes, if man followed the line of the true Spiritual Ministry of Man, with never so little courage, he would soon find that it would give him less trouble, and take less time to work a miracle, than to learn, in all its details, the least of the sciences with which men are busied, and to which they consecrate their days and the sweat of their brows. The following are the joys and rewards with which God is pleased to nourish His workmen's hopes:

Mutual reaction of all the divine powers combined within us; to produce repentance.

Reaction of the same powers; to produce resignation.

Reaction; to produce assurance.

Reaction; to bring forth prayer, in concert with every creature, past, present, and future.

Reaction; to produce intimate and entire conviction.

Reaction; for the guidance of all our thoughts, steps, and desires.

Reaction; to obtain the gift of speech (*la parole*); the Word.

Reaction; to encourage us to speak to the Word, since the Word speaks to us.

Reaction; that we may pray the Word to hear its own voice, in the groanings it utters in the midst of all our wretchedness, and all our individual bodily and spiritual infirmities.

Reaction; to obtain the investiture, and the active efficient distribution, of the ruling, judging, working, executive, and justifying powers, which this living Word, moved by its own prayer, can cause to descend in the centres and seats where it dwells and ferments within us.

This is what the Lord's workmen may do, who have gone as witnesses into the souls of their fellow creatures thus can we make God participate in all our works, and ourselves participate in His.

O workmen of the Lord, if you obtain these favours, then you may approach, with confidence, the bed of suffering, on which the Chief of the human family is still detained by the errors and pollutions of his posterity. You will comfort him in his affliction; you will relieve him by your sublime and holy works; and he will rejoice to see some of his children participate in his tender cares.

THIRD PART - The Word

The Word sustains all things for Man

If there were no power of harmony and order, which engendered itself from all eternity, we should never see order rise out of and succeed the corruption which befalls everything that constitutes the universal circle, as happens every moment before our eyes. Yes, let us proclaim with a loud voice there is an Eternal Word, the depositary of Eternal Light and Life and Measure, which continually balances, for man's sake, here below, the disorder, anguish, and infection, in which he is steeped. If man do not maintain himself constantly at the elevation where this support dwells, he falls again into the abyss of evil and suffering in the opposite extreme. There is no medium for him: if he do not use the strength of Hercules, he remains crushed under the weight of Atlas.

Yes, it requires all the Divine Light to dissipate the intense darkness which surrounds him. He needs all the Divine Virtue to balance the region of crime to which he is tied; in short, if he do not attain holiness itself, he remains sunk in abomination.

Man tries in vain to obtain these triumphs by half measures, and by the feeble speculations of his mind and reason. Those pretended expedients only deceive him; they are altogether illusory.

The vain and artificial distractions in which he daily cradles his existence, deceive him still more; the living way is the only profitable way; this living way can only be the hand of the Highest Himself, because He alone can uphold and govern all things, and He alone create a compensation for all deficiencies.

For, when it was said of the Supreme Ruler that He sustained all things by the power of His word, it was no mystical expression, calculated to leave our minds in suspense; it was positively and physically true, and that in every order we can think of.

It is quite true that, if the Word did not uphold the universe in its existence, and direct it in all its movements, it would stop at once in its progress, and return to its non-appearance:

It is quite true that, if the Word did not uphold the plants and animals, they would immediately re-enter their own germs, and these germs would be absorbed by the temporal spirit of the universe:

It is quite true that, if the Word did not uphold their play and action, all the phenomena of the Universe would cease to be manifest to our eyes.

It is equally true, in the spiritual order, that, if the Word did not uphold the thought and soul of man, as it daily upholds all things in the Universe, our minds would immediately fall back into darkness, and our souls into the abyss, over which we are enabled to float, notwithstanding our crimes, only through the inestimable and most merciful power of the Word thus, unless we would be voluntarily insane, and knowingly our worst enemies, we would not cease for one moment looking to the Principle of all things, and leaning upon the Word ; for, to do so, would be to deny our existence, and renounce all usefulness in the regions where help is looked for from the Spiritual Ministry of Man.

Metaphysicians and speculators on the Divinity. Political religion

And, woe unto you, cold metaphysicians, who make of the Divine Being, and all that emanates from Him, merely a subject for your dissertation and reasoning! Woe, woe, to you speculators, who give no foundation to religion but politics; whilst its essential foundation is the Word, without which nothing can be upheld!

You doubtless see nothing in religion but its obscure forms, which have been made still darker by the abuses that disfigure it; then, as I say, you look upon it only as a means, with the mysterious chains of which you may bind the simple; and you think they were meant for nothing else. And, in this, I excuse you; so thick is the darkness that covers the earth!

But, I do not excuse you when you make the word homage bow to your political purposes. God, the Word, and the homage that is due to them, are not results of reflection and calculation; it is a small thing even to regard it only a duty to believe in this Most High God and His Eternal Word, which has so many claims to the veneration of His creatures. This belief is more than a philosophical consequence; it is more even than a right and an obligation; it is a radical constituent necessity of your being; and your present situation is a positive proof of this, the universal destitution in which you exist being enough to make you feel that necessity every instant of your life; and, since the moment you cease to endeavour to provide for it, you fall again into the abyss.

Analogy between faults and punishments: How to discover our offence

Let us now apply the bright universal Light to the consideration of faults and punishments in general, and the principles that these faults have offended.

In strict justice, as in strict truth, there must be a perfect analogy between the punishment and the fault. And, by carefully examining man's unhappy condition here below, we ought to discover clearly the nature of his error and crime; for, the punishment and the crime must be moulded the one upon the other.

In the same strict justice, there must also be an antipathetic connection, equally marked, between the fault and the principle it offended, since the fault can only be, in all respects, the inverse and contrary of the principle; we shall be better understood, if we say it can consist only in an opposite direction to that of the principle. Consequently, by going back upon the line of the fault, we cannot fail to arrive at the principle; as, by examining the nature of the penalty and punishment, we shall not fail to learn the nature of the offence, of which they are the results.

We must begin with the punishment, since this has to teach us what the offence was. The next process must be to walk backwards along the line of this offence, to arrive at the principle. Thus, our first duty is to cease our complaints, and go through all the degrees of our punishment, with resignation; if we would arrive at a true knowledge of our disorder.

Our second duty consists in a lively, ardent activity, without a look to the right hand or to the left; because this alone can dispel our darkness, and bring us back into that life from which the offence or lapse (*altération*) separated us.

Our confinement in a dumb world shows that our offence was against the Word

When we examine our punishment, we remark that its most prominent character consists in this, that we are kept shut in, and tied to an universe, which, though upheld by the Word, is without speech; and this is a double punishment for us; making us feel, on the one hand, the shameful disproportion there is between ourselves and the dumb creatures around us; and, on the other, how distressing this dumb universe must be to the Word itself; since this Word would be, and ought to be, manifested everywhere, and freely correspond with all that exists.

Now, the first of these punishments is demonstrated not only by the actual state of things, but also by man's conduct towards his fellow-creatures.

Although the conversation of men is very far from the true Word, nevertheless, when men are together, if they did not enliven the atmosphere with their discourse, that feeble shadow of the Word; if they did not thereby animate a little the sepulchre in which they are, they would know nothing but the cold wearisomeness of death.

The second of these punishments also demonstrates a living source, incessantly seeking to revive all things by means of individual speech (*parole*); for, without such a source, man would not enjoy this individual speech, of which he daily makes so puerile a use, and from which he has so little profit to expect, so long as he is unregenerate.

Thus, we may say, we are clearly enlightened as to the punishment that has been visited upon us. But, seeing the necessary analogy that subsists between the punishment and the offence, we ought to conclude that, if we are punished by a dearth of the true Word, it must surely be against the Word that we have offended.

By the second law, or, as a consequence of the analogy between the offence and the principle, it results that, if, in our speech (*parole*), we were to proceed in an inverse direction to that in which we went at the time of its corruption (*altération*), and in which we walk every day, we should again arrive at that grand, fixed, and luminous Word (*parole*), with which we feel we need to dwell, and with which we should dwell in joy, instead of in the sufferings which now torment us.

The Word, or true speech, requires an apprenticeship, like other talents; Silence

But how should men attain the active enjoyment of this universal instrument, this Word, which, though so highly important, and greatly to be desired, is, yet, the only talent, or, so to say, the only trade they exercise, without the preparation of a long apprenticeship, such as they pass through in cultivating other talents? For, I repeat, what men say everywhere, and all day long, must not be mistaken for the Word (*parole*, true speech) ; they may be vain and ignorant enough to think it such; whereas it is absolutely its inversion.

In fact, the Word is learnt only in the silence of every thing in this world; there only is it to be heard; and, when we speak, whether to others or to ourselves, of anything belonging to this world, it is clear that we act contrary to the true Word, and not for it ; for we thereby only degrade ourselves, and naturalize ourselves with the world; which, as we have just said, being without speech, is therefore at once the mode and the instrument of our punishment.

Let us not, however, forget another fact, equally true, and incomparably more comforting: that is, the feeling that if sin deprived us of every thing, and left us in a state of absolute destitution, it is necessary for our cure that everything should be again given to us by Infinite Universal Love; otherwise our cure would never be absolute. Now this universal gift, which Love again bestowed upon the world, is comprised altogether in the wonders of the Word, it being the loss of these riches which kept us in want. But we can now learn this speech (Word) of the Spirit, but very slowly, as we see children learn human speech. We ought also to learn it in a natural way, insensibly, as children learn it. Hence the Gospel precept: "Except ye become as little children, ye shall not enter into the kingdom of heaven".

What the Word teaches: God's alliance with Man and Nature

Let us look with admiration, in this spirit, at all the Word has brought to our knowledge: the following is an extract of what we shall learn thereby.

It was by Word that God made His divine contract of universal alliance with all that exists in immensity.

It was by Word that God, in His restorative processes, formed His general temporal spiritual alliance, at the different epochs of His gracious work, manifested in the origin and creation of Nature ; in the promise made to sinful Adam; in His different elect leaders who have proclaimed His laws and ordinances on the earth, both before the middle time, and since then; and in those He will send till the end of time, and at the end.

By Word, also, God makes a special spiritual alliance with individual man, planting in him the germs of different gifts and virtues which attract each other, and assemble together by that attraction, till they acquire, by their strength and harmonical activity, such an affinity to Unity, that this Unity comes and joins them, and consecrates them with its sanction.

By Word, God rules the course of His general temporal spiritual alliance: when this alliance has acquired a sufficient amount of strength, by the attraction of its powerful divine elements, the Word allows it to explode, and itself passes in the torrent of that explosion, in order that its salutary substances may the better penetrate into the regions which await them ; and here is one of the wonders of active numbers, which, though nothing in themselves, as I have said before, faithfully represent the hidden course of the Word, and its inestimable properties.

It is by Word, also, that God makes a particular and continual alliance in the earthly nature and vegetation, in which order every production is always preceded by the gradations of activity, germination, and growth, attracting each other reciprocally, and terminating in an explosion, either by florescence, or by a birth, when the eye, or centre of life in each, has dissipated the obstacles which surrounded it, and is able to take possession of its rights.

Want of a spiritual language

As these grounds of action are disseminated through Nature, so are the germs of science disseminated through all men: we only want an analogous language or speech (*parole*) to communicate them to each other. If we cultivated these germs carefully, they would themselves produce for us a language which would convey their fruits to us; but we are carried away by impatience; and, instead of waiting for the fructification of this language, we are in haste to compose different languages for ourselves, according to the different sciences we may practise.

At the same time, as these languages are barren, unlike the one whose place they usurp, they bring us no profit ; they touch not the germs out of which fruit should spring.

And men's scientific results stop, for the most part, at our composite factitious languages; and human sciences generally lodge in the outward form, not in the virtue of the words; and their scientific languages having no life in themselves, cannot vivify each other; and as they cannot vivify, they begin only by disputing and opposing, and end by destroying each other.

Thus they propagate death, which, since the Fall, has spread its empire everywhere; whereas, they ought to have seconded life, or the Word, which, since that great change, cannot make a step without having to fight for it. In fact, every generation, every vegetation, every restorative act or operation, even every thought which tends towards the region of light, forms so many resurrections and real conquests over death. Whosoever is able to penetrate so far as to conceive and feel the continual resurrection of the Grand Word, will have great thanks to give, and I shall be surprised if he is not melted, and struck dumb with admiration. Therefore, what must not be the joy of the heavenly, spiritual, divine powers, when they succeed in begetting, in the world of Truth and Light, a man like themselves, their well-beloved Son!

The Word in anguish; all things born in anguish; even life itself

The true Word is universally in anguish; and we can neither receive nor perform anything but through anguish; and everything that exists visibly is a perpetual physical demonstration of the Word in anguish; therefore we ought not to shun inward anguish; therefore, words of anguish alone can profit; they alone sow themselves and engender, because such only are expressions of life and love.

This severe law is shown, O man, in your mother's cries when she gives you birth, and your own tears in receiving it. Learn, therefore, from this, what it must have cost the Source of all refreshment to procreate itself in your corrupted spiritual form, and make itself of your species. But compare your free and active temporal life with that you had in your mother's womb, and see if it does not bring you joys of existence which make you forget your first tears; and learn from this what you may expect from the smallest impressions which real anguish may give birth to in you.

Prepare, therefore, your eyes to see, and your understanding to admire and understand, what proceeds daily from the particular anguish of the Refreshment or Word, and will hereafter proceed from its general anguish; for the results of all these anguishes are as certain as they are immeasurable.

Hence it follows, as no salutary living word can be born in us, except in anguish, that it is quite certain that the men we listen to daily speak no word (*parole*), and deceive us when they pretend they proclaim the truth; since they speak without the intervention and power of anguish.

Moreover, the words of anguish are always new, since therein lies the principle of language. Now, the words of those we listen to every day are never new, and afford nothing but reminiscences and repetitions, which have been told over and over again before.

Would you see what the sublime object of this anguish of the Word is? When man listens very attentively, Truth seems to say to him, "O Man, I can give vent to my tears nowhere but in thy bosom".

Thus, then, the heart of Man is chosen to be the depositary of God's anguish, the friend of His choice, the confidant of all His secrets and wonders, seeing that none of them can have effusion or issue except through anguish. And, after this, so tender and friendly announcement is made to Man, he realizes it, and can exclaim in his turn, "Floods of pain inundate my veins, and all my being swells with bitterness". Give thanks then, for at that moment life commences.

How to keep the fire of Spiritual life alive

The following is a sure means to prevent these first elements of your life from being extinguished. Beware of departing, even for an instant, from the radical central fire on which you rest, which ought never to cease exercising you in pain, that this pain may extend to all your faculties, and make them bring forth their fruit.

It is this fire that ought to prepare you incessantly, and keep you in fear; and, without this continual preparation, the living Word of anguish will not enter you; you will become a disgusting object, and, when it came to embrace you, it would have to turn away its head, because of your infected breath; for, if the Spirit Man is so often offended by the breath which proceeds out of man's mouth, how should God endure it?

Remain, then, constantly on this central radical fire, as an infant remains in its mother's womb, till it is strong enough to bear the light of day; or, if a less dignified comparison may be used, as a mess being cooked, remains on the fire till it is done.

Under all this there are great experimental principles and truths. The most important is, that we should know and feel which is the greatest anguish that God experiences. It is that which comes from His continual attempts to exhume Himself out of the heart of Man, and the frightful obstacles which the heart of Man opposes to Him.

For this reason, all the abyssal fire that is kindled beneath us through life, is not too much to dissolve the thick coagulations which choke us.

For, if this abyssal fire do not prepare the way, the Words of divine anguish will never enter us; and if the Word of anguish do not enter, we can never understand the universal anguish of all things, and can never be their comforters. Yes, if we have not the substance of life in activity within us, how should we be able to judge, or even be sensible of what is dead around us?

Thus, it is not merely Nature's sabbath, nor even that of the human soul, which so urgently requires our care; we have also to make the Word itself enjoy its sabbath, since it cannot be denied that, owing to the nugatory, false, or perverse use Man makes of the Divine Word, it is on its bed of suffering, not to say its death-bed; and man can bring it no relief till he feel every anguish of the Word born within him.

We see men give the name of crosses of expiation, to disappointments of temporal life, to worldly afflictions, to bodily infirmities, etc.; whilst that name, in its true signification, applies only to the spiritual pains of men devoted to the Lord's work, and called to labour in it, according to their ability or gifts.

This class of men are generally tied to circumstances which are quite opposed to the divine work they long for, for which they were made, and of which they are so little able to speak, that they would often rather allow themselves to be covered with derision and contempt, than open their mouths about it. It is to men of this class that the Gospel precept applies: "Whosoever taketh not up his cross, and followeth not after me, is not worthy of me". For, if they do not determine to bear the cross which is presented to them, and go forwards, notwithstanding the anguish it promises them, they run the risk of missing their work, and being treated as bad servants.

The spirit of the world has disguised the most beautiful meanings of Scripture, by giving them the most ordinary and vulgar applications. I am not afraid to say, that even very great saints have failed to give to this grand passage all the meaning that belongs to it; and the famous saying of St. Theresa, "Let me suffer, or die", gives only half of it. The cross is far anterior to evil; and when it makes itself felt in us now, acting in the confinement of our present spiritual trammels, it is to lead us to its own free action, and teach us, in its own boundless munificence, notwithstanding our pollutions, what the cross before evil is.

No, no! The cross is not a suffering; it is the Eternal Root of Eternal Light. It is not the less true that, if the elect have to bear courageously the painful efforts which this cross makes in them, to arrive at the region of liberty; with far more reason ought we all to bear the tribulations of this world, both bodily and spiritual, to which we give the name of crosses; and this resignation will be the more meritorious, that, in the state of disorder and discordance into which the Fall has thrown us, we are not all called to feel, at least in the same degree, the anguish of the higher cross.

I will not say that men derive no profit from their inferior way of viewing the Gospel precept in reference to the cross; I would merely have men of desire know that they may derive far greater advantage from it in another way; for it is in their disappointments and contrarieties, in things divine, with which their faith is at once tried and nourished, that they first begin to learn what the sufferings of the Word are, and they take comfort and are even glad, instead of complaining because the Word does not advance in its pains, without also advancing towards the great epoch of its deliverance.

In advancing thus, its anguish and tribulation increase more and more; the Psalms would be very different from what they are, if they were to be written now. For the Word is the divine desire, personified and in action in man. In proportion as it penetrates and discovers itself in the human atmosphere, so it is reduced to feed upon gall and bitterness. But what must be its satisfaction when it finds a soul full of faith and desire, which seeks to become really regenerate, according to the new law of spirit and truth!

Esteem, then, O man of God, no sufferings profitable but such as have the public good for object. Can the soldier who has fallen ill from intemperance or his own negligence, be considered as serving the state, when he follows precisely the doctor's prescriptions? No, he is only serving himself, seeking his own recovery; and he will really serve his country only when he goes to fight again.

Such is generally our situation here below: we are all under medical treatment, for the consequences of the great disorder, or those of our own errors; when we observe and follow all that is laid down for our spiritual health, we are therein useful only to ourselves. It is wrong to call that serving God, for it is not serving Him.

When we are regenerate, and able to fulfil the different ministries of our Master, then we are supposed to really serve God; for then we may, through the medium of our own pains, feel and know experimentally the pains of the Word: till then, we feel only our own. Let us, then, close the gates of evil and vanity within us, that the regions of life may enter.

The hand of the Lord upon Man

When the hand of God is upon Man, for his punishment, Man is bound in all his faculties. He is tormented by disquiet, and the need of action and movement, and by the intolerable torture (gehenna, hell) which retains his whole being in violent contraction ; but he remains inactive, and all for him is in suspense.

When it is for the advancement of the work and progress of the Word, the weight of God's hand torments him also; but it is with impatience for the reign of justice, and the gehenna he experiences makes him advance daily in the regions of life, luminous with spiritual activity.

The insidious prestige of the region of appearances surrounds him with its illusions; he passes by and perceives them not. Earthly passions and darkness pursue him in vain; he travels through them, and leaves them behind.

You may leave him a prey to all the wants of this life; the hand of the Lord attracts him, and his impatience for justice is stronger than his wants. You may martyrize him, he will submit; he will feel nothing but the weight of the Lord's hand, which torments him with impatience for justice.

When a vessel is launched, will any feeble ties stop her descent? She snaps them, and plunges into the deep. Or any little obstacles in her way? She grinds them to powder, or sets them on fire, and plunges into the deep.

This is what man may become when he is happy enough to feel the weight of the Lord's hand, and he is tormented with impatience for justice.

Seek and ye shall find the hand of the Lord upon you

But how will you, O man of desire, attain to feel the weight of the Lord's hand, and be tormented with impatience for justice? By making an engagement with yourself, and saying, "I will never cease praying till I feel that God Himself prays in me.

"If I am faithful to this engagement, I shall not have to wait for the slowness of my own prayer that God may pray with me, for He will pray with me from the beginning of my prayer.

"He will soon even pray with me when I do not pray: 'They shall not labour in vain nor bring forth in trouble; for they are the seed of the blessed of the Lord; and before they call, I will answer; and while they are yet speaking, I will hear' (Is. lxv. 23, 24).

"Yes, my whole life will henceforth be one uninterrupted prayer; since it will be no more I who seek God, by detached petitions of human weakness, but it will be God seeking me, in the continuity of His unfailing action.

"Must we not one day become as so many flaming torrents, incessantly shooting forth living and burning flashes from every point of all our constituent substances? Why are we told that our God is a devouring fire, and that we were made in His image and likeness?"

Then you will be able to say: "My soul has found the friend of its life; they have kissed each other, and will part no more. She went not into the market places, nor into the suburbs of the city, to seek this friend; she had no need to enquire for him, of the watchmen of Jerusalem.

"This friend came himself to find her, in the transports of his love; they kissed each other, and will part no more.

"These are the riches he has brought me, and poured into my heart, in the transports of his love.

"I was a soul bowed down with the weight of its own misery; despair had well nigh got hold of me; but, when I saw the Comforter approach, I heard these tender words come out of His mouth: 'Why art thou depressed? Has not God told thee to forgive thy brother seventy times seven times? If God judged thee capable of so much forbearance towards thy brother, dost thou believe Him incapable of the same towards thee?'"

Call upon Him therefore to forgive you in His turn, not seventy times seven times, only, but, according to the eternal number of His infinity; take no rest till you feel that He has sealed your pardon, and Himself kept the law, the precept, the command, He gave to you.

When He has thus justified you, say to Him, "Lord, the city shall no more be destroyed; thou requiredst at least ten righteous, to enable thee to withhold the fire which threatened Sodom and Gomorrah, and ten righteous were not found.

"Thou requiredst but one righteous to save Jerusalem, in the days of Jeremiah, and not one was found. (vi. 13.).

"But now the city shall not be destroyed, if thou requirest this righteous one, for this righteous one is found; this righteous one has entered the city; this righteous one is thyself, who hast entered into alliance with me.

"This righteous one shall save the city and all its inhabitants, because this righteous one is thy divine Unity, and thy divine Unity will spread of itself, over all the inhabitants of Jerusalem.

"Thou saidst to thy prophet Jeremiah, that though Moses and Samuel came before thee, thou wouldst not forgive thy people (xv. 1.).

"But they were not priests after the order of Melchisedek; and being only ministers of the symbolical law, they could not open the holy gate of eternal mercy.

"Now this living gate is open, and this gate is thyself ; thou canst, therefore, no longer help saving the man that seeketh thee; Thou art thyself the prophet placed before thyself, to implore favour for thy people, and thou hast compelled thyself to deliver my soul when it lays its distress and misery before thee".

But the man of desire will still tremble: "Why dost thou weep, O my soul? Why dost thou weep? What is thy new cause of pain?

"If I tremble, it is because man has become the murderer of the Word, and of Truth; it is because the vital regions find nothing in him but death, and are obliged to retire; it is because his own misfortunes, his own negligences, his own pains, or rather, his illusions, prevent his feeling the pains of the Word.

"Alas! How can I but weep! Since the pains of the Word are always before my eyes, and all my substance is affliction!

"Depart from man, ye streams of infection, run from him like rivers of muddy waters; henceforward my sole task must be to prevent their approaching the Word, lest they should communicate their infection.

"I will give myself entirely to this task; I will devote myself to it with an ardour that shall know no intermission. It is the only thing recommended as necessary; and all that does not refer to this holy and indispensable duty, I will do as though I did it not.

"And thou, O Spirit of Prayer, shalt be the companion of my labour; or rather, thou shalt be its master, its agent, and its principle; and thou shalt teach me to become like thyself, the master, agent, and principle of my work, because thou wilt help me to become prayer like thyself.

"How should I not become prayer, since the Word has invoked itself upon me, and then driven away from me all the enemies of Truth, so that all the men of God might descend into me, and there celebrate their joy at having found an abode of peace?

"Oh! how they will rejoice, when they find this abode of peace! They will there keep feasts of jubilee, and sing with transport hymns of life, and they will raise their voices, that their companions may hear them, and hasten to share their happiness".

Man a steward, not a law-maker; in divine things as well as politics

Some years ago, when treating of politics, I said that it was not for man to be a legislator ; that he could only be a steward in the post committed to him. I showed that, strictly speaking, a man lawgiver was contrary to reason; that it was without example for a creature to be sent, where he would have to make laws for himself to follow; I said, moreover, that as a consequence of this fundamental and unquestionable principle, the administrative power had absorbed the legislative, in all the governments of the world; which may be easily verified by reference to facts, especially in religious history.

I can now extend this principle to Man considered in his divine post, in which, far from having any laws to establish, he ought to have no employment but to be, without intermission, the organ and minister of his Master. It is even on account of the urgency of the Master's work, and the universal vigilance and activity it requires, that those men who have attained to be employed as its organs, hardly have leisure to talk about rights of their own.

For this reason, spiritual knowledge ought to be only the daily pay of constant action; and the brilliant light communicated through chosen men, like Jacob Boehme, would even seem to belong to the next epoch after this present world, and to be the price only of the universal action (influence) which is supposed to call us, in our quality of stewards, to renovate the face of the world, and bring down the new heavens and the new earth, in which we shall contemplate the universal wonders of the Word, natural, spiritual, and divine.

Think not then, O man of desire, that you can ever have any laws to promulgate, but those of your Master.

Spiritual joys, how to receive them for the extension of God's Kingdom

And when joys come upon you in your spiritual exercises, think not that they are sent for your own sake. No, they can have no object but your Master's work, to nourish your strength, and sustain your courage. Were the Word itself to descend upon you, forget not the important intimation you have just read, and say:

"Is it for my sake thou shouldst visit me? I who have done nothing that thou shouldst come near me, but, on the contrary, everything to keep thee far from me! I will not then yield to this joy, till I feel that thou comest for thine own sake, and not for mine.

"I will not yield myself to this joy, till I feel that universal desire which animates and creates thee eternally.

"I will not yield to it, till I perceive the particular object for which thou art come, and the kind of task thou givest me to do, in the work of general improvement.

"Without this precaution not only would my joy be vain ; but my course would be uncertain, like that of a neophyte ; and I might, even, at any moment, fall again into the dark region of men in the stream".

Thus, then, O man of desire, when the Divine Word descends into you, think only of allowing it to penetrate your whole being, that it may cause the germs that are deposited there, to fructify, by visiting them with the power of its own eternal generation.

The Divine Word is so powerful, that the mere recollection of the favours you may have received from it, will enable you to drive away the enemy, as the mere shadow of the Apostles cured the sick; for this divine Word can show itself nowhere without leaving indelible signs: we have only to observe these signs more carefully, and follow them with more confidence; nothing more is required from all men, than that they should use every effort to be constant in effectual prayer for the universal recovery; that is, in a state to exercise the Spiritual Ministry of Man.

When the Word commands man to be ready, it means that he must be always prepared to answer the impulse, whenever it may invite him to the work of recovery; for the Word is the right measure itself; it tends but to restore men to their own original proportions, that they, afterwards, may cause the divine measures to revive, in all the regions where they are lost; this is the true extension of the kingdom of God; it is to be first for Himself, and afterwards for us.

How men despise the Word which governs all: their dead conversation

If we have the happiness to know, experimentally, though never so little, of the mighty power of this Word, the exclusive universality of its government, the vivacity of its action, and the suavity of its spirit, it afflicts us deeply, to see men, not only as if they were deprived of its ineffable support in their daily walk, but as not even suspecting its immortal eternal existence, and putting dead Nature, that is vacancy (*néant*), in its place.

This painful feeling is followed by surprise; for, seeing that this Word is the sole support of all order, of all that lives, of all harmony, and seeing men every day dispense with its indispensable support, or even declare themselves its enemies, we can but be astonished that they are not even worse than they are, and that they should still retain, though it be but in thought, even a trace, or any idea, of justice and perfection.

How should they advance, in the line of regularity and life, with this enormous mass of nugatory, empty, earthly, false, covetous conversation (*paroles*), which every day fills the whole world, from one end to the other? Since the great corruption, men have all fallen under the authority of dead words (conversation) that rules them despotically, and does not allow them to escape for a moment from its sway.

Look at all classes, collect all the words which proceed out of their mouths from the time they awake, till the time they go to sleep again; will you find one word that relates to their progress in true righteousness, or towards their original destination?

We will not here speak of the man of toil, who, while he tills the earth in silence and the sweat of his brow, and thereby undergoes the sentence which was pronounced upon the human family, appears, at least, by his resignation, and by that kind of dumb word, to accomplish, in an inferior order, what our virtual word ought to do in the order of spirit; we will not stop even at those words which are extorted from us by our earthly cares and miseries, and temporal sufferings, but we allude to that torrent of barren and pestilential words which we sacrifice daily to idleness, vanity, frivolous occupations, to our passions, to the defence of our false systems, pretensions, fantasies, to injustice, crime, and abomination.

Since the living Word has been withdrawn from man, he has been surrounded with an atmosphere of death. He is no longer active enough to unite his word with the living focus. Rather than bear this painful privation courageously, and wait patiently for the dayspring from on high, he supplies its absence by that flood of unprofitable words issuing out of the delirium of his thoughts. He had rather be contaminated in this way, and infect his fellow-creatures at the same time, than humbly, and in all docility, allow the healing Word to act upon him, that Word which seeks only to vivify him, as it vivifies continually all creatures to which it gave existence.

The substance if men's words will rise up in judgment against them: Watch for the sake of your fellow creatures

Man forgets that, when the substance of his words disperses in the air, it is not destroyed; that it does not therefore evaporate, but that it forms a mass and corrupts the spiritual atmosphere, as our putrid exhalations corrupt the atmosphere in our dwellings; he forgets that every word that man's tongue pronounces will one day be produced again before him, and that the air which our mouths make use of to form our words will restore them just as it received them, as every element will restore what is sown in it, everything after its kind ; that even our dumb speech, pronounced tacitly only in the secret of our being, will likewise reappear and resound in our ears; for silence has also its echoes; and man cannot produce a thought, a word, an act, which is not imprinted on the eternal mirror on which everything is engraved, and from which nothing is ever effaced.

The holy dread of an oath originally derives from a deep sentiment of these principles; for, when we penetrate to the ground of our being, we find that we can unite ourselves by our word with the ineffable source of truth, but that we can also, by its criminal use, unite ourselves with the awful abyss of lies and darkness.

There are savage nations, who, though without our science, have gone less astray than we have, who esteem nothing so much as their oaths; whilst, amongst civilized nations, the use of oaths is little more than a form, the moral consequences of which appear to be of little importance.

But, letting alone these false oaths and perjuries: when we see the great evils that result daily from the mismanagement of our words, is not this enough to teach us wisdom?

O man, if the care of your own spiritual health is not enough to induce you to condescend to watch over your words on your own account, watch over them at least for the sake of your fellow creatures; and be not satisfied no more to abuse them, as you do every day, with barren words of no profit, which drag them into all manner of doubts and illusions; but do in such sort that your words may be at once a torch to guide them, and an anchor to steady them and secure them through the tempests.

Essential laws for the management of speech

What, then, are the essential laws for the stewardship or management of your speech, in reference to your fellow creatures?

It is, to think sufficiently highly of the human intelligence, to feel that its conversation ought to be only with its own order, and that we ought to present nothing to it but what is worthy of it, and may add to its riches.

It is, to convince yourself that this intelligence of man ought to be treated a s high personages in the East are treated, who are never approached without a present being offered them.

It is, to contrive always to add to the light and virtues of those who converse with you; that your words may always show some profit for those who hear them.

It is, to converse only on solid grounds and profound truths, instead of feeding men with mere recitals and frivolous narratives; since these recitals and frivolous narratives are composed of time, in which there is only past and future; whereas great truths are always present, like axioms; they belong, not to time, but to the permanent eternal region.

It is, to distribute your words soberly, and with moderation; for it is only bad causes which demand many words to defend them.

It is, never to forget that speech, the Word, is the light of infinity, which ought to be always increasing.

It is, to always examine, before speaking, if what you are going to say will accomplish these important objects.

If you keep only on the level of those with whom you converse, the work will not advance. If you keep below it, the work recedes. Now, in observing all these laws, in reference to those with whom you converse, the advancement of the work should be your principal aim; every breath of your life should be employed for this.

The Word will direct its own ministration

I know that, in idle society, these laws of speech cannot be observed, because the Word cannot conveniently exercise its ministry there; nor is it to such I address myself. But it is for you so to comport yourself, that the Word may give you a ministry to perform, in whatever place you may be; for, if you try to do it by yourself, you will only add extravagance to profanation.

Speech is the fruit of a contact or alliance; and we are never without contracting one, of some sort

All speech can but be the fruit of a thought, and every thought the fruit of an alliance ; but, as the alliances we make are so different one from another, it is not surprising that our speech should likewise take so many colours.

In fact, it is only through our alliance, or, if you will, our contact with God, that we have any divine thoughts. Our contact with Spirit gives us spiritual thoughts; our sidereal or astral thoughts come from our contact with the astral Spirit, which is called the Spirit of the Great World; our material and earthly thoughts come from our contact with earthly darkness; our criminal thoughts from the Spirit of lies and wickedness. We have power and are at liberty to contract any of these alliances; we have only to choose.

But what ought to keep us constantly active and watchful is, that, from the very nature of our being, the fire of which cannot be extinguished, we are, every instant, pressed to contract one or other of these alliances. What is more: we never are without contracting one, of one kind or another. In short, we never are without engendering fruits of some kind; since we are always in contact with one of these centres, divine, spiritual, sidereal, earthly, or infernal, which all surround us.

Fruits of the Spirit compared with those which are natural

Now the task of Man, particularly of the Man of Truth, who aspires to become a minister of God and workman of the Lord, consists in examining well the words which correspond to these fruits, thoughts, or alliances; and this is what would pass in such a man if he is restored to his divine proportions, through the process of regeneration

Not a desire, but in obedience;

Not an idea, which is not a sacred communication;

Not a word, which is not a sovereign decree ;

Not an act, which is not a development and extension of the vivifying rule of the Word.

Instead of this, our desires are false, because they come only from ourselves.

Our thoughts are vague and corrupt, because we continually form adulterous alliances.

Our speech, or words, are without virtue or efficacy, because we allow them to be blunted every day by the sour, heterogeneous substances to which we continually apply them.

Our acts are insignificant and barren, because they can but be the results of our word.

In this melancholy list, there is nothing for the work. There is nothing for the glory and consolation of the Word, since there is nothing for the real Spiritual Ministry of Man.

Power of the enemy during night, in the absence of speech. Brave men afraid in the dark

The power to cast out the enemy, although, by virtue of our speech, one of our primitive rights, remains not only in suspense, but, from having fallen so long into disuse, has come to be considered as an imaginary thing; and here, independently of idleness, which draws worldly people together, we get an insight into the reason of their love for late hours, and their turning night into day; they are far from supposing that this inclination, to which they yield, has a very deep root.

If man were in his true law militant, he would watch much more at night, to drive the enemy away, than by day: this was the original object of the nocturnal prayers of religious affiliations, and this is still practised materially in our military encampments.

For, in both orders, it is in the night-time that the enemies commit their greatest ravages, as, in fact, it was during the sleep of the first man that he became his adversary's prey, and the divine covenant was forgot.

Without rising to this spiritual law militant, if man were, in his natural law, pure, he would sleep peacefully through the night, and derive from his rest a renewal of strength for his labours. Such is the case with the man of toil and the peasant, who, generally, are little troubled by the enemy during their sleep.

But the man of the world who feeds only on vacuity and corruption, and does not work, has no such quiet nights; and, as he pursues those false substances with which he allows himself to be continually impregnated, and over which the enemy's rights extend - which rights he enforces during the hours of night, more than in the day - this is why worldly people who are without the Word (true speech), and who run away from themselves, yet seek each other so eagerly during the night hours, because thereby, without knowing it, they diminish the force of their enemy's attacks.

It is, moreover, well known, that some very brave men, who continually face danger and death unmoved, will not enter a church, or a grave-yard, alone at night.

No doubt, these brave men have not all their rational principles developed; but the development of their reason would not alone enable them to triumph in such cases, if there is a real ground for the feeling of timidity which darkness inspires; and, what the savans call development of reason, in this respect, consists, not in their overcoming the obstacle, but in persuading themselves that it does not exist.

To speak the language of truth, we must say that this fear has positive grounds, and that what will raise us above it is that we should turn to the luminous eye of the Word, or the Spirit, which is developed and nourished with all the light that belongs to it.

There we shall learn that Nature was given to man to serve as a type and figure of the supreme truth which he can see no more; that when he is deprived of this type by darkness, and has not recovered his speech (*parole*), he is doubly separated from the truth; that having neither the copy nor the original near him, he is in complete privation, and pursued by vacuity with all its horrors. But this solution, though correct, is yet not the deepest. The following is deeper, and not less true.

Nature, a prison for the enemy, a preservative for man

Nature was intended to serve as a prison for the enemy, still more than for man; for to man it was given for a preservative also. When this preservative is not before his eyes, the thought of the enemy is secretly awakened in him; perhaps the enemy may more easily approach him when this obstacle is less active, and men cannot draw from their preservative all the support they would, were it visible to them. Thus, in this case, the presence of the smallest person is reassuring, because their combined forces can dispel the enemy. It is, then, this secret dread of the enemy which pursues men in the dark; and this dread can only be completely dissipated by the sense of a spiritual power, which they can find only in being truly born again, or in alliance with the Word.

When we recognize that the darkness of Nature acts so powerfully upon us, and the sight of it gives such a feeling of security, how can we avoid the conclusion that it was given to man, as much for his preservation and safety, as for the purpose of separating him from the Great Light?

The root-worm of Nature

It has also been remarked that fear has, in some people, produced worms. This opinion, which was advanced by Dr. Andry in his Treatise on the Generation of Worms in the human Body, quite agrees with true principles. They who have had opportunity to consider and understand the fundamental forms of Nature, are aware that the worm represents its root; showing the degradation this Nature has experienced, and the efforts it vainly makes to deliver itself from anguish, by circulating continually.

The healing power, which applied a refrigerant to this disorderly root, thus caused this root to be concealed from us during our animal existence. It is, as it were, absorbed by the harmonious, beneficent influence of this refrigerant. But when, from any cause whatever, this comes to be disturbed, and lose its dominion, then the root-worm naturally takes the rule, and shows itself. Now, of all our passions and weaknesses, fear, which is the one which most readily deprives us of speech, is also the one most apt to disturb the refrigerant, and consequently to give our root-worm and its productions a pre-eminence they would not otherwise have had, i.e., if we had been in possession of our speech.

Power of healing: Mesmerism, etc

As for the power of healing, which, however, should be considered but as a secondary privilege, even in our regenerate state, we may say, it becomes one of the snares which the enemy lays for us, when, in exercising this power, we make use of any extraordinary means; especially, if we use them of our own mere human will. When man does this by the Divine power and authority, he is perfectly in order, both as regards himself and the patient, because then the Supreme Will rules in both. We may add that then only can he be sure of success. When he proceeds by means of magnetism and somnambulism, he may injure his patient, even in curing him, for he knows not whether his sickness may not have had a moral object which will be neutralized by a premature cure; and therein the operator exposes himself greatly, because he ignorantly obtrudes himself into a higher ministry; he has, besides, always reason to doubt the result.

When he proceeds only by means of ordinary medicines, he does not sin, even though he be ignorant; because, as he then uses substances only of the inferior order, he acts only on the material man; then, if the sickness have a moral cause and object, the remedy will be without effect, because the moral order is higher. Thus, the common physician who employs his science prudently and modestly, committing the issue always to the Great Ruler, is more in order, and safer, than the magnetizer, who uses means of a higher class with too much confidence, levity, and pride.

Duties and responsibilities of literary men

From observations such as these, we learn to see how far man is from his object, when he abuses, as he does daily, a privilege of a higher order than that of curing bodily disease; I allude to that universal balm for the cure of our spiritual ailments, which ought to flow continually from the mouths of men of learning, and pens of writers, and which, in the way they dispense it, bears no better fruit than the Word does in the frivolous conversation of men.

So it is to you, poets and men of letters, I now address myself: you are looked upon as the lights of men's minds; you are supposed to supply by your gifts what is wanting to ordinary mortals. With what caution then should you not act towards them, if you were persuaded that men had to fulfil here on earth the sublime office of ministers of the Truth?

Misdirection of literary labour. Partisans of form and style

The sole aim of men of letters, the charm that attracts them, is style. When they can have it said of their works, that they are well written, they seem to have attained the height of their desire. This principle has taken such root amongst them, that one of their chiefs has not feared to say that style was every thing. Yes, for those who have only their external sense developed, and who find themselves full when this sense is satisfied; this belongs to our fibrous system, which is that of the present age. . . .

As for these noisy admirers of style, then, it is generally true that their outward senses only are struck, and are capable of being struck, owing to the direction they have given to their faculties. Their inner man is for very little in their pleasures, often for nothing at all. Their imagination is everything; and this, less in its rational and judicial character than in its sensible quality, which, in them, comes nearer to what is sensitive and conventional than to the living truth. Fine verses, beautiful periods, are enough to transport them; it matters not whether they result in falsehood or truth.

I, who render sincere homage to true literature, and who would see it applied to its legitimate object; I, who believe its powers to be as vast as the infinite itself, and that it was intended for the enjoyment of boundless privileges, it pains me when I see its partisans lower it to such inferior triumphs and restrict it to the balancing of words, when it ought to be employed in collecting the grand thoughts disseminated and lost in our desert, since our woeful dispersion. And when I see literary men, especially poets, confine themselves within conventional rules of versification, and the art of writing, and then glorify themselves for the happy, though transient sparks which, occasionally, they present to our eyes, it seems to me like a strong man tying all his members with chains, and thinking these trammels do him honour, when, notwithstanding their weight, he succeeds, now and then, in moving a finger.

The privilege of true literature is to be ruled by the laws of the Spirit itself, and to participate in the fecundity of the Word. This kind of literature is above all trammels, and has power to go to the very sanctuary of truth, to study what it ought to say, and how to express it.

But, what happens to these ardent partisans of form and style? When a work comes before them, which, in its form and diction, departs from their received conventions, they explain it by considerations of locality and climate, or condemn it at once by a judgment from which there is no appeal.

The pearl under their feet

Wandering, as we do, over the surface of the earth, we often walk over precious stones, concealed at a little depth beneath our feet, and we see them not; so it is with the literary, and men of the world, who are like them; when they read the writings of the friends of Truth, they see only sand and dust, and nothing of the fecund germinations under the surface. Oh, how hidden is God's work! Beginning with what is under the veil of Nature, down to what is concealed in the last ramifications of social things, and the darkness and ignorance of men.

This is why the bold expressions, the forcible and extraordinary images which fill the sacred books, and those of the friends of truth, have appeared, to vulgar eyes, as excusable only by attributing them to Oriental style. Why do these expressions appear so strange to these men of the stream? It is because they have lost the affections which would have produced these expressions in themselves; it is because they have buried themselves in lower regions, where contrasts are more tame, shades almost uniform, and the impressions they produce almost null.

Suspend your judgments, you who ought to be our guides to the Ministry of Truth!

Prophetic descriptions

Contemplate the great traveil of the Spirit and the Word; the shocks of agitated worlds falling one upon another, with a fearful crash; behold rivers of milk and honey descending from the eternal Jerusalem, to console and comfort the faithful servants of Truth.

Behold the enemy of this Truth incessantly trying to convert these wholesome streams into corrosive acids and poisons, that those servants may not be comforted, but driven to infidelity. Behold the human soul even rejecting these presents which are sent to it, and turning away from the feast of jubilee to feed upon serpents. Behold an awful justice destroying every where, with violence, all the agents of disorder, which appear as if coming from under the earth!

Behold the universe of Truth, deploying its wonderful powers, to attest its existence to the world, and compel it to confess there is a God! Behold, on the other hand, the universe of Falsehood, deploying its illusions and imposture, to attest that there is no God!

If you can remain cold and insensible before such a spectacle; if your thought, if your tongue, is not tortured, and do not take a corresponding style; then you will be right to consider the style of Scripture as the effect of climate.

But, if you elevate yourselves so as to be admitted by the Spirit to the living acts which compose these pictures; if you are present in spirit, like the prophets, at those terrible scenes which made the hairs of their heads stand on end, or at those enchanting ones which opened the divine marvels before their eyes, you will be no more surprised that men of God have drawn these pictures in such vivid colours, seeing you cannot help using the same colours yourselves, and you will think yourselves happy in finding them ready to your hand; - such will be your estimation of the things you have to describe.

Our writings take their colours from our affections

The art of writing, if it is not a gift from above, is a snare, and perhaps the most dangerous one our enemy can lay for us. He thereby seeks to fill us with pride, by tempting us to contemplate ourselves in our works; or else, to retard our progress by making us wait a long while for what we would write, and the way to write it. If we write only as we are led by inferior powers, he is too near to them for his influence not to be felt.

Our own affections are the substance that the spirit that rules us makes use of, whatever that spirit may be. When the pure Spirit wants to teach us, he takes the colour of these affections himself, to communicate his mind to us. St. Peter was hungry when the Spirit announced to him, in a figure, that he should not refuse to have intercourse with the Gentiles; and the angel took for emblem a cloth full of all sorts of quadrupeds, wild beasts, reptiles, and birds of the air.

With what care then should writers watch over their affections! For the spirit of lies can make use of them, as well as the Spirit of Truth, and lie neglects nothing to draw us to the foot of his altar. But, if we are careful to preserve order and purity in our affections, they will all attain their ends, without injuring each other; - on the contrary, they will mutually watch over and support each other.

The Redeemer also was hungry in the wilderness; the prince of lies availed himself of this affection to tempt him; but this law of matter, to which the Redeemer was subject, did not obscure, in him, the light of the Spirit; and the law of his intelligence triumphed over the ambuscades which the enemy laid for him, in a pure law of his matter.

Poets, men of letters, recognize here all that the Spirit can introduce into your most brilliant productions. All those images and figures you make use of are almost all composed and engendered from the habits, localities, manners, and affections of the people with whom you live.

They also, and still more frequently, descend from your own habits, haunts, manners, and affections; for every man is a people, a nation, a world, in himself. This is why you find it as easy to represent falsehood as truth.

Evil of depicting the faults of humanity

If, from the style, we pass to the substance, we shall see that writers, critics, even moralists, appear to be all occupied in describing the vices and defects of humanity; one would say that their only endeavour was to fill us with hatred towards our species; or, at least, to give us nothing but contempt for them, by showing only what is objectionable and repulsive in them. They little think how much they thereby injure both themselves and us.

In the first place, their pride is all that is gainer in this work; for it is hardly possible for them to know so well the faults of others, without secretly glorifying themselves, and intending to show, by such remarks, that they themselves are exempt from those faults.

A loving tolerance would tend to cure those faults,
and men would bow to their teachers

Secondly, these writers do not know how much more they would do for their own glory and our happiness, if they gave us rather the pleasing features of the human species, which may always be recognized, even in the mire in which it is buried. Our loving faculty and our tolerance would be gainers; and this ray of love which they kindled in us, would perhaps suffice to consume a good part of those poisonous and destructive weeds, which they are so fond of remarking upon, in man's domains.

Illustrious writers, renowned men of letters, you have no conception of how far you might extend your legitimate empire over us, if you thought more of directing it to our true profit. We should, of our own accord, offer to place ourselves under your yoke: we should wish for nothing better than to see you exercise and extend your gentle rule. The discovery of a single one of the treasures contained in the human soul, embellished by your rich colouring, would give you a sure title to our suffrage, and ensure your triumph.

The language of universal intelligence is the great desideratum

You say you want only to be understood: Well, can you succeed in this better than by trying to introduce our spirits into the regions of universal intelligence?

You would thus speak of, by, and for this intelligence; and, as it is the natural and eternal language of all that breathes and thinks, you would thereby exercise the true Ministry of the Word, and fulfil the expectations and satisfy the wants of all creatures. Now, this want is so deeply rooted and so imperious, that, if you succeeded in satisfying it by making yourselves understood, in thus speaking the language of universal intelligence, there is not a creature in existence that would not bless you.

Writers barely skim the domains of Truth, and prevent us
from entering in. Their hypocrisy

But, literary professors, and those generally who feed us with works of imagination, do not pass beyond the outskirts of Truth; they go round and round the domain continually; but they seem careful not to enter within, nor to allow their hearers to enter, lest her glory alone should shine.

Of all the celebrated works of the imagination of men, there is hardly one that is not built upon a frail and worn out foundation; to say nothing of those that are grounded on a blasphemy, or, at least, an impiety, the offspring of a proud hypocrisy. For, writers who speak of a providence, a morality, even of religion, are amenable to this reproach, if they are not in a condition to give an account of those great subjects of their speculations; if they bring them forward only to serve for ornament to their works, and food for their pride and if their morality is not grounded specially on a radical and complete renovation of our being, which is the only way we have for fulfilling the true object of our existence.

Writers cannot teach what they do not know. Secret of their false success

But, how can an author teach this doctrine if he do not understand it himself?

Unfortunately, what the frivolous or lost spirit (and where is the spirit that is not so?) asks from writers is, that they should enable him to taste the pleasures of virtue, without that continual and painful process of renovation, which we find it so difficult to resolve upon; and exhibit to him the unhappiness of crime as being secretly connected with the force of destiny, thereby allowing him to repose in his faults, and dispense with his primitive and original law, which would teach him even to master his destiny.

The charm which most of our novelists afford us arises only from this. They save us the fatigue of being virtuous by warming us with some images of virtue; they dispense us from uniting with our Principle, and allow us even to put Him aside altogether, by so constantly identifying us with what is not He. Thus, by indulging our cowardice, and making a smooth path for us, in the dark material order, they secure our suffrage, and their own success.

For this reason, the times most noted for great writers are not those of most progress in wisdom. An author makes an idea attractive by giving it a new turn: the reader catches it with great pleasure: but, the one satisfied with having advanced a fine maxim, and the other with feeling it, they both alike dispense with putting it in practice.

Sursum corda! Rescue the pearl out of this mire

When will the march of the human mind be directed towards a wiser and more profitable end? Must it ever be that literature in human hands should be the art of veiling falsehood, vice, and error, under a graceful or piquant exterior, instead of being the pathway of truth and virtue? How can Truth accompany such a course?

I say to you again, O clever writers, and celebrated men of letters, when will you cease to use your rich gifts so perniciously, so foolishly? Is gold intended only to ornament dresses for the stage? Should the thunderbolts that you might command, for the overthrow of the adversaries of our well-being, be expended in fireworks for the amusement of the idle crowd? In well-ordered states superfluities only are given to such things ; and all the useful productions of the country are to provide plenty and safety to the citizens, and means of defence to the government.

You say you endeavour to excite in our hearts, and transport our souls, with vivid emotions! Where can you find any thing more vivid than in the grand drama of MAN, which has never ceased to be played from the beginning; in the picture of those real pains and frightful dangers which assail the heedless family of Man, ever since his fall?

You would there meet with scenes ready made, yet always new, and which consequently would have a far greater hold upon us than all those which you compose with the sweat of your brows, and which feed you as well as ourselves with artificial images only, of the true emotions which you might awaken in us.

The Word, here, developing all its marvellous power before us, would make you indeed masters of all our emotions, and, at the same time, our benefactors. But how should you cause these prodigies to penetrate our souls, if you do not begin by familiarizing yourselves with them?

It is true that God, sometimes, lends us our own thoughts, that is, He leaves us to ourselves, like a master who gives some moments' relaxation and liberty to his servants, after they have done their work. One might even suppose this was the case with the vast majority of thinkers in the world, who, in fact, look like so many schoolboys in vacation. But these scholars, these servants, are in vacation, and at play, without having first attended their class, or done their master's work: they consume their moments of liberty in disputations, quarrels, and fighting one with another; often even speaking evil of their tutor, or plotting schemes of outrage against him.

What if I were to speak here of the scientific class of writers, who persist in leading our minds to nothing but superficial results, instead of directing them to the Principle and Centre? But I have said enough of them in different parts of this work.

As Man ought to be the sign of his Principle, which is God, every thing in his existence and in his ways ought to be Divine; everything should be DEOcratic for him, in his progress, and in all his measures, social, political, speculative, scientific, literary, or other.

Who does not perceive the darkness that is spread over the earth by the obscure speculations of man when left to his own spirit? And, in these deviations of literature, and the sciences, what has become of the Word? What has become of even the language of men?

Words have become in human languages, what thoughts have become in men's minds. They have come to be like so many dead burying the dead ; often, even the living; or, at least, many that would willingly live. So man buries himself every day with his own perverted words, which have entirely lost their meaning. And so he buries the Word likewise.

Religious literature

I have been considering polite literature only, so far, the chief object of which is to amuse; I have barely alluded to what we may call religious literature. We shall now devote ourselves more particularly to this, because it is still more closely allied to the Spiritual Ministry of Man, and the Word.

Writers of great talents have tried to describe the glorious results of Christianity. But, though I frequently read their works with admiration, yet, not finding in them what I think their subject requires, and seeing that they often give us eloquence in place of principles, I read them, at the same time, with caution. Nevertheless, if I make some remarks on their writings, it will certainly not be in either an atheistic or unbelieving spirit. I have long fought against the same enemies which these writers attack so courageously; and my principles, in this respect, have only been strengthened with age.

Nor will it be either as a man of letters, or as a scholar, that I shall offer my remarks; I leave this field to them, with all that can be gained in it. But as an amateur of Divine Philosophy, I enter the lists; and they ought not to distrust a colleague, who, under this title, loves, like themselves, the truth above all things.

Christianity and Catholicism or Churchism

The principal reproach I have to bring against them is, that, at every step, they confound Christianity with the Church (*Catholicisme*). From whence it follows, that their fundamental idea not being *d'aplomb*, they necessarily subject those who would go with them to many a jar, who are accustomed to travel on smoother roads.

For instance, I see literary professors of celebrity attribute to religion the works of a famous Bishop, who, on many notable occasions, greatly departed from the spirit of Christianity.

I see others, at one time, upholding the necessity of the mysteries [sacraments, etc.]; at another, trying to explain them; again stating that Tertullian's demonstration of the Trinity may be understood by the most simple. I see them boasting of the influence of Christianity on poetry, yet agreeing, in more than one instance, that poetry feeds only upon error.

I see them adrift on the subject of numbers, rejecting, with reason, the futile speculations which have flowed from the abuse of this science, and yet saying that three is not engendered; from which it would follow, according to the expression attributed to Pythagoras, that this number must be without a mother, whilst the generation of no number is more evident than that of this number three; two is clearly its mother, in all orders, natural, intellectual, or divine; with this difference, that in the natural order, this mother engenders corruption, as sin engendered death; in the intellectual, it engenders variability, as we may see by the instability of our thoughts; and, in the divine, it engenders fixity, as recognized in the Universal Unity.

In short, notwithstanding the brilliant effect their works may produce, I do not find that substantial nourishment in them that our intelligence requires, namely, the true spirit of Christianity; though I find the spirit of Catholicism.

Now, true Christianity is anterior, not only to Catholicism, but even to the name Christianity itself; the name of Christian is not once found in the Gospels; but the spirit of that name is very clearly expressed, and it consists, according to John (i. 12), in the power of becoming the sons of God; and the spirit of the Children of God, or of the Apostles of Christ, who believed on Him, is shown, according to Mark (xvi. 20), by the Lord working in them, and confirming the word with signs following.

In this point of view, to be truly in Christianity, would be to be united with the Spirit of the Lord, and to have perfected or consummated our alliance with Him.

Now, in this respect, the true genius of Christianity would be less in being a religion, than as being the term and place of rest of all religions, and of all those laborious ways through which men's faith, and their need of being purged from their stains, oblige them to walk daily.

And it is very remarkable that, in the whole of the four Gospels, which are founded on the Spirit of true Christianity, the word religion is not to be met with once; and in the writings of the Apostles, which complete the New Testament, only four times.

Once in Acts (xxvi. 5 - [in Eng. version; also, Gal. i. 13, 14]) - where the writer speaks of the Jewish religion.

The second, in Colossians (ii. 18) where the Apostle incidentally condemns the religion [Eng. vers. Worship] of angels.

And the third and fourth, in St. James (i. 26, 27) where he merely says: "If any man bridle not his tongue, but deceive his own heart, this man's religion is vain"; and, "Pure religion, and undefiled before God, the Father, is to visit the fatherless and widows in their affliction, and to keep himself unspotted from the world"; examples in which Christianity seems to tend more towards its divine sublimity, or place of rest, than to clothing itself in the dress we are accustomed to call religion.

Here, then, is a table of differences between Christianity and Catholicism.

Christianity is nothing but the spirit of Jesus Christ in its fulness, after this Divine Physician had ascended all the steps of his mission, which be commenced at man's fall, when he promised that the woman's seed should crush the serpent's head. Christianity is the complement of the priesthood of Melchisedek; it is the soul of the Gospel; and it causes the living waters which nations thirst for, to circulate in that Gospel.

Catholicism [the Church], to which the title of religion properly belongs, is a way of trial and traveil to arrive at Christianity.

Christianity is the region of emancipation and liberty: Catholicism is only the seminary of Christianity; the region of rules and discipline for the neophyte.

Christianity fills all the earth alike with the Spirit of God. Catholicism fills only a portion of the globe, notwithstanding its title of universal.

Christianity carries our faith up to the luminous region of the Eternal Divine Word; Catholicism limits this faith to the written word, or tradition.

Christianity shows us God openly, in the heart of our being, without the help of forms and formulas. Catholicism leaves us at war with ourselves, to find God hid under ceremonies.

Christianity has no mysteries; the very name is repugnant to it; for, essentially, Christianity is evidence itself, and universal clearness, Catholicism is full of mysteries, and its foundation is veiled. The sphinx may be placed at the outrance of temples built by men's hands; it cannot be seated in the heart, which is the real entrance to Christianity.

Christianity is the fruit of the true: Catholicism can only be the dressing.

Christianity makes neither monasteries nor anchorites, because it can no more isolate itself than can the light of the sun; and because, like the sun, it seeks to shine everywhere. Catholicism peopled the deserts with solitaries, and the towns with religious communities; the former, to devote themselves more easily to their own salvation, the latter to present to the corrupt world some images of virtue and piety, to rouse it in its lethargy.

Christianity has no sect, since it embraces unity, and unity being alone, cannot be divided in itself. Catholicism has seen a multitude of schisms and sects spring from its bosom, which have promoted the reign of division, rather than that of concord; and Catholicism, even when it supposes itself in the highest degree of purity, can find hardly two of its members who believe alike.

Christianity would never have made the Crusades; the invisible cross it carries in its bosom has no object but the relief and happiness of all creatures. It was a false imitation of Christianity, to say the least, which invented the Crusades; Catholicism adopted them afterwards: but, fanaticism commanded them;

Jacobinism composed them; anarchy directed them; and brigandism executed them.

Christianity has declared war only against sin; Catholicism, against men.

Christianity marches only by sure and continuous experience; Catholicism marches only by authority and institutions; Christianity is the law of faith; Catholicism is the faith of the law.

Christianity is the complete installation of man's soul into the rank of minister or workman of the Lord; Catholicism limits man to the care of his own spiritual health.

Christianity continually unites man with God, as being by their nature two inseparable beings; Catholicism, while it uses the same language, yet so feeds man with mere forms, that it makes him lose sight of its real object, and contract many habits which do not always turn to his profit or real advancement.

Christianity rests immediately on the unwritten Word; Catholicism rests on the written Word, or Gospel, in general; and on the mass, in particular.

Christianity is an active and perpetual, spiritual and divine sacrifice, either of the soul of Jesus Christ, or of our own; Catholicism, which rests particularly on the mass, presents only an ostensible sacrifice of the body and blood of the Redeemer.

Christianity can be composed of the holy race of primitive man alone, the true sacerdotal race. Catholicism, resting particularly on the mass, was, as Christ's last Passover, at the merely initiatory degrees of this priesthood; for, when he said to his disciples, Do this in remembrance of me, they had already received power to cast out devils, to cure sicknesses, and raise the dead; but they had not yet received what was most important for the fulness of the priesthood; since the consecration of a priest consists in the transmission of the Holy Spirit, and the Holy Spirit was not yet given, because the Redeemer was not yet glorified (John vii. 39).

Christianity becomes a continual increase of light, from the moment the soul of man is admitted into it. Catholicism, which has made the holy supper its highest and most sublime degree of worship, has allowed a veil to be thrown over this ceremony, even inserting, as I have observed before, in the canon of the mass, the words *mysterium fidei*, which are not in the Gospel, and are contrary to the universal light of Christianity.

Christianity belongs to eternity; Catholicism to time.

Christianity is the term; Catholicism, with all the imposing majesty of its solemnities, and the sacred grandeur of its prayers, is only the means.

Finally, it is possible that there may be many Catholics, who, yet, are unable to judge what Christianity is; but it is impossible for a true Christian not to be able to judge what Catholicism is, and what it ought to be.

Christianity and Art

When credit is given to Christianity for the progress of arts, and particularly for the perfecting of literature and poetry, it is an honour which it is very far from claiming. The Word did not come into the world to teach men to make poetry, or to distinguish themselves in literary composition; it came, not that man's spirit might be exalted in the eyes of his fellow creatures, but that the Eternal and Universal Spirit might shine throughout infinity.

How is it that Christianity has no need of all these talents of men? Because it dwells amongst divine wonders, and, to sing of these, it has no need to seek how to express itself; they supply everything, the affections, the idea, and the expression. And Christianity alone can answer the remark that eloquent writers have made: "We know not where the human mind has found it; no way is known to such sublimity!" For, in this order of things, the human mind has sought nothing; the Spirit of Christianity has given all.

The origin and spirit of art and literature are pagan, not Christian, nor Catholic

But, more: Catholicism, to which the name of Christianity has been too readily given, even Catholicism is not what has produced the development of literature and art. Neither by it, nor in its fold, have modern poets and artists been formed: they studied the *chef d'oeuvres* of antiquity, which was pagan, and tried to copy them; but, as they lived in the midst of institutions of Catholicism, it was natural that their works should bear very generally on religious subjects. Nor is it surprising that, on approaching these religious subjects, they should discover some of those real beauties with which they are indirectly connected, and some of the treasures of the Word, of which the Bible is full; and that they should have endeavoured to apply these treasures and beauties to the kind of art they cultivated, hoping thereby to add to its glory; as, in fact, every art has been embellished by them.

But, so far is it from true, that Catholicism was the principle and cause of the embellishment of the arts and literature; that, on the contrary, it was these arts and literature that suggested the idea of their being employed for the embellishment of Catholicism. For, Catholicism, admiring, with reason, those *chefs d'oeuvres* of art and literature, soon sought to appropriate them; the one for the ornamentation of its temples, the other for the nourishment of the eloquence and glory of its orators and writers.

In fact, if there had been no Phidias and Praxiteles, is it at all certain that we should have had a Raphael and a Michelangelo, and their *chefs d'oeuvres*, the subjects of which they chose in the religious order? If there had been no Demosthenes and Cicero, who knows if we should have had a Bossuet and a

Massillon? If there bad been no Homer and Virgil, a Dante, a Tasso, a Milton, or a Klopstock would probably never have thought of clothing the religious events they celebrated with the colours of poetic fiction because the purer genius of Catholicism itself would have opposed these fictions and works of imagination.

But, if the empire of Constantinople had not been overthrown, would Catholicism at all have boasted of so many marvels and geniuses of all kinds, of which it became the centre and focus after that event? And, if Italy had not received the brilliant inheritance, would France, which, in respect of writers and orators, has been the brightest crown of Catholicism, have attained so high a degree of glory of this kind?

We may confidently reply in the negative, and affirm that, without the age of Julius II. and Leo X., Catholicism would not have developed the talents, and gathered the laurels, which distinguished it under Louis XIV. But, as all these adventitious supports, these arts, and models of antiquity, in eloquence and literature, contributed only a borrowed light or life to Catholicism, inclining it rather towards human glory than to that solid and substantial glory of which they knew nothing, they could not bring it any lasting advantage.

So their relations being frail and precarious, literature and art were not long before they left Catholicism behind, and carried off the crown for themselves. The more progress they made, the more Catholicism receded; and we have seen how much their empire increased in the eighteenth century, and how much Catholicism declined; and, even now, notwithstanding the efforts of government to re-establish the Church, they are still far from yielding the field: - Now this is a triumph they would not have gained so easily over Christianity, or the Word.

If we go farther back, we shall see that arts and literature were always subsidiary to Catholicism, and never its wards or pupils. During the first centuries of our era, the holy fathers, who already retained little more than the reflection and mere history of true Christianity, lived amidst the literary monuments of Greece and Alexandria; they derived from thence the impressive, though unequal character of their writings.

They even took from celebrated philosophers of antiquity many particulars of an occult doctrine, which they explained only by the letter, as they no longer possessed the key of true Christianity. Thus, they were, for the most part, these philosophers' disciples, when they ought to have been their masters.

Catholicism takes the complexion of the age and circumstances

When the dark ages came, when fine arts and belles lettres, and numerous monuments of the human mind were destroyed, Catholicism also lost what embellishment it had received from them; having no fixity in itself, being ever moveable, and dependent on external impressions, it was unable to resist the flood.

After being erudite with the Platos, Aristotles, and Ciceros, it became arrogant and rude with the rude and arrogant nations which inundated Europe. It became barbarous and savage with the savage and barbarous; and, not having, on the one hand, either the gentle light, or, resistless power of Christianity; nor, on the other, the restraint of letters, and example of polished nations, it became remarkable only for the fury of its fanaticism, and the delirium of its despotism. It may be said that such was its existence for nearly ten centuries.

Literary art totally disconnected from Christianity as well. Religious literati

If, from all these facts, it appears that Catholicism never had any relation to the arts and literature but that of dependence, what shall we say of Christianity, which not only never had any direct relation with them, but never was in any way dependent upon them? To realize the immense distance there is between arts and literature on the one hand, and Christianity on the other, we need only repeat that, in these works of man, it is man's spirit, and sometimes less than this, which does all; and that, in Christianity, the Eternal Word rules alone.

I know how little acceptable this idea will be to religious literati, even believers, notwithstanding their efforts to glorify what they call Christianity; but the course which the most remarkable amongst these learned believers have taken obliges me to insist more and more upon it, because, while they seem to believe in Christianity, they perhaps really only believe in Catholicism.

One of these eloquent writers says, with tender sensibility, that he wept, and then believed! Alas, that he should not have had the happiness to have begun by being sure! How he would have wept afterwards!!

Nevertheless, he seems more advanced than most of his compeers, who are devoted, heart and mind, to literal Christianity, or Catholicism, which is the same thing.

In the midst of the ecstasies that the famous poets he reviews excite in this writer, flashes of truth and candour escape him, which demonstrate that, naturally, he agrees entirely with me; and that only by accident he deviates from my system. This we see clearly in what he says on the history of mankind, as briefly told in Genesis. He cannot restrain himself from exclaiming, "We find something so grand and extraordinary in this scene of Genesis, that it eludes all critical explanations; admiration wants words, and art returns to dust". I will add, on this subject of art, would to God it had never come out of the dust; for it ought to have no other place of abode, and it ought always to leave the field free for the Word.

Let us see what art really has done by approaching these high truths.

The eloquent writer in question is transported at Adam's awaking from his sleep, and says that Milton would never have reached these heights if he had not known true religion: and I answer that, if Milton had known true Christianity, the Word, he would have painted Adam in other colours.

Art has no secrets but to make comparisons between subjects with which it is acquainted. Art teaches that a child is a creature that "awakes to life, opens its eyes, and knows not whence it comes". After this pattern Milton drew Adam's picture: he makes him only a great child, with this difference, that he gives him a sublime sense of his own nature, and eminent powers for giving names to things, which the child does not possess; yet, the father having had them, it would be hard to say why the child should not have them also, since the fruit should be as the tree.

Now, from the child and the savage, materialists and ideologists have drawn their systems of sensation, origin of language, etc., and, stopping there, they have ended by animalizing our whole being. But the Bible (for we speak of this here), which it is pretended was Milton's guide, shows Adam in another aspect.

In the first place, we may believe that, in coming out of his Maker's hands, Adam was not subject to sleep, since it was only after he had given things their names that the Creator sent a sleep upon him, during which the woman was taken out of his bones, or his strong essences.

Secondly, it is probable that this sleep, and extraction of the woman from his side, was the consequence of some change already commenced in Adam ; since the Creator had said (in the first chapter), when the creation was ended, that" all that He had made was very good"; and then He says (in the second chapter), that "it was not good for man to be alone".

Thirdly, whether this giving of names was performed by Adam on his leaving his Maker's hands, or only after that change had commenced, it is certain, according to the text, that it was anterior to his sleep.

This being the case, Adam must have then enjoyed great light and vast knowledge, since the Creator had established him over all the works of His hand, and installed him in the garden of delights, and charged him to cultivate it, committing all the plants with which it was filled to his care, even the tree of the knowledge of good and evil, of which He forbad him to eat.

Thus Adam had no need to awake unto life, but, on the contrary, it was he who awoke life in the creatures ; which is very different from what happens with children; but art concealed these things from Milton, and left him to his imagination.

It was, also, according to art, that he describes the loves of Adam and Eve, supposing them to be in their first heavenly state, which they were not. For he recognizes their sexes, and celebrates the consummation of their marriage, which could take place only according to the law of animals, and which produced such bad fruit in the person of Cain.

Now, how could they know pure love, if they were already under the animal law? And how could they have known animal love, if they had not known their bestial organs, since we see, in man, that his epoch of love is when his bestiality speaks? But how could they have known this bestiality if they had not been guilty, since, according to the text, it was only then they knew they were naked? And, if they were guilty, what becomes of their heavenly loves, their purity, and their innocence, of which the poet draws such brilliant pictures?

Doubtless, they had not then that immodest modesty, which is only a secondary sentiment derived from education; but they had a deep sense of shame, arising from the comparison of their present bestial state with that they had just lost; for then their eyes were opened to their vile, degraded state, and closed to the divine wonders.

Milton knew nothing of the gradations of the sin of our first parents. One of these gradations may, indeed, have permitted the enjoyment of some delicious moments in the garden of Eden, after the change had commenced; but they were then more careful about their Sovereign's commands, and the prohibition He had laid upon them, than about their own charms and loves; and, when this degree had passed, they would be too much occupied with their laborious and painful situation to converse very quietly and tenderly together; a thing suitable only to the blind and idle lovers of our world, who have nothing else to do.

Milton, then, copied those loves from the loves of earth, although he embellished them magnificently. Yes, his long description of the loves of Adam and Eve proves that the poet had but half dipped his pen in the truth. The Scriptures are more concise in details of this nature. In the case before us they merely say that Adam knew Eve, that she conceived and brought forth Cain, saying, "I have gotten a man from the Lord". I repeat, then, that as Christianity, or the Word, would not be honoured by having contributed to the birth of all these fictions of Milton, so it is far from claiming them.

It is not that, as an amateur of belles-lettres, I do not admire Milton's poetic talent, and the magnificent scenes his pencil produced; I am even well pleased, in the cause of religion, that he traces to us some shades of celestial happiness, and pure love, which serves for its basis; and, for the sake of these sweet pictures, I forgive his anachronisms: but, as a lover of truth, I regret that he, as well as all his compeers, does not describe things more exactly, poets being supposed to speak the language of the gods. The poet's license allows him to fill up, at his pleasure, the canvas of the history of men; but this is not permitted in the history of Man, of whom the Truth alone has a right to speak.

These few examples will suffice to show the immense distance there is between Christianity and the art of the religious literati, and to fix the limits of the influence of Christianity on poetry. Our remarks will apply to any of the great works our eloquent critic passes in review; to say nothing of the fact that many of their authors, notwithstanding the splendid religious colouring of their pencils, not only did not believe in Christianity, that is, in the Eternal Word, but they did not believe even in Catholicism, which should have been its representation on the earth.

Sacred narrative not embellished by the poets. Racine

Generally speaking, I find that when poets and literary men handle the treasures of Holy Writ, they alter them without embellishing them; either mixing false colours with them, or weakening them by diffuseness, not being guided by the true spirit of Christianity; and they have never shone so well as when they have been satisfied with giving these treasures in their original simplicity and literal integrity. Why is 'Athalie' considered a *chef-d'oeuvre* of perfection? Because, in this work, Racine did nothing but copy Scripture.

Learned critics may extol the art with which he contrived his poem as they will, the vulgar know nothing of these secrets, but are quite alive to the simple and sublime beauties contained in Scripture; and the more nakedly these are presented the more they are sure to be struck by them. Only see what an effect these words produced on the stage, which are to be found on every page of the Bible: "I fear God . . . I have no other fear!"

Literary art unprofitable even on the stage

But, if we would judge how little profit these riches, in the hands of the literary, bring to Christianity, we have only to see the small effect which the finest thoughts and maxims, and most appropriate to every true want of our being, produce upon the stage. The spectator who hears them, but who, like the poet, has only the outward man open in him, experiences a slight impression, a sort of sentimental emotion, which affects him for the moment; but, having no deep roots, and being very like a muscular sensation, it terminates at the extremities of his nerves by a clapping of his hands, and evaporates in the air. So, when the piece is over, the spectators disperse, to plunge again in their customary vanities, without so much as remembering what they felt, still less profiting by it.

Now, what passes with the spectator at the theatre, happens likewise to the reader of fine works of poetry and eloquence, founded on the riches of the Bible, or the sacredness of Catholicism. It would be still worse if they spoke of true Christianity, or the Eternal Word, and Eternal Liberty; for, most assuredly, not a word of their discourse would be understood. And, on this subject of the Word, I again refer them to the German author of whom I have frequently spoken in this work.

The aim of literary art is to give emotion and receive praise. Truth suffers

Literary men, in general, whether they write for the stage, or sentimentally, any way seem to aim at nothing but the art of moving us, without at all thinking of the purpose for which our emotions must have been given us. As they seek to please us, and make us praise them at the same time, they are careful to lead us only into such emotions as suit their purpose. The spectator and the reader understand them; if they were led into more serious emotions, such as would constrain them at all, they would not listen to them; and the writers, on their side, have no objection to amuse them with figures of the truth, but they would fear to take them to the truth itself; for then they would have no more to do, seeing that the truth itself would do all.

So Truth shudders continually at the little profit she receives from the marvellous talents which great writers and poets display, who, if they sometimes approach her confines, it is only to absorb and bury her in the region of vain appearances, which is not her own; and what I here say of the literati generally, applies unfortunately, but too well, to religious writers also; therefore, in their hands, their science has come to be merely an art. With this art, its forms and precepts, and its stores of rules and formulas, we might undoubtedly produce, in a manner, some works, if not of solidity and grace, at least correct, as a piece of music may be played with dice; but true genius, especially religious genius, does not shut itself in formulas. In a word, they have studied how to give us emotions, and tickle us, as restaurateurs study the art of producing sensations on our palates: both of them would be afraid of using anything that would produce sensations too strong, and that would be likely to effect a purification and renovation of our digestive organs; they leave these cares to those who take charge of our health; yet, from the way we are living in this lower world, it may be granted that dispensers of health are much more needed than restaurateurs.

The reason why literature and poetry, even of a religious character, yield so little profit to the cause of Truth, is, that those who cultivate and profess them, do not so much as imagine that this Truth might really be their guide, and that themselves ought to be nothing less than her organs and ministers; and, conceiving nothing grander than a fine poem, they really believe that man has nothing more glorious to do on this earth than to carry off the palm from all competitors in that race.

The laws of Truth are independent of art and forms, of poets and critics alike

In this persuasion they exert themselves, and redouble their efforts to fix rules and laws, whilst all they required would be simply to follow those dictated by

Truth, from all eternity. They labour hard to bring their own industry and their own mind into action; whereas the first thing they should do, ought to be to forget this dark mind of man, and very humbly to implore the favour of Truth, that she would condescend to admit them into her service.

It is very doubtful, I admit, whether she would then require them to make poems; and, if it should so happen, it would be only after having effectually laboured in her work; for she would order them to celebrate facts which concerned her only; deeds of which she had made them agents, and which would therefore be their own doing; seeing that no bard can sing of deeds so well as the doer himself. For this reason, a lover of religious poetry has said that a poet,

> *Qui du Suprême Agent serait vraiment l'Oracle,*
> *Ne ferait pas un vers qu'il n'eût fait un miracle!*

When, therefore, I see our eloquent writer extol the great address with which Milton seized the first mystery of Scripture, wherein the Most High, allowing Himself to be moved with compassion, grants salvation to mankind; when I see him speak of the grand machinery of Christianity, and tell us that Tasso wanted boldness, and touched sacred things only with trembling; when I see him observe that all Christian poets have failed in describing heaven; some through timidity, like Tasso and Milton; others through fatigue, like Dante ; through philosophy, like Voltaire; or through superfluity, like Klopstock, I cannot refrain from saying to him in my turn

"Does Truth require address? Can Truth fail? Can Truth be mistaken? If Christianity had inspired all those poets, would you have had those faults to find with them? I reproach them with these faults, as you do but then I conclude that they had no positive experience of all those sublime subjects which they attempted to describe; I conclude that their own thoughts furnished them with as many falsities, on these subjects, as realities; I conclude that Christianity was not their guide, or that they had not attended to her lessons, and that they copied even badly; for Christianity knows no mixture, and states nothing but according to real facts, and experimental science, above the reach of falsehood, and all phantoms of human imagination; and because, what machinery it possesses, it trusts only to those who really believe in it, and are in condition to value it, and set it in motion.

"Do not therefore compare things so remote from each other as poetic productions and Christianity, for it would be an offence to the latter to make it a party to the fabrication of lies. Have you not scope enough to develop your beautiful picture of the benefits conferred by religion upon the world, in the moral ideas it has introduced into all classes of society, and even into politics; in the admirable and useful institutions it has founded, such as the orders of chivalry, hospitals, and charitable establishments of all kinds; in the splendid comparisons you may make between Christian people and those who are not Christian; or in the touching accounts of our missionaries? All these are things in which religion shows itself in act, and has nothing to feign or invent; whereas poets feign or invent every thing, without the necessity of performing any thing, or showing any virtues, since all their endeavour is only to enchant us.

"As for the failure of Christian poets, in their pictures of heaven, I agree that you have given good reasons for it; also that, in general, it is much easier to draw pictures of misery; but, St. Paul gives a far better reason, in telling of the ineffable things he heard in the third heaven, and in keeping silence thereupon namely, that human tongues could not express them".

Invocation of poets, addressed to the astral heaven only

What afflicts me is, to see poets wishing to describe what they do not know, and what they could not speak of, if they did. I know that poets have sometimes felt the necessity of being guided by Truth, for they are supposed to invoke her under the name of their muse; but is not this only in idea, and because it is etiquette, even with religious poets? And, do they very firmly believe in her existence at all.

It was, no doubt, the secret feeling of the necessity of Truth, which made Boileau say, at the commencement of his "Art Poétique",

> C'est en vain qu'au Parnasse un téméraire auteur, etc. ... .
> S'il ne sent pas du ciel l'influence secrète,
> Si son astre, en naissant, ne la formé poète.

But the German author I have mentioned will tell those who read him what heaven is to be understood by these words of Boileau, by showing us the universal power of the astral kingdom under which mankind have fallen since sin entered into the world, and which we must pass through, and subjugate, if we would overcome: which is the more difficult, that the enemy has occupied all the positions and rules in all the kingdoms of this world, as he himself said to the Lord, in the Gospel.

We may judge how often Milton may have been under the influence of this astral heaven, since he could work at his poems only at certain seasons of the year. Now, if Milton, who, besides this astral influence, also received directly some higher lights, as parts of his writings would seem to indicate, - if this author, I say, was often the victim of this lower astral influence, which is always blind, and sometimes false and corrupt, what must we think of others, who, like him, were subject to the astral influence, without having the compensations that he had?

The marvelous is everything in an epic.
The highest order of the marvelous

I regret to see our eloquent writer reproach Milton and Dante for having made the marvelous the subject, and not the machinery, of their poems; as if there were nothing marvelous but magical machines; or, to speak more correctly, as if every thing were not magical, and therefore marvelous, from the radical eternal Source of all things, to their complete development in every region, and their final return to their principle; and as if the marvelous were not therefore really the principle, the subject, and the machinery of every truly epic work.

For, if the poet chose for his subject some merely historical fact of earthly order, and wished to connect with it some kind of the marvelous other than that of fables and fairy tales, he would have no choice but to begin by raising his heroes to the rank of demigods, as all epic poem makers do; then, entering into the spirit of true Christianity, which makes of man nothing less than a son of God, and an image of God, he might, without antiphrasis, and he ought even of necessity, to develop all the marvelous machinery which constitutes the marvelous existence of all being, from God to the animalcule, and which, by its lively and constant action, entertains the ineffable harmony of all things. Now in this way, what could they offer us more marvelous than the active treasures of the Word?

Descriptive poetry

As to this eloquent writer's persuasion that Christianity has given birth to, and been favourable to descriptive poetry, by extending the harmonies of religion to natural objects, I think that in this, he has judged things rather as they might be, than as they are.

Our most distinguished authors in descriptive poetry have drawn rather from the natural sciences, and the prevailing taste for physical knowledge, than from religious causes.

On this account, descriptive poetry will probably have done more to retard the reign of Truth than the mythological system of antiquity. In fact, mythology, by placing imaginary genii every where in Nature, presented at least an image of the real powers by which Nature is governed, under the eye of Eternal Wisdom; instead of this, our poets, who only go with the stream, offer us, here and there, no doubt, and as in extract, some traces of religious teaching, but we can never be sure that, for them, they were not quite problematical; they give us physical descriptions and details in abundance, as the learned in material things always do, and thereby bring us nearer to darkness, rather than nearer to light.

There is another kind of description which seems to be equally abused: namely, those of clever literary critics who strain themselves to dissect beautiful passages of great authors ; and I cannot refrain from telling them: "if these passages are beautiful in themselves, I do not require your assistance to enjoy them; still less do I require your dissections; I should have less pleasure if I knew the reason why I have it. You cheat me by chilling my enjoyments, as descriptive poets of Nature do every day, by giving me their personal fictions for her realities"...

Demonstrative evidences of God and the soul. Atheists and materialists

Again: Before showing so eloquently, as our author does, the pre-eminence of religion, or Catholicism, over all other religions, he should begin by demonstrating true and primitive Christianity or the Word; for it seems to me that, in his answers to the atheists, he omits precisely what is most essential.

The principal difficulty, in my opinion, is, not to prove to unbelievers the existence of God, nor even that of the soul; especially if proofs are taken in the Spirit-Man. Many philosophers, taking this light for their guide, have proved these two facts, by reasons such as the sect of atheists require; that is, such as positive minds may compare with what they call demonstrations of $A + B$.

And there is nothing to wonder at in this, since, in spite of all the reveries of atheists and materialists, the only inability which we can recognize in God, is, that He is unable to conceal Himself; and the soul of man, which is His image, shows itself continually in all our acts, even in the very effort we make to deny it.

But it is not these two points which obfuscate the refractory, so much as the whole religious edifice which it is sought to raise on these foundations; and, to prove these two points, is not to prove the positive consequences which are deduced from them.

In fact, reason and logic prove merely the existence of God and the soul. The object of religion should be to prove their mutual relations, and bring them together; this union cannot take place without an inward concurrence on our part, and the voluntary action of our being. The mere belief in the existence of God and the soul demands no such concurrence.

Inadequacy of ordinary teaching for the conviction of Deists

For this reason, it is easier to cure a materialist, or an atheist, than a deist. In truth, how can a deist be persuaded of the natural source of religion, its utility, or its necessity, but by showing it as grounded on the dark and infirm condition of fallen man? But how shall we do this, after all the mischief which human philosophy has done to man? Where shall we find men in condition to lead their fellow creatures this way'?

We need not then be surprised, that the daily efforts made in behalf of religion bear so little fruit. Let us at once confess that, to combat materialism and atheism, the ordinary religious teachers are so far provided with but feeble arms, since they prove God only by the universe, and souls by theological books. How then would they prove them if there were no books, and no universe ?

These teachers do not study eternal things; they do not study the Word; they do not study its universal action, nor why this action alone gives life. How then should they see the Divine Source of thought and immortal man? How should they see his connection with his Principle? How should they perceive the profound aim of religion, and teach us to admire our God, in His restorative economy, and sublimity of Wisdom?

Demonstration which religion requires. Proof positive

It remains then to demonstrate directly to the refractory the great lapse or change that has happened to the human family, and the nature of this change; the help which Supreme Goodness has sent from the beginning, and still sends continually, for the solace of mortals in their misfortune; the character of this help or of religion in general; and, lastly, the rights which the ministers of this religion claim exclusively to direct their fellow-creatures, and the means they pretend they possess, to give rest to troubled souls, and enable them to fulfil the Creator's laws.

Now, religious philosophers have not proved these important articles by their $A + B$, as they have the others; yet, if all these things are true, they also must have their positive proofs, since everything must make its own revelation.

But these proofs must take a new character as their object becomes more substantial, and employs a greater number of our faculties. Nevertheless, they ought no more to depend upon the will of men than the other two; nor should they repose upon any literal expressions; still less, on the dogmatic teaching of others; they ought to bear their own evidence in themselves.

Intellectual mathematics

Our eloquent writer has acknowledged that there is an intellectual geometry; and, whatever may be said, I believe this intellectual geometry was more familiar to certain ancient philosophers than it was to Leibnitz, Descartes, Newton, or even to Pascal, who came nearer to it than the other three.

Thus, if there is an $A + n$ to prove the existence of God, and the immateriality of the Spirit-Man, there must be an $A + n$ to prove our degradation, and consequently religion, which is its remedy; as there must also be an $A + B$ to prove the efficacy of this remedy, which cannot fail to be specific; for if the will of free beings may neutralize it in regard to themselves, and prevent its operating for them, they cannot prevent its operating against them. Now, all these kinds of proofs, though different from each other, must each be positive in its kind.

Rational, affectional, and experimental proofs positive

The first of these proofs, or that which has for object the existence of God, and the Spirit-Man, may be called a rational and intellectual proof-positive; because it belongs, in fact, to simple reflection and reasoning.

The second, which refers to our degradation, and, therefore, to religion, we will call a sentimental or affectional proof-positive, because it necessarily requires that man should put in action a new faculty, besides that of judgment; as the medical faculty makes a man sensible that he is attacked with a serious illness, thereby causing him uneasiness and alarm about the danger he is in, and points out, at the same time, the remedy that may be useful to him; whilst, to know and possess medicinal science, the student has only to make use of his reason.

Lastly, the third proof, the object of which is to demonstrate the powers of the ministers of religion, and the superiority and efficacy of religion itself, we will call an experimental proof-positive; because it is a question of facts; and because, taking possession of all our faculties, it confirms the two preceding proofs, the sentimental proof-positive and the intellectual proof-positive. If we transpose these different kinds of proofs, or employ only one, where all are required, how can we expect the adversaries to submit?

It is not very difficult, as I have asserted, to demonstrate the necessary and exclusive supremacy of One Superior Being, as well as our radical connection with Him; without which we could not so much as question His existence, nor even think of Him.

In fact, we can really call great a being only who is so much so that none other can surpass, or even equal him. Now, in this sense, there is none great but God; because, Himself being all, it is impossible for any other being, not only ever to exceed Him in greatness, but ever even to attain to an equality. For this reason, after God, all greatness can be only relative; and, for us, everything is only proportional; but, at the same time, and for the same reason, we must have been gifted with some positive means of demonstrating His generative influence in all creatures, and His restorative influence in ourselves; and of showing, by the fact itself, and not by books, the exclusive supremacy of the Being of beings, and the effective relations which the Word continually seeks to establish with us.

The sublime is God, and what connects us with Him

It was, no doubt, this idea that led me to say, in 'L'Homme de Désir', No. 166, that "the sublime was God, and all that connected us with Him". This intelligence came to me after having heard a celebrated Professor say that the sublime was indefinable.

I have since read in the works of the same Professor "what is beautiful, or great, or strong, admits the more or less; the sublime does not", etc.

I here saw that our ideas coincided, except that I am persuaded that what we both believe of the sublime may be extended to the other qualities, virtues, &c., which he excludes as well; for, in God only these things are positive; and the Word is the universal proclaimer of these positive sublimities.

I may here add an important remark, which is, that nothing can really appear to us sublime, but by communicating to us an extract of what passes in the superior, divine region, which is the source of all sublimities, the source of everything. Augustus captivates us in saying: "Cinna, let us be friends; it is I who ask thee:" because this is the positive and constant language of Eternal Truth to Man; and the same may be deduced from all other examples of the sublime, in words or deeds. They do nothing but lift the veil, and open the inexhaustible focus of all the sublime acts and thoughts in which our being has its roots. Now, if we are borne never so little towards that region, so as to hear its language spoken, as this is the language of our own nature, it is not surprising that it should enchant us.

We see God in every thing

On this principle, which would deserve being treated *ad hoc*, and is capable of being extended , by reason of the infinite number of subjects it embraces, and testimonies which depose in its favour, we can understand why Malebranche said that "we see every thing in God"; but we conceive also that his idea might be conveyed under a less gigantic form; and, if not simplified, at least brought more within reach of our weak minds, so as to shine upon them with a softer light than that dazzling flame which blinds them.

This form would be to say: "we really see God in every thing"; and, in truth, we should see nothing in any object whatever, if the Principle of all qualities, that is, God, did not move actively in it, either by Himself or His powers.

Thus, sonorous bodies are without sound if deprived of communication with air, which must necessarily penetrate them if they have to give a sound. For the same reason, we may say that sound itself would not be sensible, or manifest to us, if there were no universal generative sound in every partial sound; which is the true reason why music has always had such power over men.

Different mediums of the sublime; Christianity the highest

Thus the different examples of the sublime, or partial glimpses of the universal generative focus which reach us, carry us far beyond what they show us.

Therefore, of all the means afforded us for the enjoyment of the sublime, none is more sublime than the Word, or true Christianity, which is nothing less than our very union with the Spirit and Heart of God; and we might draw from thence a direct proof that Christianity is divine, since the tree is known by its fruit. But this fruit can be gained only by experience; that is its A + B. It cannot be established completely by the intellectual A + B of reasoning.

226

The bel-espit's estimate of the sublime

At the same time, the admiration which literati and rhetoricians evince for what they consider sublime, confirms me in the persuasion that these *beaux-esprits* dwell habitually in very inferior regions; and that when they meet with any ideas or expressions a little more elevated than usual, they experience an impression which fills up their usual vacuity, and seems to raise them to the highest degree of the sublime, only by reason of the constant privation they are in, in the barren regions which they inhabit.

If they knew the truly sublime region for which man was made, they would reduce to their true value all those particular examples of the sublime at which they go into ecstasies, and consider them only as child's play; on this subject, suffice it to refer them to the prophets.

Inconsistencies of men of letters. Human literature a snare, when misapplied

As to what these *beaux-esprits* and men of genius may think of these positive and experimental proofs of which I have been speaking, we know what we may expect. They put upon one level those who call themselves atheists, and those who, though in their senses, become illuminati, prophets, thaumaturgists, from vanity, pride, or curiosity. They say that any strong passion may give to the mind a spice of madness. Do we not know, moreover, what they say of the spectre of Athens, and the phantom of Athenodorus, two narratives which they laugh to see told seriously by Pliny, and which they believe may be taken as the originals of all ghost stories, which have been repeated and forged over again in different ways; seeing that any one may relate, according to his own fancy, what they believe never happened?

O learned and eloquent men, who take the chair to rule the world, I am far from intending to plead with you for these questions of fact; but I would that, in your capacity as teachers of nations, you began by learning questions of right. Your affirmations about facts, for and against, would then have more weight and, till then, they leave us to view them as mere crude opinions, which may be as fantastic as phantoms themselves; and from this we may judge what progress you have made in the course of divine philosophy and true Christianity, or, what is the same thing, in the Ministry of the Word.

I will then here repeat what I have reproached the literati with, especially the religious; that, attaining, as they sometimes do, either by their natural gifts, or their efforts, to the region of truth, they dissipate the treasures they find there, by applying them to subjects in a lower region; and reduce the domains of the Word to the art of describing and writing gracefully and with regularity; thus continually sacrificing the substance, which they do not know, to the form.

This is what led me to say that human literature in general was one of the enemy's snares; and that he uses it with great address, to delay men in their march, while giving them to believe that they are very advanced, as, in fact, they are, in their art, beyond ordinary mortals.

Man's thoughts and words are sharp swords, and corrosive juices, which were given to him to break and dissolve the infected substances around him. When he fails to apply them to their real purposes, they corrode and destroy him, because they cannot remain inactive. Therefore action is so useful to man; and it is so profitable to him to be employed in the active work of the Word, which is true Christianity.

We now proceed to address those who, by their calling, are specially charged with the Ministry of the Word.

What have Ministers of the Word done? Withheld the key of knowledge?

You Ministers of the Word, then, do you think yourselves free from reproach? You, who have placed the Word under tutelage, and impoverished your ward, without enriching yourselves - might it not say, that, if you obtain nothing from it, it is because you ask it for nothing; and, if you ask for nothing, it is because you think you possess already?

Have you not degraded that Word, by reducing its stewardship to symbolical institutions, sermons, and outward pomps; by offering us none of the wonderful fruits of its fertile domains; and by teaching that the time for its wonders is past; as if this Word were decrepit, and as if our need of its fruits were not as urgent since your rule, as it was before, and as it will be to the end of all things? Have you never done to this Word, what the Saviour reproached the Jews with; namely, taken the key of knowledge, and not only not gone in yourselves, but prevented those from entering who would? Have you never paralyzed God's work, by restraining men of faith and desire, who, through your gifts and your light, should have become workmen of the Lord?

You see what human industry produces from the raw materials of Nature, by means of the splendid discoveries of Science. Has it never struck you what prodigies you might have expected from the soul of man, if, instead of constraining its movements, and retaining it in bondage, you had seconded its divine aspirations, and opened to it the sublime regions of liberty where it was born?

Have you never, by your institutions, compelled the Redeemer to go back into the Temple, the destruction of which he proclaimed beforehand, and into which, after his resurrection, he never went, although, after that event, he showed himself frequently to his disciples?

Have you never neutralized the means of cure for the human soul, by telling him vaguely to destroy the old man within him, without teaching him how to make the new man come to birth; which is nothing else than the renewal of the divine contract; a renewal which you ought to second effectively by every means in your power?

Worldly reason and right reason should not be proscribed alike

Have you never done like those pious, mystical, and spiritual professors, who forbid us to walk according to reason?

But why do they forbid us to walk according to reason? It is because they have not observed, that, if there is a human reason contrary to the truth, there is a human reason in its favour. They are prudent and wise in prohibiting the former; for, in fact, it is the enemy of all truth, as is easily seen by the outrages against truth, committed by the doctors in the outward sciences, which are at once the objects and the results of the mere reason of this world. The principal property of this kind of reason is, to fear error, and mistrust truth: ever occupied in scrutinizing proofs, it never leaves the mind time to taste the sweetness of living enjoyments, and is always suspicious, which prevents the taste of truth ever reaching it. This is what leads learned societies into unbelief at last, after keeping them so long in doubt.

But they are no longer wise and prudent, if they forbid us the use of the second kind of reason; for this, on the contrary, is the defender of Truth. It is the piercing eye that continually discovers it, and tends only to disclose its riches ; and, far from reason, in this respect, being objectionable, it would be a crime not to follow it, since this gift has been presented to all men, with the one and sole intent, that they should make use of it; the Lord knowing that by humbly presenting this reason to the focus of universal Light, it would suffice to teach us, and lead us to all things.

The light of Truth is evidence itself: Belief in it, irresistible. Blind belief

How, indeed, could the Supreme Ruler require us to believe in Him, and all His wonders, if we had not essentially the means requisite for their discovery? Yes, the Truth would be unjust if it were not everywhere clearly and openly written before the eyes of man's mind. If Eternal Truth requires that we should believe it, it is because it is given us to assure ourselves at every step of its existence; and that, not on the mere testimony of men's assertion, - even ministers of this same Truth, - but by direct, positive, irresistible evidence.

The belief you sometimes instil into the minds of proselytes, how useful soever it may be to them, is very far from the certainty that would rest on evidence. It is not uncommon to meet with men, over whose belief we may exercise some dominion; it is not even uncommon to hear it said by people in the world, that nothing is more easy than to believe; some indeed are to be found who pretend they can believe whatever they like.

I will grant this of blind belief, because this consists in discarding the universal and seizing only a point. This dispenses with all comparison ; and for this sort of belief, the more we descend into minutiae the more ready people are to believe; which explains the fanaticism of the superstitious, which is always in exact proportion to their ignorance.

But I deny it in regard to that certainty which is the very opposite of blind belief, because we can arrive at this certainty only in proportion as we rise towards the universal or the ensemble of things, seeing that when we compare things in this ensemble, and there discover the unity or universality of the law, it is impossible not to have the certainty. And, in fact, this certainty is the opposite to blind belief, because it is in direct proportion to our elevation and knowledge.

Thus, I grant that nothing is easier than to believe, but it is not so easy to be sure! Men of the world, from time to time, throw out specious propositions that they believe to be peremptory, because nobody answers them. They are a sort of chemical reactives which they introduce by the side of truth, and by which they try to precipitate it to the bottom of the vessel. But we see that it is not impossible to escape their subterfuges.

In general, men plunge into blind belief, into doubt, or even into scepticism, only because they do not go beyond the imperious and dark opinions of men, their incoherent systems and their passions ; in a word, because they look only to men, in whom everything is diverse and in opposition. If they considered Man, they would there find the root of all virtues, all light, all harmony; in short, they would there see the divine system itself, and find themselves in such uniformity of principles and certainties, as would soon make them of one mind. Of our two human reasons, therefore, let us not discard the one which has power to attain the Truth.

Scripture estimate of the understanding. Mystics

Those who read the Scriptures will see how they value the understanding; how they threaten to deprive those of it who depart from the right way, and promise this light to those who love the truth. They will there see how God's elect, commissioned to proclaim His Word, reproved the people, the ministers of religion, and individuals, all alike, who neglected to make use of this understanding or divine reason, and discernment, which was given to us only to continually separate light from darkness, as the Spirit of God Himself does.

Here then you see, O ministers of holy things, what the work is, which Truth has a right to expect from you. Consider, if you will, the course that respectable mystics have taken. But be not one of those timid pietists who forbid us the use of the light which man has received by his nature. It is not uncommon to see some of these mystics, women and men, who describe wonderfully the most perfect state of souls, and even the exact regions or impressions through which the true workmen of the Lord have to pass.

But these mystics appear to be called into these regions only to describe them, without having the active vocation of true stewards ; they see the promised land, but do not till it; others often till it without seeing it; these would even be afraid of distracting their minds by stopping to contemplate it; such is their eagerness to make it fruitful. Their post is not in partial or particular regions. We may judge of this by considering the nature of desire.

The nature of desire: the principle of movement

Desire results only from the separation or distinction between two substances, analogous in their essences and properties; and, when men of maxims say that we cannot desire what we do not know, they prove that, when we desire a thing, there must necessarily be in us a portion of it, which therefore cannot be considered as unknown to us. It is certain also, as I have often said, that every desire exerts itself to attain the end that attracts it, as we may see in whatever order of things we choose to look for instances; which ought, at once, to rebuke our idleness, revive our courage, and condemn those who check it.

I may add, that desire is the principle of all movement, and therefore an incontestable fact that movement and desire are in proportion to each other; and that, from the First Being who, being the first desire, the divine One, or Universal desire, is also thereby the motive of movement itself - to the Stone, which is without movement, because without desire.

Man's soul the receptacle and envelope of the desire of God, and may know all the desires of God

I may also add that each desire acts on its own enclosure or envelope, to manifest itself; and the higher the order, the more susceptible is the envelope of feeling and participating in the desire which is enclosed within it; and the reason why Man may be admitted to the sentiment and knowledge of all the divine wonders is, because his soul is the envelope and receptacle of the desire of God.

On the one hand, the splendid natural destiny of Man is, that he can only really and radically desire what alone can really and radically produce all things. This only thing is the desire of God: whatever else attracts man, he is but its slave or plaything; he does not desire it. Then, the greatness of his ministry is, that he cannot act really and radically, except under the authority which alone is equitable, good, consistent, effective, and in conformity with the Eternal Desire, and which is communicated to him positively every moment. As for all other orders that he daily receives, he provokes them himself from self-interest, and often from pride, and more as a sovereign than as a servant. So almost the world over, servants put themselves in their masters' places.

I cannot conceal here that the divine desire that makes itself felt in the soul of man, has for object to establish the equilibrium between the soul and God, since a desire comes from the separation of analogous substances which want to be united. Now this equilibrium is not a dead, inert effect, but an active development of the divine properties which constitute the human soul, inasmuch as it is an universal divine extract.

But if these notions were extinguished in the human soul, it belonged to you, the ministers of holy things, to revive them there: if this desire in men was weakened, it was for you to strengthen it, by showing them all its advantages.

What a magnificent part were yours, thus working to accomplish, in this high order, the reunion of what is separate from and desirous of its own! You see that a mere animal desire, such as hunger, has for object to establish the equilibrium between our elementary bodies and Nature, to enable them to manifest and fulfil all the elementary wonders or corporeal properties of which Nature made them, inasmuch as they are an extract of Nature. What might we then not expect from this desire, in another order, and from that sacred want, of which the Most High composed our essence?

Listen, O Man! Your body is a continual expression of the desire of Nature, and your soul is a continual expression of the desire of God. God cannot be an instant without desiring something; and He cannot have a desire which you may not know, since you ought to manifest them all. Try, then, continually to study the desires of God, that you be not some day treated as an unprofitable servant.

Difficulties of our re-union with God

But there is a high reason why our re-union with God, from whom we are separated, is made so laborious; and this reason, which explains why we are obliged to act so forcibly and perseveringly to reach God, is grounded on two difficulties

The first is, that since the great Fall we are in a real prison, which is our body, which ought to have been our preservative; and, instead of diminishing the weight of their shackles, to the best of their means and abilities, most men help their souls to become of the same nature as their prisons, by materializing themselves as they do. Thus the human soul having thereby become prison itself, we may judge what its lamentable condition at present must be.

The second difficulty, which is of immense weight, is that God, like all other beings, concentrates Himself; it is that, by His own central attraction, He tends continually towards Himself, and to separate from all that is not He; it is that, by this means, He makes Himself continually a world apart, shut up in His own Universal Spherical Envelope; the form we see taken by all particular worlds, and all bodies, down to globules of water and mercury, which also take this form of envelope.

Worlds to be overcome: the specific for accomplishing it

Now, as we have been confined by sin, in a world which is not divine; as, moreover, by our defilements, illusions, and ignorance, we make for ourselves a world still less divine, we may judge what efforts it must require to cancel these false, dark, heavy worlds which surround us, and get an opening into the divine world, into which it would be so sweet, as it is so necessary, for us to enter. The great efforts we must make for this may be imagined, if we reflect that all these worlds, concentrating themselves, each in itself, tend continually to separate from each other.

Yet we must not be discouraged; for this divine world, which tends to concentrate itself, also tends to universalize itself, because it is All, or at least, should be All; this is its right. Thus our labour, well understood, would have for its main object to attenuate all these false worlds with which we incessantly surround ourselves, and allow them to dissolve; because the universal, or divine world, would naturally take their place, as all places belong to it ; and these results would be both prompt and facile, since we should therein concur with the tendency of that Universal World itself.

Now, what is the true specific for accomplishing this marvellous work of attenuating the false worlds that surround us, or which we create for ourselves every day, and opening the divine world which would fain take their place? I ask again, was it not for you, the ministers of sacred things, to teach us what this specific is, and prove to us that it consists in the virtues of the Word? Yes, the Eternal Word raises its voice, and acts only to exterminate these worlds of illusion, these Titans which scale heaven daily, and to cause the divine and real world, whose organ and principle the Word is, to reign over all.

Succours given to man in his contest: their great efficacy

I know that obstacles are innumerable, difficulties immense, and dangers almost unceasing; but there are also aids of all kinds, granted universally to man, that he may defend himself everywhere, gain the victory, and fulfil every intention of his being, without the enemy getting anything but shame.

Although we waste our words daily in innumerable secondary occupations, and upon inferior objects, which do not at all advance us in the true Spiritual Ministry of Man, yet, if we do not exceed the measure of our wants, or depart from justice, these very occupations may be useful to us as preservatives.

In fact, the numerous diversions, affections, and attractions, suggested to us daily by the labours and cares of life, whether physical, or social and political, are so many succours which are continually presented to us, to stop us on the brink of our precipices; without which our spirits might plunge in at any moment. They are so many dikes and palisades along the edge of these precipices, near which we walk in our passage through this lower world.

There is not a moment of our existence that is not met with such support, and these supports enable us to traverse our infected darkness without experiencing the frightful disgust and intolerable bitterness that awaited us there. Thus, when man allows himself to fall into crime, or mere acts of weakness, it is, most assuredly, because he has not made proper use of those succours; for it is a truth that he was surrounded with all he required, if not to go forward, at least not to fall.

Without here rising to those sublime principles of morality, which teach us that before yielding to illusions we ought to look about us to see if some useful work may not be found to which we might apply ourselves; we see here, at least, from whence derives that commonplace morality which teaches us to shun idleness, whether of body or of mind; we also here see why there is generally less corruption amongst men employed than amongst those who live in idleness and inactivity; also why there are fewer insane in the occupied class than amongst the idle; and fewer amongst those who are occupied with natural and material objects than amongst those employed in works of mere imagination; and why, lastly, there are fewer people addicted to evil sciences amongst the inferior and busy order than amongst the great and idle.

Not only are these succours and supplies our ramparts against the enemy, but if we use them zealously, with a pure intention, they always connect us more or less, each according to our measure, with that delicious magism which the truth carries with it, and which its Word filtrates everywhere, even though we may not know it; so that, on the one hand, impregnating us with their living juices, and, on the other, rendering us invisible and unapproachable by our enemies, they afford us safety and happiness everywhere, and neutralize the bitterness which is ever ready to break through our enjoyments.

There is no state or situation in life to which this doctrine will not apply. Painful and pleasant situations may, alike, here find their prescription and the regimen suitable to their cases; for the pleasant states have their drawbacks, as well as the painful; they have them even more, and therefore have greater need of these supplies, and require still more to be under surveillance.

The Word itself is with these succours

Now, as the Word is always secretly united with these supports, every one may attain to a participation in its vivifying action. Therefore, by preserving ourselves from idleness of spirit in the pleasant states, and from idleness of body in the painful ones, we should insensibly connect ourselves with the Word, and perhaps become naturally its ministers.

For this Eternal Word passes incessantly from death to life for us. This, indeed, is its mode of existence; it is, in itself, a continual prodigy, always being born anew: as it acts everywhere, and continually, in this manner and character, it everywhere diffuses this same active impress and colouring over all it does and all that is, whether visible or invisible.

This is our compass, our vessel, our harbour, our city of refuge. Let us go to this guide, in spirit and in act; let us unite with Him, and He will everywhere cause us to be born out of death into life, through Him and with Him; and everywhere make us participate in His property of being a continual prodigy; and the enemy will be obliged to let us pass without levying any tax upon us, or upon our present or our future happiness.

The sensible favours of the Word lead to the "best possible state" here below

We need no more ask what awaits the good man, even here on earth, when he fulfils punctually and with resignation the decree which condemns us all to fight if we would conquer. What awaits him is nothing less than the favours of the Word, since this is what he would have enjoyed if we had remained faithful to the divine contract. It is, then, true that, if we conducted ourselves wisely, not only should we have no doubt of there having been a former state of perfect order for us, which we might call a primitive "best possible state" (*optimisme*), but we should even discover around us a "best possible state" of a secondary order, which would fill us with consolation in our painful situation and trials here below.

But if, generally speaking, the radical basis of our being inclines us willingly to believe, whether from need or from conviction, in a primitive optimism, in which everything was good, we find it more difficult to believe in a secondary optimism, when we see so much evil around us. Yet this would not be long questioned, if we would but open our eyes to the source of life and love which ever seeks us in our abyss; and we should be obliged to confess that, if we do not learn to know this secondary optimism, we shall never know that which is primitive.

For want of distinguishing between these two kinds of optimism, reasoners, or rather unreasoners, have stammered so much about good and evil. We all descend from the primitive optimism; we all tend to return to it, but do not allow ourselves time to make the journey; and, in spite of the inconsistency, we persist in thinking that we have arrived, while we are only on the way. It is very true, that, notwithstanding we have deviated so far from the primitive optimism, it is still possible for us to perceive it and see it coming into birth every where, through the secondary optimism. For the divine Word still opens in us the gate of divinity; that is, of holiness, light, and truth. The enemy has also a word, but, in speaking it, he only opens the gate into himself. The more he speaks, the more he infects himself; and as he is always pronouncing this word falsehood, he is always infecting himself. He does nothing but spill his own poisonous blood and drink it. This is his perpetual labour.

Three degrees of the Word given to Man

A pure word was, on the contrary, restored to the first man after his crime; one still more glorious and triumphant was restored to him in the middle of times; what then will that be which shall be restored to him at the end of time, when the Word will give itself in the eternal plenitude of its action?

We see that all here is love; and, as the Word is the continual and universal hymn of Love, this Word fills all the ways of man with gentle progressions, appropriate to every degree of his existence. This is why all commences, for the human soul, by sentiment and affection; and why all must also end there.

Our understanding or intelligence is opened only after our inner being has experienced the first sentiments of its own existence. This is known at the age when man begins to think. At this epoch we feel a new centre born in us, a moral sensation which we did not know before.

The intelligence is not then long in giving signs of its presence, but this is only after the moral centre has been opened.

In a more advanced age, the sap rises forcibly to the region of our understanding; and, at this moment, we have most need of guardians to direct its course, and preserve us from the dangers of its impetuosity; for, without much care, our moral centre would be soon darkened or deteriorated. Then it is that the savans put ideas before morals, which they make to depend upon them; as they also make ideas to depend on sensation and outward objects.

But, if this moral centre of sentiment and affection has the initiative by natural right, it follows that every thing must return to it at last; as we see that the food we take fulfils its object, and is useful to us, only so far as its juices and properties are conveyed into our blood, the focus of our life.

We must confess that all the flashes of intelligence which men acquire by reasoning, are of use only so far as they penetrate the moral focus, whither they bring whatever property they possess. It is a tribute and homage that they all have to render to this source, coming to bear witness, by the fact itself, to the nature of their relations with it. In short, the understanding may aid us to recognize the fruits of the secondary optimism which surround us in abundance, but the moral principle may enable us to feed upon those of the primitive optimism: such are the services which the stewards of the Word might render us.

Will the devil cease to be evil?

Thinkers, who believe in the universal source of love, may hence conceive how all things must terminate for the man of desire, in Love and the Word. They will also see why this material world cannot last for ever: because it is only a picture, an active one, no doubt, but without love, and without word, or speech; that is to say, it must one day return into the Love and the Word, from which it was separated by crime.

If we would extend this to the enemy of all truth, who was himself the cause of the deviation of the universe, and of its being, as it were, exiled from Love and the Word, we must observe, that, unfortunately, this enemy is not without speech; which is the reason why he works out his own deviations, and his own exile.

Besides, those who teach the final return of this guilty being, do not reflect how impossible for them it is to get any positive idea on these great subjects, in this world. In fact how wonderful and profound soever may be the knowledge they acquire of the divine and the infernal regions, yet, so long as they are in their material covering, they can attain neither to the God Principle, or what we call the heaven of heavens, nor to the chief Wicked one, or what we call the hell of complete devils. In these things, here below, we have results only, of these two principles; because the object of our bodies is at once to keep us deprived of God, and to serve as a rampart against the devil.

The true source of all these judgments of man is, that, without being God, he is, nevertheless, an universal being; and consequently, that he cannot feel a single point of his being, without finding himself, image-like, in a universal good or evil. It may be said, also, that it is this idea of universality which induces Him so readily to save all sinners; he does not see that, if there were but one man saved, this idea of mercy, which does him honour, would still be true, because there is not a single man who is not an universality.

Destination and predestination

On the other hand, he has plunged into inextricable labyrinths on the subject of predestination. But, you stewards of sacred things, might you not have saved him from this, by showing him the difference between destination and predestination?

Destination seems to be taken in a good sense only; Predestination has two faces. God often gives destinations to men, and, in this way, there have been elect of all kinds; but He gives them no predestination, because, in its most favourable acceptation, this word implies a sort of constraint which would detract from liberty, and, in its opposite direction, it implies a sort of fatalism, which would seem contrary to justice.

This word is an abuse. God may have said to several; "I choose you from your mother's womb", and "before the world was"; but it was man's spirit which clothed this election with the word predestination; the weak have still further altered its meaning, and the fanatical abused it.

From his origin, Man might have said that he was predestinated to manifest the Divine Being; and yet he has not manifested it. Since his fall, when he is called to the work, he merely resumes his original destination; and if, in this case, he is comparatively higher than his fellow creatures, he nevertheless only returns to the primitive line in which he ought always to have walked, and therefore does not come under the name of predestinate, in the sense it commonly bears; for he is still far lower than he would have been if he had remained in his glory, and far lower than he will be at the end of time, if he arrives there regenerate.

Man's power over God

Instead of this discouraging system of predestination, might you not, on the contrary, have taught us that it is man, who, by his love, may, in a manner, govern God?

For, the hasty do not perceive that God is guided, not only by our wants, but even by our desires. He is to us, not only like a clever physician, who follows, step by step, the course of an illness, and regulates his remedies every moment accordingly; but also like a tender and watchful mother, who studies all our tastes, and who, if we are eager to please her, has nothing too costly for us, and sees nothing in us but the cherished object of all her indulgences. Where is the mother who is not entirely possessed by her son, and ruled by him, when he behaves towards her as he ought?

Let us not be surprised then, if, far from being harsh and unjust towards us, if we were wise, God should, on the contrary, seek only to anticipate us in every thing, and if our love should acquire over Him a mighty rule, and possess a magical attraction, to which He were always ready to make every kind of sacrifice, even that of His own supremacy and glory.

Yes, yes, it is a positive truth, that, if we would, we might, govern God by our love; and that God is grieved that we leave Him so much authority, when He would use towards us nothing but friendly complacency and benevolence.

Read Isaiah xli., beginning at the 8th verse, and you will see that God not only called Abraham his friend, but, on account of this friendship, lavished every attention and kindness upon him.

Read 2 Chron. xx. 7: you will see in Jehoshaphat's prayer, that Abraham was regarded by his people as the friend of God; as Judith also says it (v. also St. James ü. 23).

Read the Book of Wisdom of Solomon (vii. 27) you will see God make use of this name friends in speaking of holy souls. Lastly, in the Gospel of St. John, xv.: where the Lord is pleased to call his disciples his friends.

Was it not your office, O ministers of holy things, to open these truths to our minds?

Whatever is sensible is an expression of Being

The Primary Essence may really dwell in us, and take pleasure in us, when we really make ourselves His friends; for this reason we are, when regenerate, a true and living copy of the Being of beings, since it is the character of this Being Himself which then asserts itself in us.

All spiritual sensibilisations, which are but productions of Divine Operations, have for object to notify His existence and presence; the regions would otherwise forget Him; as we should ourselves, on account of the sublimity of His existence; and this truth may be applied to physical sensibilisations, and to the existence of our corporeal being, as well as to that of all Nature, since each of the sensabilisations which we see, and hear, and taste, is nothing but a notification and expression of Being, whilst, otherwise, we should slumber near Him, and be as if we were without Him, so separate and distinct, though not distant, is He from us.

Let us not then be surprised, on becoming regenerate, at feeling the seven sources or powers, the fundamental pillars of all being, born again in us; or the seven organs of the Spirit form themselves, and moving there; since the Spirit wishes to be known, and we are chosen to be its living witnesses. If spiritual sensibilisations are only indications of the eternal operations of the Primary Essence, we must be spiritually sensibilised before we can know this essence.

And, when we are spiritually sensibilised to this degree, then the tongue is silent ; it can say nothing more; and it is not necessary it should speak, since Being itself acts in us, and by us, and with such measure, wisdom, and power, as to surpass all human language.

In this picture we see how Man proves God, and may be useful to Him; since he ought to be His universal witness. We also see how dear man must be to Him, by reason of this his sublime destination. For, as I have often shown, it is certain that, if there were no God, we should have nothing to admire; but that, if there were no immortal spiritual soul, God would have no permanent object that could be the focus and complete receptacle of His love.

Progressive names, states, and processes, in the
representation of Divinity

As for the different names of Man, we have already seen that his present name is pain or sorrow: this name must resound through our whole being, before we can reach the gates of the Word and Life. But, the second name that Man finds at the gates of Life is holiness, the Hebrew root of which means to renew. When he has the happiness to cause this name to be born in him, then he may hope to enter into the Spiritual Ministry of Man; seeing that the Word desires nothing better than to have workmen; and he who shall understand the dignity of this name, the clarifyings it effects, and the delightful and splendid services it enables us to render to the universality of things, will know what is the happiness and glory of being a man.

He will then take no rest till he has put himself in condition to be employed: for, to be really useful in the universal regions, it is not sufficient to have arrived at a lively permanent sentiment of one's title as a spirit, if we attain not besides to be employed as such in the divine, spiritual, heavenly, earthly regions, and in the Israelite living-grammatical (*grammatical-vif*), patriarchal, prophetic, etc. fields, against evil, vanity, and darkness. He will not be stopped with shame at being obliged to teach his essences and spiritual organs this element of the universal language, seeing that he hopes to teach it one day to every thing that does not know it, yet groans for that knowledge.

The work of holiness in man

This second name, holiness, engenders in man every other partial name, the need and properties of which he will find in the divers talents and employments that await him in his course, according to the various functions and improvements he may meet with to do. And when the Spirit-Man applies himself courageously to his work of regeneration, and develops his faculties, there appear to gather round his head, from different points of the spiritual horizon, as it were, active and living vapours, which come to establish abundant and fertilizing springs above him.

The fire of these clouds ferments; it explodes; the springs open, and a thousand rivulets of heavenly dew descend upon man and overflow him; these vivifying rivulets penetrate and saturate him, as rain does the fields of Nature. Man's zeal and desire are the first centre and focus of these wholesome clouds; it is he who attracts and fixes the divine and spiritual vapours which he has power to command and convoke, so to speak, from all the countries in which God acts, that is in the universality of all things. This is one of man's highest privileges, and what shows him most convincingly how he was invested with the right of being the image and representative of Divinity.

God has produced eternally, and still produces, the essences of these vapours: man, as God's image, has the power to collect them, and render them sensible, and form regions of them, of a strength that nothing can resist. It is, in a manner, to repeat their generation, that is, in the lower visible degree; the higher degree being reserved for God alone.

Spiritual deluges over the mind of Man. Spiritual Noahs

Yet, what obstacles are opposed to these rights of the man of desire! To what distressing limits they are confined! God truly said to the men of Noah's day, that there would be no more deluge; because, according to the laws of Nature and Justice, when the germ of sin which had invaded corporeal forms, and as such was analogous to water, had made its explosion, and drawn down the corresponding punishment, it could not reproduce the same disorder, and the punishment of a deluge by water could not be repeated. But God did not therefore say that there would be no more spiritual deluge; and, in fact, far from believing this kind of deluge cannot take place, we may say that it is continual and universal, when we behold the floods of error that cover the minds of men.

And the different Noahs who are named to preside over these deluges have to endure and stem the torrents of suffering which come upon them, traversing their being in all directions. They do not complain when they feel themselves thus assailed; they are glad that these torrents accumulate upon them, and rise and press one on another till they make irruption in all the faculties of their being.

They wait with lively faith and delicious hope, for the waters to flow off through the channels which are open within them; for the earth to resume its fertility around them; for the olive-branch to appear, brought by the dove, which is the Word; that they may restore to the desert and barren regions, the animals they have collected in their holy ark, the races of which they are so eager to see perpetuated.

Why does evil still exist in the universe?

Nevertheless, amongst the spiritual afflictions which the man of desire experiences in the course of his work of regeneration and his ministry, there is one which, at first, seems to him very heart-rending, and he is surprised that he cannot abridge its duration by his will; it is, to know that, whatever we ask of the Father, in the name of the Redeemer, may be obtained; and yet the ways of the world are not made straight, human iniquity is not yet abolished, and Nature not yet redeemed.

Sometimes this man of longing is pleased with the sweet prospect which his mind presents to him, persuading himself that this great work must be possible according to the promise. Sometimes even he feels himself moved with holy aspirations, leading him to believe that he might, by faith, succeed in realizing some part of this sublime work, and then he is filled with joy. But when he enquires scrupulously on this point, this is the answer he receives.

God rules over all in patience, love, and wisdom

All God's ways are ways of love; the powers of God are, in truth, without limit, and can do all things, except what is contrary to love. Now it is in love that God temporizes; it is because He loves all things, that He wills that all shall have the means and the time that are requisite to fill themselves with Him, that nothing may return to Him empty of Himself. By doing violence to the process and to time, He might, certainly, cause all the dark and false appearances that hold the spirit captive, to disappear; but He might thereby cause this captive spirit to disappear likewise, if it is not yet saturated with the divine tincture. Now this tincture can penetrate only by degrees if it were to do so suddenly, and all at once, it would push the spirit into extremes beyond its strength, and which it could not resist.

Thus, the long suffering of God tempers even the designs we form for the advancement of His kingdom; thus the man of desire, whatever his zeal may be, can walk in the ways of wisdom, only in so far as he is penetrated with the sentiment of that universal love which disposes all things gently; and when he feels strongly moved to "make straight the crooked ways", he must carry his desires into the bosom of Eternal Love, who alone can know what is best for the accomplishment of His own wise and beneficent divine will; he must retire into the depths of his heart, and there, moaning like a dove, sigh in silence for the extension of the kingdom of the Word and of Life; he must there traveil in pain and patient waiting, and never forget that if, through guilty man, evil flooded the world, it can be only through man made righteous that the reign of goodness can recover its place.

He must, in a word, take care lest he listen only to his own imprudence, blind to his own darkness, privations, and well attested impotence, while he fancies he listens only to justice, and that he has a right to exact from God more than his present mission permits him even to beg from Him.

Let him then reflect that God's continual occupation is to separate the pure from the impure; and all time is consecrated to this great work. This is what He does with us from the moment of our birth, even of our incorporation, since, from that instant, He seeks gradually to deliver our souls from their prisons; and yet He accomplishes this work only at the end of our lives: and even then it depends upon how we have lived.

The Spirit of Wisdom, and Spirit of Charity, which should animate men

We have seen, more than once, that the spirit of the divine operation, on man and the universe, is a perpetual sacrifice, a continual devotion of the Word, sacrificing itself incessantly, to substitute the divine substance in all creatures, for that which is their disquiet and torment. As we proceed from God, this spirit should animate us every moment of our lives, if we would be His image and likeness, and revive the divine covenant within us. And we should be wise, not from virtue only, but from equity, and regard for the title we bear, as well as for the honour of Him who granted it to us, and whom we are commissioned to represent.

If all these motives were insufficient to make us wise, then we ought to be so out of charity to other creatures and regions which are related to us, since we cannot cease to be wise without causing them to die, instead of giving them the life which they expect at our hands. Now, if we are not sufficiently elevated to give them life, let us, at least, not so debase ourselves as to occasion their death. Happy will it be when we are able to rise a degree; for, from that moment, all virtues will flow out of us, and we shall, from duty, promote the happiness of all creatures.

The wise man works for his own repose, when he daily wipes out the stains that darken Man since his sin; and seeks to cause the fountain of life, which alone can give him peace, to descend into him. This is the term to which every man who would be just, must tend. The man of Charity goes farther; he is not content with his own happiness, he wants the happiness also of what is not himself ; and here this spirit of charity has two distinct characters, one spiritual, one divine.

By the former, man seeks the peace of his fellow creatures; by the latter, he seeks to make even the Word itself keep its sabbath, and here it is that many are called, but very few chosen.

Ought not you, O ministers of holy things, to have taught us these truths, which are so weighty and so little known? For, who, here below, believes that we are the great overseers of God's domains, commissioned to work for His repose? Alas, it may be said that man labours for the very opposite, as if he sought only the enemy's repose; whilst we ought to be occupied altogether in healing the wounds which he incessantly makes in all regions and things; and everything shows that we may attain this high employment by attaching ourselves in spirit and in truth to the ministry of the Word; for if there is, on the one hand, a downward progression of abominations of man and his enemy, from the beginning of the world, there is also an ascending progression of divine riches developed before us since the same epoch, and which will not cease to be developed till the end of time.

Dangers and horrors concealed under divine goodness, to be overcome and dispersed by charity

If we reflected on what is concealed under this universal material world, we should thank the display of divine goodness that it has been so active as to hide this horrible sight from our eyes.

If we reflected on the unhappy condition of the human family, visible or invisible, we should thank the powers of Nature for having spared our sight this heart-rending picture; and we should thank Supreme Wisdom for permitting that man and woman should now be able to join love and light in themselves, under the veil of the Eternal SOPHIA; because every holy marriage that is made is celebrated throughout the human family, and fills it with joy, as our earthly marriages give joy to families in this world.

If we reflected what the anguish of the Word must be, we should thank it for its generous charity, in devoting itself to our repose; and devote ourselves to its repose, in our turn.

By thus marching in these ways of love and charity, we should ultimately banish all evil and pain everywhere, and recognize the immeasurable preponderance of good. It is quite true, that the devil is so wicked, that, but for the divine ground or goodness which has come into man, we should not even know that there was a God; but it is also true that men are so surrounded with divine goodness, that, without the wickedness of man, we should not perceive the existence of the devil.

Wonderful revelations of Wisdom, notwithstanding the hardness of Man

There are such grand manifestations of the Word in the world, independently of traditions, and independently of the superb tableau of Nature, that, when I look at these grand openings that Wisdom in her bounty has disclosed to some of Her servants, I cannot contain my astonishment at so much prodigality! I might be almost tempted to believe that she does not know the state of brutality, ignorance, and gross hardness, in which men are steeped, in regard to the progress of truth, and the fecundity of the spirit.

In fact, in spite of her universal oversight, I believe she does not perceive the lapses and wickedness of men, till they fill up their divers false measures; because then this extreme deviation from right penetrates to the order of the Most High and stimulates Justice, which otherwise would like to rest eternally in its covering of Love.

The habitual state of God and spirits, in regard to men, is to believe them less evil than they are; because, as God and spirits inhabit the abode of order, peace, virtue, and goodness, they convey this colouring of perfection, which is their perpetual element, to all that exists. Though they be deceived, in some sort, continually by the oft-repeated abuses of mankind, they do not the less lavish new favours upon them the next minute; a truth of which the two Testaments of the Jews and the Christians present an uninterrupted chain of evidences; a truth which ceases to surprise when we gain an idea of the eternal generative Root, which never ceases renewing itself.

This manner of God and spirits towards man is not contrary to that oversight which they continually exercise over him to preserve him, to warn him, and guide him, in the ways which Wisdom may open for him; because these are all works of love and beneficence, and their natural element.

They always begin with him in this way, far from suspecting evil in him; and he must be completely bound up in disorders for them so far to see it as to leave him to himself and the consequences of his faults; and even then they are not long before they give him fresh marks of attention and attachment.

To know these things is nothing: the doer of the Word only can realize them

The two progressions of evil and good are within our being, and thereby we have relations with all worlds, where we may exercise the Spiritual Ministry of Man. But it is nothing to know these things; what is essential is to realize them. The savant is nothing in God's eyes; the workman it is whom He values and rewards. At every step we advance in our work we gain new strength, and the man who follows the living paths of his regeneration may reach the holy Mount, to learn the Lord's commands.

But there the impatience of justice seizes him, when he beholds the abominations to which the children of Israel have addicted themselves.

He breaks the tables of the law, because this people are not worthy to hear it. In his anger he exterminates the sinners who entice the human soul to prostitute itself to the Gentiles, and are in arms against the Word.

He hurls his lightnings against the giants which would assault heaven, and make themselves its masters "O my people, what has thy God done to thee that thou art enraged against him? What iniquity have your fathers found in me, that they are gone far from me, and walked after vanity, and become vain?"

Accordingly as we ascend this mountain we put on Elijah's mantle, which we may inherit during this life, and by means of which we may bring down fire from heaven; divide the waters of the river; cure diseases; raise the dead; for nothing but this Elijah's mantle, or our pure and primitive garment, can preserve the Word in us, as an earthly garment preserves our bodily warmth. Our animal being cannot contain this living Word; our virginal bodies only can hold it.

Embalming bodies for the resurrection

The custom of embalming bodies of the dead, filling them with costly aromatics, is a transposition of that principle which requires our bodily and spiritual resurrection. If we were wise, it is certain that we should have no other task in this world than to labour continually to revive the pure body and spirit of truth within us, which are there, as it were, extinct, dead; so that, at our physical death, we should be found perfectly embalmed in all the corporeal parts of our first form; not like earthly mummies, which are without life or movement, and turn to dust at last, but as carrying with us the living incorruptible balm, which will restore their primitive activity and agility to all our members, and that in everlasting progressions, like infinity and eternity.

Now, for this we need not wait for our physical death. The prophet Ahijah could not see, because his eyes had grown dim on account of his great age; yet he was able to recognize the wife of Jeroboam, and her errand, when she came to him disguised to consult him about the sickness of her son, whom she was afraid of losing.

Yes: if we are not lost, and bound by our enemy, we may so open the pores of our spirits, hearts, and souls, that divine life may penetrate them all and impregnate us with the pure element, and, in spite of the decay of age, to which our material organs are subject, we may exhale the perfumes of the world to come, and thus be walking organs of the light and glory of our Sovereign Original; and such was our primitive destination, since we ought to be united with and animated by the Spirit and Word which itself produces all these things.

By following the steps of the great workmen of the Lord, we should adorn our true bodies with all the works in which we took part, or which we performed ourselves, as the Redeemer adorned his glorious body with all the works he had manifested, whether personally, or through the patriarchs and prophets. Hereby we assist in adorning that same glorious body in which the Redeemer will show himself at the end of time, " when he shall come to be glorified in his saints, and "to be admired in all them that believe in that day" (2 Thess. i. 10); and hereby we contribute to the destruction of that man of sin who has been preparing of old, and who is composed of the sins of men.

The enemy is not satisfied with having robbed us of our primitive body; he would rob us also of our elementary bodies to cover his own nakedness, because he receives no help from this physical nature in which he is confined, and experiences nothing but roughness and harshness from it, these being the first qualities he awakened in it; and only by clothing himself one day with our elementary bodies, can he put a climax to his deceptions and abominations, and to the illusions of those who put not their whole confidence in truth.

Who are commissioned to teach the deep things of God?

It is you, the ministers of holy things, who ought to teach us these deep things. You know that the Lord said to the prophet Jeremiah (xxvi.): "Stand in the court of the Lord's house, and speak unto all the cities of Judah which come to worship; thus saith the Lord: If you will not hearken unto me, to walk in my law, which I have set before you, to hearken to the words of my servants the prophets, whom I have sent unto you, both rising up early and sending them, but you have not hearkened, then will I make this house like Shiloh, and this city shall be a curse to all nations".

Well! Ye ministers of holy things, the Lord has placed you at the entrance of the souls of men, and ordained you to make known his laws and commandments.

You ought, therefore, to stand at the entrance of the souls of men, and proclaim all the words which the Lord has commanded you to speak; for if He has chosen man to be God's prophet, why should He not choose men to be prophets to men?

And the prophet to man is the servant of the servants of God.

Stand, then, at this entrance of the soul of man, and tell it all that the Lord will say to you: "diminish not a word, if so be they will hearken, and turn every man from his evil way, that I may repent me of the evil which I purpose to do unto them, because of the evil of their doings" (Jer. xxvi. 2).

The Word itself must dwell with men: Prepare to receive your guest

You should teach men that, if they will not become altogether vanity, the Word itself must dwell in them; and you must make them sensible of what they have to do for the Word to dwell in them. When some dear friend is expected in a mansion, all who inhabit that mansion, master and servants, put themselves in movement: when some great commander or sovereign arrives at a garrison town, or any other large place, what eagerness every one manifests as to who shall best acquit himself of his part of the reception!

Well, then, to prepare men to receive the important Guest who desires nothing better than to visit them, every faculty of their being ought to show its zeal, and acquit itself with still more eagerness of its part, to manifest its respect and love. All that constitutes their being, and every region of their existence, must be given up to a burning, uninterrupted activity, that all that is in them may become the channel, organ, and agent of the Word, that majestic, ineffable Guest, for whom their being may be an abode, in which He will even come to celebrate His holy mysteries.

Celebrate the holy mysteries! Happy the man who has felt in himself the smallest signs of this wonderful, incomprehensible work, or had the smallest perception of this magnificent living miracle, to understand which leisure, perhaps possibility, fail, so entirely does it absorb us in pain and pleasure; and because it belongs exclusively to the Ministry of the Word!

Decline of the Light in the world, because its ministers forgot His promise to be with them

Unhappily, the Redeemer, the visible Word, had hardly disappeared from the earth, when the Light began to decline; and the ministers of holy things, falling into discussions about earthly laws, were reduced to go by votes; because, besides this Word, there is no fixed light whatever, and they forgot that he had promised to be with them to the end of the world.

I should have been very disconsolate if Paul had wavered in his faith, after his election, because his election was made after the earthly temple was closed, and the divine opened. I am not so affected by Peter's denial, which occurred before either; nor by the anger of the gentle John, who forbad others to cast out devils in his Master's name, because they did not follow him, and wanted to bring down fire from heaven to destroy the Samaritan village, which would not receive him because he was going to Jerusalem.

The Master teaches us what was then the ignorance of his disciples; they "knew not what spirit they were of". Let us not lose sight of the progressions, and temporal and spiritual epochs, to which the Redeemer himself was subject.

But you who have entered the stewardship of the Word, only after every door, spiritual and divine, has been opened, do you not think you have sometimes laboured to shut them? Why, in your solemnities, do you give merely as a commemoration, what ought to be given only to an ever-increasing real work in us? For them to be truly religious festivals, the spirit that presides over these solemnities should, by your means, make us rise at each period to the same degree of virtuality which divine things attained at the corresponding epoch in the world.

Spiritual signification of religious festivals

Thus, in the time of the Jews, at the feast of Tabernacles, the inward invisible man should have ascended with the consecrated minister's assistance to the region of the spiritual and eternal tabernacles, towards which we ought all to tend in this world.

Thus, at their bloody sacrifices, they should have risen inwardly to the inward sacrifice of their whole earthly being, so that their burning will, rising through this sacrifice in which the victim is their own selves, they might unite with the holy desire and sacred love of Supreme Wisdom, who seeks but to renew her old alliance, or first covenant with us.

Thus, in celebrating the sabbath, they should have risen in spirit above the six actions or elementary powers which now imprison man, and unite their intimate being with the seven universal sources from which it derives, whose virtual representation it is, and from which it ought never to have separated.

Thus, the children of the new law, at the festival of the Nativity of Christ, should, through your ministry and example, cause the Redeemer to be born in themselves, and open the door for him to fulfil his mission in them individually, as he fulfilled it for the whole world.

Thus, at the festival of Easter, they should strive that he may rise again from the sepulchre in them; where our corrupt elements, our darkness and pollution, keep him buried.

Thus, at the festival of Whitsuntide, they should labour to revive in themselves the understanding of all the tongues which the Spirit incessantly speaks to all men, but which our dense matter prevents us from hearing. Every yearly return of each of these festivals should work in the faithful a new development, till he attain the degree of regeneration that may be accorded to him in this lower world.

Functions of the divine ministry

Are you not afraid that the use you teach of these memorable and salutary epochs may leave but a barren impression on his memory, and delay the man who may seek, under your wings, to become a workman of the Lord? Yet, where shall consolation and rest be found, if no servants are trained for the Lord? The Word waits for men reinstated in the divine ministry, to exercise its functions, each according to his degree and position.

Now, this ministry consists in being filled with the divine fountains, which engender themselves from all eternity, that by nothing but his Master's name man may cast all his enemies into the abyss; that he may deliver Nature from the chains which bind her and keep her in bondage; that he may purge this earthly atmosphere of the poisons which infect it; that he may preserve men's bodies from the corrupt influences which pursue them, and the diseases which assail them; that he may still more preserve their souls from the malign influences which affect them, and their minds from the dark images which shroud them; that they may bring rest to the Word, whom the false words of men keep in mourning and sadness; that he may satisfy the desires of angels who look to him to open the wonders of Nature; lastly, that the universe may become full of God, like Eternity.

This is what might be called man's natural breviary, or daily prayer; a profound truth, which the outward Church has perhaps not thought it its duty to teach, but which it preserves at least figuratively, in making its breviary one of the most imperative duties of a priest; and this is the employment which man may hope to have in rising towards his Principle, and daring to beg that He may go out of His own contemplation to the assistance of Nature, Man, and the Word. The Spirit waits for this epoch with groanings ineffable.

The ways of the man of desire

Such, O man of desire, are the paths you travel, and you not only perceive real traces of your positive destination, but you know from experience that every moment we spend not for God, is spent against Him, since the sole object of our existence is to help God to return into His kingdom, and establish Himself universally on His throne. Therefore, you will cry out continually

"Weep, O prophets! Give free course to your tears, ye souls of desire, because the time is not yet come when the Word can pour out its riches on the earth: it weeps more even than you, because it finds itself so counteracted in its love.

"My mind is resolved with a holy and firm resolve, to give itself altogether to the advancement of its work; it settles to it, and swears never to turn away from it; my thought will apply its fire to everything that is combustible and foreign to my essence,

249

"And keep it in the midst of all these combustibles till they are heated and inflame, and an universal explosion takes place, the sound of which shall be heard every moment, as long as I live.

" Why should not my thought's fire effect such an explosion, as I see an evanescent fire in the clouds causes them to explode?

"And shall man's thought, a living ray, proceeding from a fire still more vital than itself, be less privileged than this natural fire, which, when once the eyes of the Divinity are turned away from it, will cease to exist?

No, no! "Have a sense of your dignity, your greatness; give yourself altogether to your work and your advancement. The enemies of both are at hand; if they are not now identified with yourself, they have seized the post that was made for you, and omit nothing to prevent your entering upon it.

"Turn not aside till you have so cleansed this post, that you alone shall have authority in it, and the last traces of the enemy's footsteps are effaced.

"Be careful to light fires in every place he may have inhabited, and wherever he may have passed, to purify it; because, after having been a field of murder and carnage, this post may become a temple of peace and holiness.

"The HOLINESS OF THE WORD is the fire you must light in all the places where the enemy has dwelt, and through which he has passed; indeed this word alone will make him flee, and drive him from his post.

"Speak no other word for the rest of your days; sojourn no longer amongst the shadows of men's opinions; cease from their dark researches. You are quite sure to be in the way of life, the instant your heart pronounces THE HOLINESS OF THE WORD.

"The dark opinions and obscure researches of men will impregnate you with their confusion and ignorance; but look not back when once you have put your hand to the plough.

" Let peace reign between you and all who believe in the HOLINESS OF THE WORD, and let all diversities of opinion cease. Naaman, the General of the King of Syria's armies, believed in THE HOLINESS OF THE WORD, and when he asked Elisha, who cured him of his leprosy, if he would be permitted to go with the king to worship in the temple of Rimmon, the prophet answered him: 'Go in peace'.

"Let the phantoms and illusions of all worlds, and the powers let loose from the abyss, present themselves before you; it will henceforward be in vain, for they must find you always at your post, and know that you mean to be there eternally".

The sublimity of Man's titles; his prayer

Behold, O Man, the sublimity and extent of your privileges! The universe is in pain; the soul of man is on the bed of suffering. The Heart of God waits for you to open access for His Word into the Universe, and the Soul of Man. Thus you have power to give repose to the Universe, the Soul of Man, and to the Heart of God.

O Man, do you not hear how they all demand from you their repose; how they beg you not to withhold it ; how they address this touching supplication to you "Speak but a word and my soul shall be healed!" A prayer which you ought yourself to have continually in your mouth, addressed to Him who the first held out His arms to help you in your distress.

Speak this word, then, O Man! You will have no rest yourself till you have said it. Let man's heart be no more shut up in its cold confinement; cause the centre of the human soul to open. Such is its greatness, that the repose of all regions is connected with its own repose and glory. Not only are you thereby as the established sovereign and ruler over God's works, but you are even so constituted and established by the eternal divine charity, that your zeal and love may become the compass of the love and zeal of the Eternal Power ; that your heart may become, in some sort, the God of your God.

But, if your heart may, in a manner, be, here below, the God of your God, see what the consequences will be if you stop! Man cannot cease an instant from his sublime work, without everything else suffering from his idleness and indolence! O Man, respect your office! Let your sacred Ministry be your glory; but tremble! You are accountable for the harmony of Nature, for the repose of the souls of your fellow-creatures, and for the ineffable joys of Him who Is, and whose name is ALWAYS.

It is true that man's prayer is no less necessary for the happiness of creatures than movement is necessary for the existence of the universe. But this prayer has two periods: the one ought to be employed in attaining our posts, the other in fulfilling their duties: and neither of these ought to know a moment's suspension.

Man ought no more to rest than God Himself. Man's repose even becomes a prayer, when he is careful to pray virtually before he rests. The action of God, and that of Man, are bound together, and ought ever to be simultaneous. Man is spirit, God is spirit; Man has the power to say to God: We are both spirits: let our action be co-ordinate! Man may, under the eye of God, assist at the oscillation of the pendulum which regulates the movements of the different regions of being; he is appointed to direct it.

Do all in concert with God; bring every faculty into subjection, in prayer without ceasing.

Let man see here whether he ought ever to allow himself anything whatsoever but in concert with God. Jacob Boehme has said that even a desire was a sin. If a desire which is not shared in by God is a sin, a thought which is not of God is a snare; a project which is not from God, is an usurpation of His rights; an action which is not of God, is a robbery committed upon His universal activity; a single movement which is not of God is a crime of ill-judged ambition.

Before all, Man ought to say to all his faculties, properties, and forms: "I, as father and chief of the family, command you each to attend to your functions in me, that whenever Universal Order may come, it may find me ready. Be not an instant without contributing by your vigilance and activity to maintain order in me; use your powers constantly in this special work; you are creatures of action; as for me, I have only to employ my will, because I am the image of my Principle".

O Man, your degradation even does not dispense you from this perpetuity of prayer.

Formerly, your hands were to be perpetually raised to heaven. The divine decree condemned you to lower them laboriously to the earth, to procure your sustenance from it; but, while employed in this painful task, you may still lift up the hands of your soul towards the universal Source of light; only your bodily hands are condemned to earthly labour. Above all, beware of using them in an injustice. The man of the stream not only does not lift up his hands to heaven; not only does he not lower them to the earth to undergo his sentence; but he steals, to escape this sentence, and, by this social crime, violates at once the laws of heaven, of earth, and those of brotherhood or the family.

Oh! what injury has not covetousness done, and does it not still, to heaven, to man, and to earth! To heaven, because it destroys all confidence in the Supreme Principle, the only Powerful, and from whom you might expect living riches, instead of the dead virtueless treasures you steal and heap up with so much care; to Man, because, besides destroying his confidence in his Principle, it deprives him of industry and activity, in working out his great sentence which condemned all mankind to the sweat of their brow; to the earth, because it is thereby deprived of its culture.

The judgment of men's words

But if speech was given to Man for the sublimest of objects, what will, one day, be the fate of his word, seeing how he daily abuses it?

Every word that has not contributed to the universal improvement will have to be recast.

Every word that has served to increase disorder will be ejected.

Every word that has been used in derision and blasphemy will be cast into the corrosive pit, where it will become still more venomous and corrupt.

The Eternal Word will have to pump up again and take back into its bosom all the false, vain, and infected words of man, and, making them pass through the fire of its ineffable judgment, recast those which are yet capable of it, put aside those which have been vitiated, and cast into the corrosive pit those which are already filled with infection.

Sufferings of the man of desire, from the abuses of speech

"Lord of All", cries the man of desire, "what pain can be compared with mine, when I thus see the word with which thou hast gifted man, become in his mouth a murderous instrument, pointed against thee and thy word?

"Oh! the pain is too great for me! I cannot bear the trial thou layest upon me ; it exceeds the endurance of Nature! What, then, must be the inexhaustible infinity of thy eternal divine soul, O Power Supreme, if the human soul, which is only its reflection, can feel an approach to such pains !

"Why dost thou expose the human soul to such suffering, so that he can hardly tell his fellow-creatures of their unhappy condition? He is obliged almost to be silent on the subject of their ailments; his soul must keep its fearful anguish to itself, as thou keepest in thine own ineffable heart the anguish caused by the false and hard words of all mankind.

"Thou lovest to be taken by violence: I will give thee no rest till thou restore breath to my word, that it may groan freely for the disharmony of Nature, the miseries of man, and the anguish of thine own divine soul.

"But the only true way to obtain this favour, is to labour incessantly to restore in myself the harmony which thou engenderest and maintainest in all regions. Yes! I must labour incessantly to make my word the God of my ego and my circle, as thou art the God of the infinite circle; then, having become spirit, as thou art, I shall cease to be a stranger to thee; we shall recognize each other as spirits; thou wilt no longer be afraid of coming near to me, and holding converse with me.

"Then only shall I be alive; then only can my word make itself heard in the deserts of the Spirit of Man. To make a true and proper use of my speech, I must not pronounce a word which does not create improvement and life around me. And, not to speak a word but such as shall create life and improvement around me, I must not speak one which is not suggested, prompted, communicated, commanded".

Man's happiness, in time and eternity, depends on the holy use of his speech

How fecund is the Supreme Author of peace and order, and how inexhaustible in wisdom and treasures of goodness! He has founded man's ministry and his happiness on the same foundation, and appointed him to speak and act, only to do good, like Himself; and he cannot do good till he begin by being made happy, or vivified by the Word.

Man is destined to enjoy a permanent felicity like His; and, for this, it would suffice for him never to separate from the Word, and never interrupt his correspondence with it. For why does God nothing else but good? It is because

He can allow nothing to proceed out of Him but the living Word.

Why is He happy without interval? Because He never ceases to hear, speak, and feel the Word of Life. Why is He always serene and at rest; or why is He living? Because He speaks always, and the Word He pronounces inwardly, in His own centre, never ceases there to engender order and peace, because it never ceases to engender life.

And you, O Man! are destined to be active speech or word, according to your measure, throughout eternity, as God is so, universally. Delay not, another moment, to work with all your might to become active speech or word, even in this world: not only this ought not to seem impossible to you, but you ought even to consider it a duty; it will be only recovering what is your privilege, since you are destined to be active speech (*parole active*), eternally.

Yes! The man who unites with his Source, may attain such a degree of activity and wisdom, that every breath which proceeds out of his mouth may produce and shed abroad a glorious influence, the quintessence of the universal balm of purifying.

And Man is a creature unworthy of the name, unjust in the highest degree, and a frightful criminal, when he remains an instant without disseminating the holy active Word upon Nature, or Man, or the Truth, in affliction.

Alas! Why is this frightful, fruitless, blind waste of words, of which men are continually guilty, possible? The Psalmist said, the mouth is an open sepulchre; what, then, must this earthly region be, which incessantly receives into its bosom those dead and cadaverous words which incessantly proceed out of the mouth of man, and float in the atmosphere? What fearful darkness is that in which the human family almost entirely passes its life-long day!

Eternity is in a point of time: the present

They say that time is too short! Alas! if they but took the trouble to measure it, they would see what its immense extent is; they would be amazed at the abundance of time which God has given us so prodigally! It is such, that if we could make use of an infinitely small part of what is given to us, we should soon be placed above time. In fact, there is no man, who, in his life-time, has not had a moment sufficient to attain and embrace eternity; for there is not a point of time in which this eternity, in its completeness, is not contained. How should we, then, be ignorant of the vast extent of time, since we may measure it with eternity itself, which is its scale: instead of which, we measure it only by the broken results of time itself, which are always variable, indefinite, corrosive, or void.

Then, we perceive only its emptiness; and this is why it appears so short and sterile. Oh, if we could but feel what it is full of, how vast and fertile it would appear! The universality of things is a great balance; eternity is its summit and regulator; time is its two basins. Eternity is the pivot of time: it is only on this fixed universal point that time rests and moves.

On the other hand, they say that time is very long, and strive only to shorten it: this they do, not by extracting what is in it, but by allowing it to run on without filling themselves with the life it contains; and, when the time is gone by, they believe they have gained their end, whereas they have only run themselves out, with their vain projects and futile occupations, not to say their criminal covetousness, so outraging to their Principle.

How the present is lost in the past, and the future not gained

In fact, men do not know how to fix the present, because it is no longer near them; but, always hoping that they are going to meet something of this present, which they want, they seize with avidity all that is daily presented to their sight in the earthly, political, scientific, or merely social orders, which are filled up with such puerile occurrences as we witness. This is what makes the multitude run after sights of all sorts, from the theatre to the smallest incidents in our streets, and the small-talk of frivolous society.

But, instead of thereby fixing the present, all that their restless curiosity gathers is carried into the past. Indeed, as they gather only things of time, these, for them, at once become things of the past; and the only use they make of them is to relate them afterwards, which is the reason there are so many reciters in the world. If they occupied themselves with the real present, that which is not in time, they would turn their eyes to the future, and, instead of being mere reciters, they perhaps might become prophets.

A threefold eternity

They do not dream that there are three eternities - the suffering, the militant, and the triumphant; expressions which have been applied to the outward Church, by transposition. But these three eternities may make but one for man, and accompany him at every step.

It follows, if the threefold eternity accompanies man at every step, and man is God's image, that man does not fulfil his office, and cannot be at rest, if he partake not habitually of the treasure of this threefold eternity; and this treasure is to continually deliver himself and all creatures from death. It is only this kind of miracles that he has to perform in time: when time is no more, he may devote himself to another kind, if he have gained the privilege to do so, by his zeal and study in the cultivation of those which preceded; and this new kind of miracle will be, eternally to manifest the wonders of life.

Man is a focus of perpetual miracle

When the man of God instructs his fellow creatures, therefore, not one of his words but should be confirmed by living signs of his election, and of the virtual presence of the spirit of life in him. Thus this man ought, so to say, to be nothing but a perpetual and inexhaustible focus of miracles, which might proceed incessantly out of all his faculties and organs; since such was his property in his first estate, and such will be his final destination when he is reintegrated in the Universal Source, where prodigies and miracles will have mere delights to produce and spread abroad, and there will be no more disorder or iniquity to be seen or combated.

We have not now to ask why man should thus be a little inexhaustible focus of perpetual miracle: it is because the divine life ought perpetually to dwell in him, and open in him an entrance for works to be intrusted to him, so innumerable, that all the efforts of all men combined would hardly suffice to perform them. What then must it be, when, so far from this, there are so few who know, even by name, the important office of the Comforter, which men should exercise here below!

Yes! Divine life seeks continually to break through the doors of our darkness, and enter into us with its plans, for the restoration of light: it comes to us shivering, weeping, and, so to say, begging us to join it in this great work; at each solicitation it deposits a germ in us, a concentrated germ, which it is for us afterwards to develop. Now, to assist us in this divine undertaking, it deposits none of those germs in us, without, at the same time, depositing an extract of the sacramental substance on which our confidence may repose, in the joyful hope that these germs cannot fail to grow, if we apply ourselves, in spirit and in truth, to their culture.

These signs would not be long in showing themselves about us, if we valued this sacramental substance as it requires to be, and if we cared for it with all the ardour it deserves and demands from us.

For it would have everything to become centre and word, like itself ; therefore it seeks continually to make us centre and word universally, that, through our means, all regions may become the same in their turn. And it never comes near us without at once dissolving some portions of the heterogeneous substances in us, which are opposed to our free and universal communion.

The Universe an obstacle to prayer; Man must purify it

It is your earthly condition, O Man, it is the world which is an obstacle to your manifesting these glorious signs, this solemn testimony - because it is an obstacle to your prayer; and Isaiah was right in calling upon the world to listen to him, for the universe makes too much noise for the Word to be heard.

Be zealous with a holy rage; take the purifying censer, go and disperse the clouds which surround you; go and dissolve the coagulated substances which cause the opacity of this universe and form the obstacle to your prayer, and prevent your penetrating to the divine sanctuary, to force the Supreme Ruler to come out of His own admiration, to the help of the regions.

Take the living torch that since it could produce all things, is able to consume all things, and go and set fire to those corrupt essences of the universe which make it an obstacle to your prayer. Is it not you, O Man, who are yourself the cause that these corrupt essences should have so accumulated as to weigh so heavily upon you? Ought you not therefore to help in clearing them?

What do I say? Is it not yourself who should do it? Are not you the cause that these substances have spread before you like a phantom, hiding the temple of prayer from your sight? Is it not therefore for yourself to grind them to powder, and disperse them even to their last traces?

What glory, what consolation will be yours, O Man of desire, if, by your tears and your efforts, you are able to contribute to this great victory, and thus secure the repose of the human soul, and the Word! All who, like you, have co-operated in these sublime labours, will, one day, be placed, like notable and terrible swords, in the Lord's armoury; they will be hung for ever to the eternal arches of His temple; and over each of these shining blades will be written an immortal name, proclaiming their services and triumphs throughout eternity.

Prayer must do all; for the work is within

This, then, is the way that will lead you to the abode of prayer ; for prayer must invest you with these powers. Begin by driving from the universe the enemy that watches only to corrupt it, as a prisoner seeks to surprise and rid himself of his gaoler. There will be then one great obstacle less, opposed to your prayer; and the universe will show itself to you in its simple proportions, though fearfully emaciated.

What will you have to combat next? It will be that acrid fermentation which keeps the fundamental bases of Nature in a state of violence and confusion. Labour to contain and stop this fermentation; and the spirit of the universe, delivered of this frightful impediment, will become more accessible to your efforts; for you have this also to attenuate and subjugate; is it not a blind worker of evil and good alike?

When you have attenuated and subjugated this spirit of the universe, you will arrive at that eternal Nature which knows not good and evil, nor the acrid fermentation; still less the pursuits of the enemy; go through the enclosure of this eternal Nature, and you will find within, your place of rest, and the altar on which to place your offering; for it is inhabited by the Pure Spirit, Intelligence, Love, the Word, and Sacred Majesty; you will then perceive what prayer is: from these divine sources, indeed, alone can it come, flowing into your bosom, that you may pour it out over the world.

This is the work which each individual of the human species is charged to perform on himself ; this is the Work which Supreme Wisdom labours to accomplish universally; and the Lord's workmen in truth and equity are called to join in this immense undertaking. Work, ye workmen of the Lord ; relax not your efforts, in this magnificent enterprise; glorious rewards await you.

The universe crumbles at last! It burns! It is about to be demolished to its very foundations, and dissolved! Do you hear the holy eternal prayer ascending through the ruins of the world? How it presses through its barriers; how penetrating are its plaintive and mournful sounds! Pray, then, O Man, and you will hear them followed by sounds of consolation and joy.

Let the sacred regions rejoice; behold! the pure harps are advancing, the holy canticles are ready; rejoice, for the divine hymns are about to commence; rejoice, it is so long since they were heard! The chosen singer is restored at last; man is about to sing the songs of jubilee; there are no more obstacles to restrain him; he has dissolved, demolished, and burnt up all that obstructed his prayer! Blessed be the God of Peace for ever. Amen!

Be not afraid: only believe

How encouraging soever these pictures, which he has been contemplating, may be to the man of desire, pictures which call him to nothing less than to approach the divine sanctuary, and beg Eternal Wisdom itself to come out of its state of rest, and its own contemplation, to look upon and solace all that suffers, I hear this man of desire, restrained by his own humility, say to himself, inwardly:

"O Most High and Eternal Creator of all, is it for thy creature, paralyzed and disfigured by the universal crime to presume to stimulate the generative Principle of order and harmony? Is it for a nothing to call the Being of beings out of His own contemplation? Is it for death to awaken Life? No! I will not be so audacious!"

But I see him pursued with the feeling of the enormity of evil, the pain of all that suffers, and the imperious want of justice. I see him then revive his courage; I see him again take confidence in the Word that promised to give him all things, provided he would ask in His name. I see him approach the holy portals, and hear him offer these humble supplications:

"O Most High, and Eternal Creator of all! If He whom I venture to call the Elect of His own Love had looked upon me with an eye of compassion, and deigned to take up His abode with me, I should have recourse to Him to guide and sustain me in my holy enterprise; to Him I should remit all the rights which thou, in thine inexhaustible munificence, hast given me as man, and I should then be sure that there were no depths in thee which I might not reach; no light in thee which I might not kindle; no sentiment of love or beneficence in thee which I might not get to germinate, since this Elect one is but one with thee, Thou and He being bound by an eternal, indissoluble alliance.

"O Most High and Eternal Creator of all! In the name of this Elect of His own Love, I dare to appear before thee; He has taught me to know Him whom thou hast sent; He taught me to know thee by whom He was sent; in His name I will solicit thy love and beneficent zeal for all that is, as it were, banished from order and harmony. For, through Him, I shall endeavour to interrupt the peaceful transports which the intimate ineffable admiration of thine own Being continually occasions thee; through Him, I shall pray thee to suspend the delights of thine own contemplation.

"In His name, I will beg thee to exchange thy days of joy for days of sadness; to allow the radiant sojourn of thy glory to be covered with mourning, and come and plunge thy look full of fire into a cold and arid climate; and, into the region of death, thy fountain of Love, which bears with itself eternally the universal Source of Life.

"What can be more urgent than the motives which impel me to claim thy watchful interest? The question is, that Thou come to the help of Nature, of Man, and of the Word."

Who will help me here, to engrave deeply the picture of what the man of desire must become, to be able to awake the Supreme Majesty out of the divine intoxication which His own greatness, and the brightness of His own wonders, cause Him continually? He who partakes of this divine intoxication, and is seated in the midst of those eternal wonders.

The impulses of our will are given to prevent the enemy's approach.

The principles of our elementary life are given to us, not only to maintain our posts, but also to effect a breach in the ramparts of the citadel, and open the way for us to attack the enemy in his stronghold.

The active powers of Nature are given at our disposal, to consolidate our strength, and renew continually our means for fighting the enemy when the breach is practicable.

The powerful virtues of men of God of all epochs are offered us, to strengthen and support us, that our own spiritual virtue may take courage and confidence in the fight, as well as to instruct us in the marvels and grandeurs which fill the kingdom of God, which they began to know, even while they were in their earthly bodies.

The virtual sacred support of the Redeemer is granted to us, to revive within us all our former regions and powers, upon which He is pleased to take His seat, and to which He communicates His universal life.

Lose not a moment, O human soul, in reviving within you all these measures, if you have allowed them to die. Make these powers, each in its class, always advance, without looking to the right hand or to the left; for this is the way of justice.

Make your will and the elements thus prepare a way to the harmonical powers of Nature.

Make the harmonical powers of Nature open a way to the vivifying virtues of men of God of all ages, in which they have manifested, or at least proclaimed, the wonders of the kingdom of Life.

Make the vivifying virtues of the men of God of all ages open a free way for the ruling and sovereign voice of the divine Chief and Redeemer, who rules in heaven, on the earth, and in the hells; for you are a dead member, and soon will be mortiferous, if He cease a single instant to communicate His orders effectually, through His Word, to your whole being.

Then, O man of desire, being made agile, sanctified, and harmonized in your whole being, universally, you will, in your partial unity, be an image of the Universal Unity; then, through the holy analogy which will exist between the supreme Ruler and you, your soul will enter naturally into the sanctuary of this Supreme God; and when He sees it thus enter, He cannot but receive it, and drink of love for its beauty; for you likewise will be one of His marvels.

But, let not your heart forget its purpose: you will have ascended to the throne of divine Majesty only to bring it, in a manner, out of the very intoxication to which you will have further contributed by your presence!

Let a sigh still be heard in the midst of your triumph. Conclusion

Seize, then, this happy moment, when all will be divine, for and around you; cause a sigh to be heard in the midst of this circuit of happiness and joy. At this sigh, the Supreme Ruler will turn His eyes with interest towards you. When God looks upon a soul, it is to see it in its depth; and invite it by a tender foresight to express all it feels. Approach then still more closely to Him, at that moment, and say

"Lord, I bring only groans into the midst of thy heavenly delights; my voice can utter only cries of pain, in the bosom of divine joy. Deign, Lord, to suspend thy transports and joys, to listen to the just causes of my sorrows!

"The riches which thou hadst deposited in Nature are disregarded by Man, whom thou hadst placed in the world to develop their wonders to the eye of the human understanding; and, through the negligence of this careless and faithless steward, they have fallen a prey to the enemy, who has dissipated them; or he has poisoned them with his corrosive venom, so that man can no longer approach them without danger of infection from their pestilential vapours.

"The rivers of the universe, instead of circulating freely, and disseminating everywhere, their fertilizing waters, are transformed into frozen masses.

"Those magnificent productions which thou hadst created like so many instruments to transmit the sounds of pure harmony to us, are silent, because the air and the spirit have ceased to penetrate them. Hoarse and repulsive sounds, which create fear wherever they are heard, are all that compose the concert of

Nature now. In vain Man calls upon her, and urges her to publish thy glory, by manifesting the wonders thou depositedst in her bosom; she answers nothing; thy wonders remain hidden, as in an impenetrable cavern; and thy praise is heard no more by the ears of man.

"If I speak to thee of the ailments of the family of men, my groans will still increase. Thy Man, the beloved and radiant image of thine own splendour, has allowed all his colours to grow dim. Not only does he remember his original titles no more, but he has so far departed from his primitive destination, that, instead of manifesting thee, as it was the purpose and privilege of his essential constituent nature to do, he is in arms against thee, and is no more looked upon as being alive, by those who make themselves sovereigns in the domains of thought, except in so far as they see him take rank amongst thine adversaries, and serve in their armies.

"If they do not see this sign in him, - according to these imperious masters, he is dead: they consider this the only sign by which be can be acknowledged, and admitted to be a man; without it, they look upon him as an abortion, whose existence they dare not own.

"The mouth of man, which ought to have proclaimed thy glory, and sounded thy marvels every where, is no longer an open sepulchre, as thy Word expressed it, but death itself has become alive in them. It is no more dead men's bones in whited sepulchres; the bones are active, and have come out of their tombs, with all their corruption, to spread their infection; for, by electrifying themselves at the centre of iniquity, they have caused corruption itself to take movement within them.

"Human souls have become as walking corpses, wandering at liberty over all the earth, and, with their pestiferous breath, causing every being that has an idea of life to flee before them.

"Yes: let a man of desire now seek for thee in the hearts of his fellow creatures; let him look in that mirror, in which alone, on all the earth, thy features should have all been seen, and he will not find a trace of them; he will have to go away full of grief, when he finds that he no more knows where to look for the temple of his God: and thou, O Sovereign Author of all beings, unless thou show forth some new signs of thy love and thy power, thou wilt soon be without a witness or a testimony in the world.

"If these pictures are not sufficient to awaken thy pity, and stimulate thy glory, I will speak to thee of Him in whom the fulness of thy Godhead dwells, in whom thou hast deposited thine own heart, as it were, that He might come into the world, to transmit and distribute it to this very family which was so far from thee.

"Instead of receiving their portion of this ineffable gift, this inextinguishable light, the least spark of which would have revived their whole being, men try to proscribe this sovereign balm, and make it appear as a poison.

"The least corrupt amongst them keep this Divine Being in frightful agonies, allowing him no asylum within them, and leaving him to wander round them, exposed to all the inclemencies of the corrosive air of their abode of falsehood, and the sharp arrows of all the workers of iniquity. Others, infinitely more wicked, try to pierce this heart itself, hoping thereby to annihilate thine own existence.

"O Most High God, for the sake of the eternal wonders which thou hast sown in perishable Nature; for Man's happiness, in whom thou hast deigned to engrave thine image; for thy love and thine own glory's sake, turn thy regards, for an instant, from the splendour which fills thy heavenly abode, and direct them towards thy creations.

"Come and cause Nature to recover her ornaments; come and snatch the human soul out of death, by preventing him from poisoning himself.

"Alas I come to the aid of thine own heart, thine own Word, and, in pity to thyself, save men from a Deicide; for that which they want to perpetrate is a thousand times more criminal than that which the Jews perpetrated on the material body of thy Christ.

"In the time of Moses, thou sawest the afflictions of thy people, and camest down to deliver them out of the hands of the Egyptians; look now at the afflictions of all Nature, of the whole human family, and of Him whom thou sentest into the world to proclaim the good tidings and the kingdom of joy, and thou wilt not refuse to come down, and do for the relief of so much suffering, what thou didst for a single nation.

"Since thou hast permitted my soul to penetrate into thy sanctuary, and bring thither the groans of the world, the wretchedness of Man, and the anguish of thy divine Messiah, it is assuredly not alone in desiring to fix thy regards on this abyss of desolation; there are, doubtless, many others ready to fulfil thy sovereign orders, and devote themselves to the stewardship of thy gifts, and fly whithersoever thou callest them, for a work so vast and so urgent.

"If they distrust their own strength, and the reality of their call, thou wilt say to them as thou didst to Moses: 'I will be with thee, and this shall be a token unto thee that I have sent thee.'"

Then, O man of desire, wait in peace for the fruit of your prayer: you will soon feel the Heart of God penetrate all your essences, and fill them with His sorrows; and, when you feel yourself crucified in the very agonies of this divine Heart, you will return into time, to fulfil, according to your measure and your mission, the Spiritual Ministry of Man.

THE END

Parchment Books is committed to publishing high quality
Esoteric/Occult classic texts at a reasonable price.

With the premium on space in modern dwellings, we also strive - within the limits of good book design - to make our products as slender as possible, allowing more books to be fitted into a given bookshelf area.

Parchment Books is an imprint of Aziloth Books, which has established itself as a publisher boasting a diverse list of powerful, quality titles, including novels of flair and originality, and factual publications on controversial issues that have not found a home in the rather staid and politically-correct atmosphere of many publishing houses.

Titles Include:

Theosophic Correspondence	St.-Martin & Kirchberger
Secret Doctrines of the Rosicrucians	Magus Incognito
Corpus Hermeticum	(trans. GRS Mead)
The Virgin of the World	Hermes Trismegistus
Raja Yoga	Yogi Ramacharaka
Theosophy	Rudolf Steiner
Knowledge of the Higher Worlds	Rudolf Steiner
The Interior Castle	St Teresa of Avila
The Gospel of Thomas	Anonymous
Pistis Sophia	(trans. GRS Mead)
The Signature of All Things	Jacob Boehme
The Conference of Birds	Farid ud-Din Attar
The Cloud of Unknowing	Anonymous
The Rosicrucian Mysteries	Max Heindel
The Lost Keys of Freemasonry	Manly P Hall
The Secret Destiny of America	Manly P Hall
Heretics	G K Chesterton

Obtainable at all good online and local bookstores. View Aziloth's full list at:

www.azilothbooks.com

We are a small, approachable company and would love to hear any of your comments and suggestions on our plans, products, or indeed on absolutely anything.   Aziloth is also interested in hearing from aspiring authors whom we might publish. We look forward to meeting you. Contact us at:

info@azilothbooks.com.

CATHEDRAL CLASSICS

Parchment Book's sister imprint, Cathedral Classics hosts an array of classic literature, from ancient tomes to twentieth-century masterpieces, all of which deserve a place in your home. A small selection is detailed below:

Mary Shelley	*Frankenstein*
H G Wells	*The Time Machine; The Invisible Man*
Niccolo Machiavelli	*The Prince*
Omar Khayyam	*The Rubaiyat of Omar Khayyam*
Joseph Conrad	*Heart of Darkness; The Secret Agent*
Jane Austen	*Persuasion; Northanger Abbey*
Oscar Wilde	*The Picture of Dorian Gray*
Voltaire	*Candide*
Bulwer Lytton	*The Coming Race*
Arthur Conan Doyle	*The Adventures of Sherlock Holmes*
John Buchan	*The Thirty-Nine Steps*
Friedrich Nietzsche	*Beyond Good and Evil*
Henry James	*Washington Square*
Stephen Crane	*The Red Badge of Courage*
Ralph Waldo Emmerson	*Self-Reliance, and Other Essays, (series 1&2)*
Sun Tzu	*The Art of War*
Charles Dickens	*A Christmas Carol*
Fyodor Dostoyevsky	*The Gambler; The Double*
Virginia Wolf	*To the Lighthouse; Mrs Dalloway.*
Johann W Goethe	*The Sorrows of Young Werther*
Walt Whitman	*Leaves of Grass - 1855 edition*
Confucius	*Analects*
Anonymous	*Beowulf*
Anne Bronte	*Agnes Grey*
More	*Utopia*

full list at: www.azilothbooks.com

Obtainable at all good online and local bookstores.

THE CARTON CHRONICLES

THE CURIOUS TALE OF FLASHMAN'S TRUE FATHER

Keith Laidler

Morose, cynical and given to drink, Sydney Carton is one of Charles Dickens' most famous characters; a cold, dispassionate man, yet capable, in the final moments of A Tale of Two Cities, of sacrificing himself beneath the guillotine for Lucie, the woman he both loved and lost.

It now appears, however, that Dickens was being somewhat economical with the *actualité*.

Newly recovered documents, written in Carton's own hand, tell a far different tale. Sydney Carton survived his execution, only to find himself at the mercy of the monstrous Robespierre, author of the Paris Terror. His love Lucie languishes in a French prison, her husband dead, and Carton can ensure her survival only by becoming Robespierre's personal spy.

Reluctant, terrified and often drunk, Carton blunders his way through the major events of the French Revolution, grudgingly partaking in some of the blackest deeds of the Terror and, by a mixture of cowardice, bravado and luck, lending a hand in the fall of most of its leading figures. Kidnapped by the British, he finds himself a double agent, trusted by neither side. Our hero chronicles the slow decay of revolutionary ideals and, in passing, casts light on the true parentage of that sadistic villain of "Tom Brown's Schooldays", the beastly Flashman.

Praise for Keith Laidler's writing:

"Laidler's book is meticulously researched and covers a fascinating period" (The Times)

"It is a riveting story, and Laidler tells it well" (Sunday Telegraph Review)

From all good online and local bookstores.

CPSIA information can be obtained
at www.ICGtesting.com
Printed in the USA
BVHW060427150820
586436BV00004B/116